Political Obligation

Political obligation is concerned with the clash between the individual's claim to self-governance and the right of the state to claim obedience. It is a central and ancient problem in political philosophy.

In this authoritative introduction, Dudley Knowles frames the problem of obligation in terms of the duties citizens have to the state and each other. Drawing on a wide range of key works in political philosophy, from Thomas Hobbes, John Locke, David Hume and G. W. F. Hegel to John Rawls, A. John Simmons, Joseph Raz and Ronald Dworkin, *Political Obligation: A Critical Introduction* is an ideal starting point for those coming to the topic for the first time, as well as being an original and distinctive contribution to the literature.

Knowles distinguishes the philosophical problem of obligation – which types of argument may successfully ground the legitimacy of the state and the duties of citizens – from the political problem of obligation – whether successful arguments apply to the actual citizens of particular states.

Against the anarchist and modern skeptics, Knowles claims that a plurality of arguments promise success when carefully formulated and defended, and discusses in turn ancient and modern theories of social contract and consent, fairness and gratitude, utilitarianism, justice and a Samaritan duty of care for others. Against modern communitarians, he defends a distinctive liberalism: 'the state proposes, the citizen disposes'.

Dudley Knowles is Professor of Political Philosophy at the University of Glasgow. He is the author of *Political Philosophy* and *Hegel's Philosophy of Right*, also published by Routledge, as well as many articles.

Routledge Contemporary Political Philosophy

Edited by David Archard, Lancaster University
and Ronald Beiner, University of Toronto

Routledge Contemporary Political Philosophy is an exciting new series for students of philosophy and political theory. Designed for those who have already completed an introductory philosophy or politics course, each book in the series introduces and critically assesses a major topic in political philosophy. Long-standing topics are refreshed and more recent ones made accessible for the first time. After introducing the topic in question, each book clearly explains the central problems involved in understanding the arguments for and against competing theories. Relevant contemporary examples are used throughout to illuminate the problems and theories concerned, making the series essential reading not only for philosophy and politics students but also those in related disciplines such as sociology and law. Each book in the series is written by an experienced author and teacher with special knowledge of the topic, providing a valuable resource for both students and teachers alike.

Also available in the series:

Theories of Democracy
Frank Cunningham

Toleration
Catriona McKinnon

Rights
Tom Campbell

Forthcoming titles:

Equality
Melissa Williams

Public Reason and Deliberation
Simone Chambers

Political Obligation

A critical introduction

Dudley Knowles

Routledge
Taylor & Francis Group

LONDON AND NEW YORK

This edition published 2010
by Routledge
2 Park Square, Milton Park, Abingdon, Oxon OX14 4RN

Simultaneously published in the USA and Canada
by Routledge
711 Third Ave, New York, NY 10017

Routledge is an imprint of the Taylor & Francis Group, an informa business

© 2010 Dudley Knowles

Typeset in Goudy and Gill Sans by
Book Now Ltd, London

British Library Cataloguing in Publication Data
A catalogue record for this book is available from the British Library

Library of Congress Cataloging in Publication Data
Knowles, Dudley.
Political obligation: a critical introduction / Dudley Knowles.
        p. cm.—(Routledge contemporary political philosophy)
Includes bibliographical references and index.
1. Political obligation. I. Title.
JC329.5.K66 2009
320.01′1—dc22   2009006960

ISBN10: 0–415–41600–0 (hbk)
ISBN10: 0–415–41601–9 (pbk)
ISBN10: 0–203–87249–5 (ebk)

ISBN13: 978–0–415–41600–9 (hbk)
ISBN13: 978–0–415–41601–6 (pbk)
ISBN13: 978–0–203–87249–9 (ebk)

To Tom, Maya, and Gemma,
All good-citizens-to-be, and of some just state, I trust
With love from Popi

Contents

Preface

In this book I contribute to the study of one of the most ancient of political problems. As reported by Plato in the *Crito*, Socrates considered carefully the question of his allegiance to the Athenian state, asking whether he had a duty to accept the sentence of (self-administered) death imposed on him for impiety and corrupting the youth of Athens. Would it be morally permissible for him to escape to Thessaly with the connivance of his friends or does he have an obligation to obey the law of Athens? The issue of principle is as live for citizens today as it was for Socrates and for some poor souls in the modern world the stakes are just as high. I have felt it a privilege to be able to address this philosophical problem and to assist others who are troubled by these old worries. All of the text is the product of an independent mind reviewing arguments ancient and modern. That said, the most novel features are in Part I, the earlier, preparatory chapters where I discuss the form of the problem of political obligation, developing a strong distinction between the philosophical and the practical (or political) problems of political obligation and clarifying the nature of authority in general. I imagine many readers will wish to skip these preliminaries, believing that the meat of the matter is contained in Part II where a variety of arguments for and against political obligation are directly considered. That would be unfortunate, but I shall be pleased whatever pages are opened and studied. If you are an opportunist with a specific problem to ponder or an essay to address, please move directly to the appropriate chapter or sections – with my good wishes.

This book has taken too long to write, but that couldn't be helped. I was encouraged to write it for the Routledge Contemporary Political Philosophy series by David Archard who heard me read a paper on the topic of 'Gratitude and Good Government' and believed (optimistically) that I had more to say on these topics. My project at that time was a monograph on 'The Duties of the Citizen'. I kept this working title as long as I could, but finally I was persuaded by Tony Bruce of Routledge to accept the plodding version: *Political Obligation: A Critical Introduction* on the basis that it would be a better fit with the series style and find a wider readership. I hope he's right. On the advice of Matthew Kramer (for which, many thanks) I broached a strong jurisprudential literature I would otherwise have ignored. As well as broadening my education, I trust this has much strengthened the book, although some readers will view it as more boring in consequence. I was ill for a while, then struck down by the Academics' Curse – an involuntary spell as Head of Department. Over this period I have incurred many debts and it is a pleasure to acknowledge them here.

My colleagues in Glasgow heard presentations of three or four bundles of material and some of them commented carefully on drafts. I am grateful to Pat Shaw and David Bain amongst others for their help. I've given papers on different chapters of this book to colleagues in the Northern Political Thought Association, in the Hegel Society of Great Britain, to the Chinese Academy of Social Sciences (Beijing) and at the Joint Session of the Aristotelian Society and the Mind Association in Southampton (2006) and I am grateful to those present for their help. I've also discussed these issues at meetings in the Universities of Stirling, Dundee, Edinburgh (both Politics and Philosophy Departments), Leeds, Southampton, and with students at King's College, London, and I learned something on all these occasions. I'm hopeless at remembering who said what, so I would like to thank all those who attended and put sharp points to me. I should thank Dr Massimo Renzo (Stirling) for his expertise and time spent in conversations about Samaritanism which I've used in Chapter 10. I have also discussed bits and pieces of my manuscript with my students, from whom, as ever, I have learned a great deal. I should record the particular attention which was given to it by David Colledge which caused to me to make a couple of important changes.

I am also grateful to the many scholars who have contributed to the huge literature I had to study. My most perspicuous debt in this regard is, as ever, to the Great Dead Philosophers, particularly to Hobbes, Locke, Rousseau and Hegel, whose texts might as well be nailed to my desk. But amongst modern writers I judge that my greatest debt is to the work of A. John Simmons, notably to *Moral Principles and Political Obligations* (1979), but also to his books on John Locke and to his essays. I studied this work directly, learning much from it as I criticized it robustly. Even when studying other prominent modern writers on the topic of political obligation I found it hard to escape his influence since I find that it is standard practice to orientate a position either alongside or in opposition to Simmons's declared views.

I am especially grateful to the anonymous referee who gave me many specific problems to address and, in particular, urged me to revisit Margaret Gilbert's recent work on political obligation. I confess that I had read this material carefully before I composed the final manuscript and felt guilty that I hadn't found a place to give it close attention in this book. So I am very pleased to have accepted advice on where to place my discussion of this important recent contribution to political philosophy.

I am also pleased to record my gratitude to the University of Glasgow for giving me study leave to advance this project and to the Arts and Humanities Research Council, under its splendid Research Leave scheme, for funding its conclusion.

Lastly, I should thank the staff at Routledge – Tony Bruce in particular for his forbearance, and Adam Johnson and Richard Cook at Book Now for encouragement and assistance in the final stages of manuscript preparation.

As ever, I'm most grateful to my wife, Annie, for her splendid support during so many preoccupied days.

Part I

The authority of the state and the duties of citizens: the conceptual apparatus

Chapter 1

Political obligations and citizens' duties

It is fair to say that states and citizens have always regarded each other with suspicion. However just a state may be, there have been so many examples of truly awful states, states that kill, rob and pillage their citizens, that the most loyal citizens do well to be on their guard against the state apparatus being in the hands of fellow citizens who would do them harm. We should always remember that this apparatus has a sinister as well as a kindly face. Down the road there is a hospital where I will be treated if I am ill and a school to which I send my children, but over the river there is a police station from which policemen patrol the streets with powers of arrest. Beside it there is a court where citizens can be tried and punishments ordered. Outside of the city there is a prison, where citizens, having been stripped of some of their rights in the judicial process, are incarcerated, sometimes for many years. And in a nearby town there is a barracks where members of the armed forces are housed – and they are trained and willing to come to the assistance of the civil power should the people be regarded as a threat. Even a just and stable state, whose citizens properly feel secure against usurpation, may make mistakes. It may prosecute and convict innocent persons, it may become inefficient and too costly and as a result tax folk excessively. It may take a grandiose view of its remit and interfere in the lives of its citizens where it has no business. So even the most loyal citizen is right to be suspicious of the state.

The state, too, operates with a Janus-faced view of its citizens. In its day-to-day dealings, through its vernacular rhetoric, it speaks to citizens as decent and loyal, presuming compliance, allegiance and a willingness to serve. It addresses its subjects as 'good citizens'[1] and is not ashamed on occasion to demand extraordinary sacrifices. And yet it has grounds to be suspicious of these same citizens. Even where the state is providing services that the citizens acknowledge they could not do without and which they know to be costly and which they judge are best managed and provided for by the state, many citizens, individually, will seek to avoid payment, breaking the law whenever they judge that they can succeed in free riding with impunity.

If we think of the state and its citizens as characters in a relationship we can describe the interactions between them as caring, cooperative and conflictive. Or if that analogy offends (on the grounds, perhaps, that it implies a tendentious individualism – more on this later), and we prefer to think of the relation between the state and its citizens as analogous to that of a family and its constitutive members, again we shall identify care, cooperation and conflict in the dealings of family members with each other and with the family taken as a whole. States (through the voices of politicians, law officers, bureaucrats and participant members) and citizens individually, address each other in the language of prudence as they each pursue their best interests. But in their treatment of each other they also employ the language of morality (and law), each claiming rights against, and ascribing responsibilities and duties to, the other party.

I shall argue that the relationship of state to citizen can be deeply moral, which is not to say that states cannot be evil and thuggish in their dealings with citizens, nor that citizens cannot be immoral and opportunistic in their dealings with the state. The particular aspect of that relationship which we shall be examining in this book is the state's ascription of duties to its citizens – which is not to say that this moral relationship (if such there be; its existence is itself a matter of argument) can be isolated from other elements of the state–citizen relationship. That, too, is a matter for discussion and careful argument, since, for example, whether or not citizens bear duties to their states may be conditional on whether the state fulfils its responsibilities, serving the prudential interests of its citizens and doing its duty to them, in turn. But the duties, or in the philosophical jargon, the political obligations, of the citizens are our prime concern. Hence the first step in our enquiry will be to state the problem and articulate the concept of political obligation.

What is the problem of political obligation?

Here is a question: when you break the law, do you do something that is morally wrong? Of course you may well do wrong if the law that you break is one that forbids actions that are morally wrong according to some independent standard. You've stolen your neighbour's car. If it is morally wrong to steal and you have broken the law forbidding theft, then of course you've done something that is morally wrong. But have you done two things that are morally wrong: first stealing your neighbour's car and in addition breaking the law? That would depend on whether breaking the law itself amounts to doing something that is morally wrong. But is it morally wrong to break the law just because it is the law?

I put matters in this way because I expect that some variant on this question has occurred to most readers. Perhaps conscience has pricked Adam when he was just about to do something which he knew to be illegal, but which would otherwise give him no qualms, say buying a drink from the local grocers before 10.00 am. (It gave him no qualms before a law was introduced which makes it illegal.) Adam wonders why this should be so. Perhaps the phenomenon is quite the opposite. Betty has been engaged in some behaviour which gives her no moral qualms, say she has just handed over a glass of beer to her daughter, as she does at home, and she understands full well that she is doing something illegal since she is in a pub and her daughter is under-age. What strikes her is that she has no feelings of guilt whatsoever. Her conscience is silent. This strikes her as odd since she would describe herself as a morally sensitive and generally law-abiding person. Both Adam and Betty identify at least one philosophical question in the offing, although they may be ill-equipped to deliberate the matter carefully. Both of them are prompted to think through the details of the moral relationship in which they stand to the state that governs them. Whether we obey the law or break it, we can be brought up short. We can be caused to wonder whether or not what we have done or what we propose doing is morally wrong or morally permissible.

I suspect that scenarios of these types, wherein we find our anxious law-abidingness or our insouciant law-breaking to be a puzzle to us, contain the most familiar ethical format that generates the philosophical problem of political obligation. This is the occasion when agents deliberate the rights and wrongs of obedience to law. If one were careless one might identify the problem of political obligation as the general or most abstract form of the puzzles that vex Adam and Betty: is illegality *ipso facto* immorality? This would be a mistake because the problem is wider than is suggested by its most striking and perspicuous manifestations. The relationships in which citizens stand to the state and to each other as fellow citizens are deeply moral, and it is the moral contours of these relationships which will engage us throughout this book.

Let me give a few more examples of possible moral relationships in which citizens stand to their state.

(a) Suppose an aggressive neighbouring state initiates a war for reasons of aggrandizement and plunder, as Germany invaded Poland in 1939 and as the English used to invade Scotland at regular intervals. The state which is defending its territory calls for young men and women to volunteer for the armed services to resist the aggressor. (This is not a case of conscription.) Posters which display a much respected elderly warrior are widespread: 'The State Needs You' is the message as he points sternly at readers. Do the young men and women have a duty to serve? Do they deserve the odium of white feathers and charges of cowardice if they fail to respond? Some would say, and with a great deal of plausibility, that they have a political obligation to rush to the defence of their country.

(b) Suppose next that our country is a genuine democracy with plebiscitary and representative institutions making for effective participation by citizens. Do citizens have a political obligation to vote in referendums and elections even where attendance at the polling station is not compulsory? I think they do, but of course I can understand those who dispute this.

(c) Suppose next that our nation has a decent and just state. As these things go, its political health requires a loyal citizenry who recognize the importance of their active engagement. These sentiments are not easy to inculcate, however appropriate they might be in such fortunate circumstances. Success requires parents to educate their children into allegiance – which is not to say political docility. In such a state do parents have a political obligation to fetch up their children to be good citizens? My inclination, for what it matters, is to say that they do, although again I can understand those who take a very different view.

(d) Suppose finally that our basically decent and just state has been led by an over-ambitious and self-righteous Prime Minister into engaging in a war that a serving officer in the armed services deems to be illegal. His conscience tells him that he should refuse to serve, but further, he deems that he has a political obligation as a loyal citizen to protest against the war and thereby break the law governing the terms of his service. This officer may be mistaken in his judgement that the war is illegal, but surely he is quite right to believe that open disobedience may be amongst his political obligations.

I haven't introduced these examples in order to persuade readers that youngsters should volunteer for war service, that citizens should vote, that parents should regard themselves as agents of the state teaching the arts of citizenship, or that conscientious objectors should rebel. I use them to make the point that one should not think of political obligation as consisting solely in (or the problem of political obligation as concerned solely with) the obligation of citizens to obey the law. One should not even think of the obligation of citizens to obey the law as the paradigm or core obligation. How would one argue for that view against one who believed that the key element of citizenship is the duty of parents to educate their children properly? All such beliefs are at stake in a philosophical theory of political obligation.[2] Of course, one may engage in a philosophical discussion of whether citizens do have a duty to obey the law. One may perfectly well restrict one's philosophical attention to that particular issue (just as one might concentrate on any of the other cases I have listed). But if one does, he or she should not claim to be settling the problem of political obligation – the problem is much wider than that.

Obligations and duties: why this book has a really misleading title[3]

Having read the last page or two you might think it odd that one should describe the parent who educates her children to be good citizens as fulfilling a political obligation. But that may be because the term 'political obligation' is very much a term of term of art amongst philosophers. It is really just a label for a cluster of familiar problems that we broached above. Obviously we need to say more about the concept of obligation but we should be aware that the analysis of terms is not an exact science and any conclusions should be viewed with caution. It has been a commonplace of philosophical discussions of the concept of obligation that one might profitably begin by marking a distinction between the concepts of 'obligation' and 'duty'. Both of these terms are used to specify how agents ought to behave in usages such as 'x has an obligation to ϕ' or 'x has a duty to ϕ', but the first appears to be the more specific.[4] The distinctive features of obligations according to Hart are:

(1) that obligations may be voluntarily incurred or created. (2) that they are *owed to* special persons (who have rights), (3) that they do not arise out of the character of the actions which are obligatory but out of the relationship of the parties. Language roughly though not consistently confines the use of "having an obligation" to such cases.

(Hart 1955: 288, n. 7)

On this account, a paradigm obligation is that which the person who promises (the 'promiser' or 'promisor' in legal jargon) owes to the promisee.

This is as clear an account of the concept of obligation as one might find, so long as one observes the caution which is explicit in Hart's final sentence: it provides a rough match with general usage. But notice straightaway that if we accepted this analysis as creating necessary conditions on political obligation then it would be tendentious on the grounds that it begs important questions that will have to be tackled directly. May political obligations be voluntarily incurred or created? Some say that they must be; others say that they can't be, as we shall see in Chapter 4. Likewise, what are we to make of the claim that obligations are owed to special persons? Can the state be viewed as a person in this context? As for the thought that our obligations do not arise out of the character of the actions which are deemed obligatory, we shall see later in Chapter 3 that this fits very well the particular case of the authoritative command and hence the dictates of law. It does not fit so well with the obligations of the volunteer soldiers, the enthusiastic voters, the patriotic parent or the conscientious law-breaker. These obligations arise directly out of the nature of the actions the agents are obliged to perform.[5]

But then again, perhaps the mistake is to think of these latter cases as obligations rather than duties. It would certainly be more natural to say the youngsters have a duty to volunteer, the citizens have a duty to vote, the parents have a duty to educate their children to be good citizens in turn, and the officer has a duty to refuse to serve in the unjust war. In my book these are all duties of the citizen, as also is the duty to obey the law, each being orientated towards[6] the state as a political institution or one's fellow citizens as specifically citizens of the same polity; they are distinctively political duties, as against legal duties, religious duties, family duties or more broadly moral duties, although these categories may overlap in interesting ways. For this reason, the title of this book should be *The Duties of the Citizen* and you will notice that I shall use the term 'duties' much more readily than 'obligations'. It is likely that some of the duties of citizens are more naturally deemed obligations than others, and that in this loose sense political obligations are a subset of citizens' duties. But I have no real confidence in this judgement since my views on matters of common usage have long been tainted by philosophical study. True or false, I want to insist that it really doesn't matter which term we use.[7] What is important is that we don't use our intuitions or guesses concerning the linguistic nuances of these different terms to fashion philosophical arguments that beg substantive questions.

Institutional duties

The next questions then concern the concept of the duties of the citizen. We should notice first of all that it is common practice amongst philosophers to distinguish institutional duties from other moral duties, sometimes dubbing these latter 'natural' duties.[8] Institutional duties are the duties that persons hold in virtue of their occupying some specific role, office, job or position. Three important (and related) features of institutional duties are said to be:

(a) they are conventional, the product not of 'nature' but of human artifice, elements of historically contingent, socially constructed practices;
(b) they are not universal or general, they attach only to persons who are members of a given institution or who occupy a specific institutional role;
(c) their ascription is conditional on the duty-bearer's occupancy of the institutional position to which the duty is attached.

The duties of parents are different from the duties of children, though of course a person may have both as well as neither. The duties of the teacher are different from the duties of the student. The duties of the shop steward are different from the duties of the union member, but notice that there may be overlap; both have a duty to pay their dues as long as they remain members of the union. Priests have duties as priests, soldiers have duties as soldiers, and citizens have duties as citizens. These are all institutional duties, being incumbent upon their bearers in virtue of their location in a contingent social practice, and they contrast with the moral duties which persons have regardless of any institutional affiliations – their duties not to kill or steal, their duty to care for people in distress, for example.

This distinction is useful but, at bottom, unclear. This should not be surprising since the key notion of an institution or social practice is not well defined. To see this, consider an example that has been very important in the literature – that of promises. Is the duty to keep promises an institutional duty or a 'natural', moral, duty? It has often been argued that promise-keeping is an institutional duty, constitutive of the institution or social practice of promising, promise-making and promise-keeping. It is well known that Hume believed that 'the rule of morality, which enjoins the performance of promises, is not *natural* . . . a promise is not intelligible naturally, nor antecedent to human conventions' (Hume 1965: 516 [Bk III, Part II, §5]). Perhaps just as famously, John Rawls treated promising as a social practice in his important article 'Two Concepts of Rules' (Rawls 1955). If Hume is right (re: (a) above), it looks plausible to say that the duty to keep promises is an institutional duty. With respect to (b) above, I, for one, may well not have a duty to keep any promises since I don't fulfil the institutional role of promiser, not having given any promises which are outstanding at the moment. Which is to say (re: (c) above) that I don't meet the necessary condition on promise-keeping – that I have made a promise which requires keeping. All three marks of institutional duties can be identified in this case.

On the other hand, to start with Hume: how do we know that there was ever a time when it was *unnatural* (meaning what?) to promise, understanding that to mean minimally to tell other folk what one would be doing with the intention that they can rely on one's performance in the planning of their own business? Note that however sophisticated the philosophical articulation of what it is to make a promise might be, one can promise by nodding one's head – or maybe, a expressing a grunt – so long as all the contextual understandings are in place. Mutual advantage is one explanation of why one might do this, but how many other reasons might one not have? What conventions are necessary for this ploy to succeed? I shan't chase this hare any further since everything now depends on how we are to understand conventions. With respect to the second mark of institutional duties, that they attach to institutional roles, offices, positions, jobs even – sociological stuff like that – what social role need one occupy to have the duty of a promiser apart from the fact that one is a person who has made a promise? Similarly, with respect to the third mark of an institutional duty, that having the duties of a promiser is conditional on one's having made a promise – of course that's true, but then having the duty of truthfulness is conditional on one's making statements, and *that* duty doesn't seem to be institutional.

I would not argue to the death against a philosopher who insisted that the duty to keep a promise is an institutional duty, but I would want to know what purpose is being served by that categorization, and in particular I would want to know whether this implies that the duty to keep a promise is not a straightforward moral duty.

For similar reasons the duties of the citizen appear to be institutional duties. We know that citizenship is not a universal condition. A person may be a non-citizen, stateless, for many reasons and in different ways: perhaps because the conventions which might establish her citizenship have broken down, as in dysfunctional states (today Somalia, tomorrow . . .?); perhaps, amongst members of a small nomadic tribe, the claims that various states have made on their allegiance have never been recognized although borders have been established on a distant drawing board (and perhaps dismantled) and the tribe has been moving back and forth across them. Many poor folk are in transit, seeking rather than recognizing the duties of citizenship, desperate to satisfy the conditions that some decent state might impose upon them as a condition of membership.

Let's agree then that the duties of the citizen are institutional duties. But we should be wary of the implication that since the duties of the citizen are institutional duties they are not thereby moral duties of a familiar kind. This is a conclusion that A.J. Simmons reaches. He argues quite generally 'that no positional duties [institutional duties in my terminology] establish anything concerning moral requirements' (Simmons 1979: 17). As I see matters, there are three possible views on this issue: first, one might argue that all institutional duties are moral requirements, having some moral force; second, one might argue, following Simmons, that no institutional duties have any moral force; third, one might argue that some institutional duties have moral force, whereas others do not. Against the first claim, it is sufficient to notice Simmons's examples: 'the

Spanish Inquisitors, a leader of the Gestapo, and a member of the Ku Klux Klan' all have institutional duties. It would be absurd to suggest that their respective duties – to torture heretics, to exterminate Jews and to lynch Blacks – are moral duties in any sense and to any degree. The second (Simmons's) view can also be rejected on the basis of examples. The duty of parents to care for their children is an institutional duty, and so too, I would like to believe, is the duty of children to obey their parents. These duties are quite straightforwardly moral duties, how-ever they might be qualified by the parties' age and conduct (and they are as *nat-ural* as 'natural duties' could be). They are not derived from other duties. They are not, for example, particular cases of persons exercising a duty of care towards the young and vulnerable, otherwise every parent would have the same duty to look after everyone else's children. There may well be such a duty, but it is not the specific duty of the parent.

I favour the third view, that some institutional duties have moral force, some do not. The duty of the KKK member does not have moral force. The duty of the parent towards the child does have moral force. How do we mark the difference? And once we have marked the difference, how might we decide whether or not the duties of the citizen are moral duties? In the first place we should accept that institutional duties to do evil cannot be moral duties. There are two cases: the first case is where doing evil is integral to the duty as specified. It was the duty of Gestapo officers to progress the extermination of the Jews. That is an evil task. It can't be a moral duty. The second kind of case is more nuanced. Suppose a goal is morally permissible but the only way to secure this goal is by doing evil. The goal of the Currency Integrity Agency is the protection of the currency; the only means available to secure the integrity of the currency is to torture the one member of the counterfeiting gang who has been caught. (Let's not make the case too horrible; the counterfeiter will not respond to questions, but has a very low pain/disclosure threshold.) I judge that the member of the Agency with the institutional duty to torture the counterfeiter (as his boss so instructs him) does not have a moral duty to do so. What of cases where the goal is an undisputed good – the preservation of the lives of many citizens? Very crudely, some philoso-phers say that the ends can justify the means; others say the ends cannot justify the means if the means have a distinctively evil quality. Each of these views has the capacity to characterize the one way to accomplish the good end as the wrong thing to do. For the former, the only way to achieve the good end is too costly on balance; there are better things to do than achieve the nominated good end. For the latter, the only way to achieve the good end is morally impermissi-ble (e.g. if it violates human rights). If the only thing that can be done to achieve the undisputed good is wrong on either count, one can't have a moral duty to do it.

Second, we should distinguish the non-moral institutional duties from the institutional duties that have moral force. Again, we can argue by example. It is the main duty of a goalkeeper to save the opponents' shots. Suppose Peter turns out to be hopeless in a really important game. He's failed to keep out a couple of shots he should have saved. He hasn't done his job. He has let his team down.

He will be heavily criticized for his performance. He hasn't done his duty. But he hasn't done anything *morally* wrong if he has simply had a bad day. (Things would be different if he was a professional goalkeeper with a hangover or exhausted following a night on the tiles, or worse, one who had been bribed to let in the goals.) By contrast, there are two ways in which institutional duties may have moral force. The first way (which Simmons recognizes)[9] is attested when a person has assumed a moral duty to perform an institutional duty. Say she is a President of the United States who has voluntarily undertaken the job, indeed swearing the proper oath of office that she will fulfil the appropriate duties. If she then fails to respond to an international crisis because she's dallying with a handsome young man who works in her office, she has violated a moral requirement. But that is the requirement that she keep her oath of office, not the institutional duty to respond to an international crisis. Her oath is the *ground* of her duty, as Simmons puts it.

The second way in which an institutional duty can have moral force is if some moral requirement is integral to the role, position or office. I have already given an example of this in the case of the parent. In the jargon, it is constitutive of being a parent that one has a duty of special care for one's own children. This doesn't have an independent ground in a wider duty of care, as noted above, and the duty certainly does not derive from any agreement to assume such a duty at the moment of the child's conception or birth. I would argue that the same is true of other institutional duties of care. A teacher has a special duty to educate the students in his class; a doctor has a special duty to treat the sick: both of these duties are quite distinct from the general duty of care which the stranger has, for example, to rescue the infant from drowning in the paddling pool. Of course in the normal case these will be duties that the teacher and the doctor have voluntarily undertaken as they chose their respective vocations. But the moral force attaching to the fulfilment of their duties attaches directly to the duties in question. It does not derive from some prior act of commitment at the moment of their appointment, say the teacher's signing a statement of the conditions of employment or the doctor's swearing the Hippocratic Oath. One could perfectly well be a teacher or a doctor without doing these things.

Granted as claimed above that the duties of the citizen are institutional duties, the pertinent question is whether or not they are moral duties, and if they are moral duties, on what basis? Are they moral duties on the basis of some independent grounds or is the moral force of these duties integral to them, on the basis of the kinds of duties they are? Let me answer these questions in reverse order. They may well be moral duties on some independent ground. As we shall see later, if it turns out, for example, that persons have actually consented to assume the duties of citizenship, other things equal they have a moral duty to fulfil these duties. There may well be other independent grounds which hold in the particular case. Citizens may have taken benefits from the state and, in consequence, considerations of fairness or gratitude may require that they should assume at least some of the duties of citizenship. Whether or not arguments such as these succeed in establishing that some or all of these duties are incumbent on some or all citizens as moral duties will come out in the wash as we examine them in detail in later chapters. Equally, we shall have to wait and see whether or not the duties of citizenship might not be moral duties which are integral to the station of citizen. Of course if the state is unjust and imputes to its citizens duties to do things that are evil, then these institutional duties cannot be moral duties. But what of the just state? We shall need to examine whether or not it is an integral feature of the just state that its citizens' duties (their political obligations) are moral or natural duties. That issue, as with the independently grounded moral duties of the citizen, is entirely open.

Moral (and other kinds of) duty

We shall be studying the duties of the citizen. These are institutional duties, but the feature of them which is of cardinal importance is that they are moral duties. We have so far *assumed* that if the duties of the citizen are duties, then they are moral duties, whether their moral force is integral to them or whether it is established on the basis of independent moral principles. But this assumption needs to be defended. Perhaps the duties of the citizen are duties, but not moral duties. Thus far we've argued that the duties of the citizen *may be* moral duties, depending what sort of story is told about their source, but we haven't shown that they *must be* moral duties. Perhaps they may be like the duty of the goalkeeper to keep out the opponents' shots – duties of some kind or other but definitely not moral duties.

The term 'duty' has a distinctive moral flavour, for sure, but one can't insist that all duties are moral duties as the goalkeeper example teaches us. We can perfectly well understand how prospective actions might be regarded as duties but not moral duties, regardless of the moral odour hereabouts. Perhaps the duties of the citizen are like the duties of the goalkeeper – just things they should do – but carrying no moral force, embodying no moral requirement.

I think this view is mistaken. The idea that the duties of the citizen are not moral duties is encouraged by the fact that there are varieties of duty other than moral duty and, in particular, by the close linkage of the concepts of political obligation and legal obligation. Some duties, as noticed above in the case of the goalkeeper, are morally neutral. They function as requirements on the conduct of the holder of a position within some institutional regime, but persons who fail to fulfil them have not committed a moral wrong. Other cases are the occasion of great dispute. Religious folk may deem themselves to have duties in accordance with the tenets of their faith. They recognize a duty to attend church or mosque. They may have a religious duty to render unto Caesar the things that are Caesar's, as their Saviour or prophet teaches. They may well think of this as a moral duty, believing that all persons have a moral duty to witness the Christian or Moslem faith and that unbelievers live deeply immoral lives. They equate sin and immorality; it is not just that the commandments of religion and the principles of morality overlap in many cases. If moral wrong-doing amounts to the violation of the commandments of God, which commandments specify our religious obligations, then one's religious obligations are equivalent to one's moral duties. But others take a different view of their religious duties, particularly those who do not view their faith as available to all mankind. It may be a religious obligation of Jews to visit the synagogue but it cannot be a moral duty incumbent on all mankind, and may not even be an institutional moral duty for all Jews. It is perfectly possible to believe that the doctrines of one's faith encode one's religious duties but to distinguish these sharply from one's moral duties, again recognizing that there will be overlap when the dictates of religion and morality coincide. The idea of a religious duty which is binding on the faithful quite independently of their moral duties is quite clear.

In a similar fashion, it is a commonplace that the requirements of law and morality may be co-extensive. There is a view of law that goes further and identifies the law of the land and the moral law, just as some religious believers identify the law of God and the moral law. (And in traditional versions of natural law these different views are connected – God being the source of both law and morality.) An implication of this view is that if a particular law of some actual state is immoral or unjust, requiring citizens to behave in an evil fashion, then it is not a true law. On a natural law account one's duty to obey the law will be a type of moral duty. Let us put this view aside for the moment – we shall come across it again later. According to the opposing *positivist* position there can be evil laws if they meet whatever formal conditions on legal validity hold in a specific legal system.[10] This yields a straightforward concept of legal obligation: x has a legal obligation to ø if and only if there is a valid law which commands x to ø.

On this very rough positivist account of legal obligation one can see immediately that legal obligations are institutional duties. And there have been plenty of examples of evil laws which give rise to them. One example, which was prominent in the literature of jurisprudence in the Hart--Fuller debate concerning natural law and legal positivism, is the Nazi law requiring persons to inform on their spouses if they denounced the Nazi regime in the privacy of their own homes.[11] Assuming that it is an evil thing to inform on one's spouse for uttering such sentiments, this law could not have generated a moral duty. If this legal obligation is *ipso facto* a duty of the citizen (a political obligation) in virtue of its being a requirement of the state, then the duties of the citizen are not a type of moral duty. There are two ways in which one might respond to this. First one might concede that this argument demonstrates that some of the duties of the citizen, some political obligations, are not moral duties or obligations. Specifically the citizen's duty to comply with an immoral law is not a moral duty. (Further, and by implication, the citizen's (generic) duty to obey the law, taking that duty to be the duty to obey all laws severally and collectively, whether they are immoral or not, cannot be a moral duty either.) This leaves open the possibility that other duties of the citizen might well be moral duties, the duty to serve in a just war, for example. It also opens up the question: what kind of duty might the non-moral (indeed immoral) duty to obey the unjust law be? The only possible answer is that it is a legal obligation. The second way forward is to preserve the distinction between legal and political obligation and retain the connection between political obligation and moral duty. Then one can insist that it makes no sense to describe the citizen's obligation to obey an unjust law as a political obligation and, *a fortiori*, a moral duty. This is plausible, since nothing is added to the thought that one has a legal obligation by describing it as a political obligation, too.

What then are we to make of the obligation to obey the law? That isn't a legal obligation. (There is no master law that states that citizens must obey the law.[12]) It has standardly been thought of as a political obligation, indeed the cardinal political obligation. There are two options available: we can continue to deem the obligation to obey the law a political obligation but, as suggested above, deny that it is a moral obligation, that one has a moral duty to obey the law. It must be some other kind of duty. Some philosophers would be happy with this, having suggested that political obligation is a distinct kind of obligation. It's not moral obligation or legal obligation or religious obligation – it's political obligation, *sui generis*.[13] I confess: I just do not understand this view. Its proponents accept that political obligations are requirements and that something has gone wrong when these requirements are not met. Generally sanctions or some other critical response are due. How are we to characterize this wrong-doing? What I cannot see is how political life might impose requirements on a population which are neither legal nor moral nor the duties of a job (nor simply prudential). What could the normative pull of such a requirement be? How might such a requirement (or the concomitant thought of failing to meet it) motivate you or me? How might the duty of the citizen to obey the law be morally neutral in the fashion of the duties of a goalkeeper? We shall have to revisit this issue.

The alternative position is that we further specify the political obligation to obey the law as the obligation to obey *just* laws, more generally the duty to obey the laws of a just and decent state. This is the proposal that I favour and shall defend in more detail in Chapter 5. For the moment I shall conclude that if x, as a citizen, has a duty to ø, then there is a *moral* reason for x to ø. Alternatively, if x has a political obligation to ø, then there is a *moral* reason for x to ø. That said, I should emphasize that nothing that has been said so far has shown that there are any such duties. States (or to be more accurate, the politicians or officials who speak for them) may assert that citizens have such moral duties[14] and citizens may recognize them, but states and citizens alike may be mistaken. Whether or not their beliefs are correct depends upon whether there are substantive arguments available that can serve as a plausible grounding.

Prima facie duties and *pro tanto* reasons

There is a final item of philosophers' jargon that we should cover. Take any element of the list of possible citizen's duties that I gave earlier – but we might as well keep the duty to obey just law in our sights. Is that an *absolute* duty such that, if the law states that ø-ing is illegal, then it is *always* morally wrong for citizens to ø? Such a claim looks both plausible and implausible. It looks plausible because we have specified that it is a condition on there being a citizens' duty to obey the law that the law which requires citizens not to ø is a just law. We have excluded the possibility of citizens having a moral duty to comply with an unjust law, to perform an evil action. If it is not evil not to ø, and if there is a moral reason for citizens to do their duty as specified by the law that requires them not to ø, surely it must be morally wrong for them to ø?

The question is not rhetorical because the answer is surely 'No. It is sometimes right'. Here is an example that supports this view. The law forbids theft. Suppose that in a café Emily overhears a couple of hit-men discussing the tactics of the contract killing they will carry out as soon as they finish their cup of coffee. Emily deduces, correctly, that the only way she can prevent the murder is by stealing their car, then 'phoning the police so that they will be arrested. So she steals the car and 'phones the police, the villains are arrested and the life of the prospective victim is saved. As described, Emily is a law-breaker. The law forbidding theft that she has broken is a just law. Has she done wrong? Let's agree that what she has done is illegal.[15] Surely she hasn't done anything that is morally wrong. But haven't we just stated that it is morally wrong for citizens to break a just law?

There is a simple answer to this puzzle. Emily does have a citizens' duty not to steal in virtue of the law against theft and so she has violated a moral duty in stealing the car. But she has not done anything that is morally wrong since the duty to obey the law is outweighed by her moral duty to prevent a murder and save a life. This is a familiar case of conflicting duties. One could hardly say there is a moral dilemma here. Emily doesn't have to think very hard to work out that the right thing to do is to break the law, given that she can save a life thereby. There are many cases which have this structure. We can safely conclude that it can be morally permissible to break the law in cases where, as described, citizens have a moral duty to obey it. There is no practical problem in the case I described since it is quite straightforward to work out what is the right thing to do, but there is a philosophical issue: how can we describe the position so as to avoid the seeming contradiction in claiming that it is morally permissible to do something that is morally wrong?

Sir David Ross introduced the concept of *prima facie* duty to explain what is going on, all the while accepting that this terminology is seriously misleading.[16] It is fair to say that all commentators have agreed with Ross on this point, not least since, as he himself states, the term falsely implies that *prima facie* duties are duties at first sight, duties which may well turn out to be illusory on closer inspection. This is *not* the problem in the cases we have in mind (though of course one *could* construct a concept of *prima facie* duty which meant just this – *prima facie* duties as the product of fallible moral nostrums). The moral duty of citizens to obey the law (if there is one) is not a duty in appearance only, in those cases where it is outweighed. It remains a genuine duty. The same is true of all other moral duties which are outweighed in the circumstances of a particular case. I speculate that there is no moral duty that has not been in practice, nor could be in principle, outweighed by a competing duty or by some other weighty moral consideration. Ross put his finger on a philosophical problem, discussed it in a manner that is both perspicacious and confusing, and bequeathed a technical terminology which is unsatisfactory but probably ineliminable.[17]

That said, I shall try to avoid it in favour of the more recent and more helpful term 'pro tanto reason'. A pro tanto reason is a reason that always carries some weight in the balance of reasons concerning how one should act. If no other reasons bear on the case, then one should act as the reason dictates, as one should also do if it outweighs any competing reasons.[18] But even when the pro tanto reason loses out, as reasons favouring an alternative course of action are taken to be stronger in the balance, it still retains its force. On this account a moral duty to ø is a pro tanto reason to ø. Thus although it may be best to break the law on a specific occasion, that an action involves breaking the law always counts as a reason against doing so given that one has a moral duty to obey. Hence correctly breaking the law may be a matter for regret, in the same way that one would think it a matter of regret that one had to break a promise although that was the right thing to do in the circumstances.

When I write of citizens' duties in what follows I shall take these to be pro tanto moral reasons. They are not absolute reasons; they do not dictate what one should do, all things considered. Hence there is no philosophical problem in claiming that citizens have a moral reason to do their duty, yet acknowledging that doing their duty is not always the right thing for them to do. Citizens' duties or political obligations are moral requirements but not absolute. We can perfectly well conclude that citizens have a duty to obey the law (and sometimes a duty to break the law) without having to deny that it is sometimes right to break the law (and sometimes right to obey it, despite the contrary duty).

Thus far I have been explaining the use that I shall be making of the concepts of duty and obligation as these feature in claims that citizens have duties as citizens, or equivalently, political obligations. In the next couple of chapters we shall turn to the state to examine the nature of the claims it makes on citizens and the authority with which it directs their conduct. In Chapters 4 and 5 we shall discuss how such claims might be vindicated.

Chapter 2

The state and its legitimacy

Books galore have been written about both of the topics of state and government, and the history of political philosophy is replete with definitions and analyses which are the recognizable outcome of special pleading on behalf of some favoured doctrine. Rousseau is a celebrated culprit. For him, the 'state' is the body of people, each of whom, as citizens, compose the sovereign of a directly democratic republic, and every one of whom as subjects must obey its laws. By contrast, the 'government' is the executive branch of the republic, the civil service which has the task of putting into effect the laws of the sovereign. Rousseau had his own reasons for employing this idiosyncratic vocabulary (not least that he was thus able to put monarchy and aristocracy (types of government, both, as he defined them) in their proper place as forms of executive service to the people) and no harm is done so long as one reads him carefully and attends to his definitions.[1] Outside this specific context these definitions are tendentious.

Probably the most familiar definition of the state is that of Max Weber: 'a state is a human community that (successfully) claims the *monopoly of the legitimate use of physical force* within a given territory' (Weber 1946: 77). This is at best a partial specification of the leading characteristics of one conception of the state, but the focus on violence or coercion is something to keep in mind. In referring to the state we can pick out a collection of people, a political and legal apparatus, and a circumscribed territory. Nowadays, most states have the character of being nation states, a unitary body with a history and an identity through time.[2] I think we can operate with a rough-and-ready conception of the state so long as we recognize that there will be puzzle cases. There are political oddities – in Europe, relic city-states or principalities, and even a set of discrete religious enclaves in Rome in the form of the Vatican. There may be no recognized or acknowledged unity amongst a collection of people, and historically independent social groups may clamour for secession. The political apparatus may be alien and imposed, as is found in the colonial territories of an imperial power. There may be international groupings, alliances or federations such as the European Union which exercise some of the distinctive functions of the state. We should not be surprised if such strange political items generate problems concerning authority, legitimacy and citizens' duties, but these will not be at the forefront of our attention.

There is one analytical point that should be clarified at this stage in the argument. Our topic is the duties of the citizen. To whom are those duties owed? Clearly when speaking of the duties of the citizen I don't have in mind all of the duties that citizens bear. I'm not thinking of the duty I owe Helen to keep the promise I made to return the book I borrowed. In some sense, still to be specified, we shall be discussing the duties of the citizen *qua* citizen, and I believe the natural way to think of these is as duties that citizens owe to the state. This seems obvious in the central case of the duty to obey the law which is frequently imputed to citizens. Some philosophers have had qualms about this on the grounds that it seems to invoke the state as an independent entity, attesting an exotic metaphysical commitment. Not wishing to elaborate or defend the existence of such a strange object, they have preferred to regard the duties of the citizen as owed not to the state but to fellow citizens generally. If the state is to be spoken of as an individual which imposes and is the object of duties (which it invariably is) this may be viewed as the employment of a *façon de parler*, a convenient fiction, a literary device which reaps the advantages of personification whilst abjuring the metaphysical costs.

My view is that this strategy is metaphysically squeamish. I suspect the motivation for such scruples is not the ontological cleanliness imparted by Occam's Razor, but a fear of any taint of that kind of social idealism embraced by Hegel and his British followers, notably Bradley, Green and Bosanquet. This is unfortunate since if there is any philosophical corner that is best illuminated by the tradition of absolute idealism it is social philosophy. The key thesis here is that the state is a mental (or spiritual, or intentional) phenomenon: as Hegel put it, a manifestation of objective spirit. It is a substance as objective, if not as physically obtrusive, as any stone available to be kicked, its reality constructed out of the understandings and intentions of the citizens who compose it and its constituent institutions (together with any foreigners who recognize its distinct existence when they visit or speak to its representatives). It is, as Hobbes said, an 'Artificiall Man' or an 'Artificiall person'.[3]

The use of these terms by Hobbes reminds us that one need not be an absolute idealist to personify the state or identify it as a real entity in some sense which entails that it can, for example, bear responsibility for its actions. In modern times John Searle has explained the reality of the state as that of a social union performing status functions through its collective intentionality,[4] and Ronald Dworkin has argued that the state or political community can be personified in a non-reductive fashion without any spooky metaphysics.[5] It is important for the argument that follows that the state can be intelligibly personified since I will present the arguments through which duties are purportedly imputed to citizens as a dialectic conducted between the state and its citizens, a dialectic wherein the state advances arguments and the citizen reviews them. None of this, however, is to deny that it may be a conspicuous feature of some of the political duties of the citizen that they are best understood as owed to at least some fellow citizens severally, with the state acting as an intermediary administrating the norms. This may be true of the duty to make transfer payments, e.g. taxation to fund pensions for war widows. But these are nuances that can be explored later. Nor should readers take my construal of the duties of citizens as duties owed to the state to refute or exclude from consideration carefully articulated philosophical theories which analyse political obligations as obligations owed by each citizen to every other citizen.[6]

I take it that we can operate with a loose conception of the state, so long as we bring to the surface any implications that have relevance for the argument in hand. I want to say the same about the concept of government. The term is often used as a synonym for the state, where the state is understood as a legal or political entity. As against the state, 'the government' is a resolutely political notion; it is not itself territorially bounded and its constituent members are political agents or functionaries, never mere subjects (though in a direct democracy all subjects will be actively participating citizens). Although governments can have an identity through time that perdures before and beyond any specific group of office-holders, the most frequent use to which the term is put is to refer to the political administration of the state at some particular point or period of time. Generally, when I use the term, I refer in these ways to something more specific than the state, as in 'the government of the state of Israel'.

The most significant feature of the state for our enquiry is that highlighted by Weber; its exercise of a monopoly of violence is a consequence of its capacity to wield effective coercive powers. This is the nasty face of the state, expressed in laws backed by sanctions, police forces, armed services, courts and prisons. States do things which in the normal run of human affairs are impermissible. They threaten their citizens, fine, imprison, publicly shame and exact compulsory service from them. In some jurisdictions they inflict corporal punishment and the death penalty. To point up the nastiness, all of these activities if performed by ordinary citizens and not by agencies of the state would in the normal course of events be taken as violations of citizens' rights – human rights even. Of course the state may have more attractive features. It may organize the administration of necessary services, providing health, education, a transport infrastructure, consumer protection, lighthouses and much else, but these services have to be paid for and this is achieved by the compulsory taxation of income, wealth or purchases. Altogether, these are formidable coercive powers. Such powers and their possession and exercise by anyone or any institution stand in need of justification. When people claim or believe that the possession and exercise of these powers is justified, they use the language of legitimacy. What is it to claim legitimacy on the part of the state?

The state which justifiably exercises coercive (and other) powers is deemed legitimate (or perhaps lawful) and a legitimate state is often glossed as a state with the right to rule its citizens. The state rules its citizens by imposing duties or obligations upon them. So a state which is legitimate may properly exercise its right to impose duties or obligations on citizens. It defends these impositions by citing its authority to do so.[7] I take it that these statements are truisms, but that is because they bear a wide range of interpretations which can be manipulated to meet objections. Whether and how they can be clarified and articulated in a fashion that makes them philosophically acceptable, whether and how they can be analysed and manipulated into the formulation of a philosophical theory – these are different questions entirely. We need to examine further the legitimacy of the state. We can make a start by drawing some distinctions, since several different conceptions of legitimacy seem to be in play.

Legal legitimacy

The most straightforward account of the legitimacy of a sovereign state will explain legitimacy in terms of the state's meeting some actual (or *positive*) legal standard. Such legal standards may be of different sorts. We can distinguish internal and external standards. The simplest kind of internal standard is represented by constitutional laws which dictate the form of the decision-making process, and, most importantly, state the rules that determine which shall be the governing body in a system that makes explicit provision for a change of rulers. The latter rules yield the most conspicuous test of legitimacy. There are familiar cases of tyrants who illegitimately change the rules of succession in a way that is not provided for by the constitution in order to stretch their period of office or to install a family member or favourite as their successor. There are also cases of genuine dispute over the legitimacy of the succession of a sovereign, or some part thereof. When George W. Bush was elected President of the United States in 2000, many lawyers challenged the legal propriety of the Supreme Court ruling that permitted votes in several districts in the state of Florida to be tallied without a recount, despite the technical flaws of the voting machinery. What was at stake in this dispute was the legitimacy of at least the executive branch of the sovereign (the President and his administration) and for some, the legitimacy of the Supreme Court in light of its decision in the case.

In other cases it may not be the legal legitimacy of the state that is directly in question, but the legitimacy of specific provisions, the legal validity of its laws. If a government does not follow the rules laid down for the regulation of its own conduct – say it issues instructions directly to its subjects in some domain where the constitution requires that complex processes of legislation be followed (in UK terms, for example, it issues orders in council in matters that should be the subject of primary legislation) – such directives will not have the imprimatur of legal validity. The same would be true of *ultra vires* activities, e.g. legislation or legally sanctioned activity on the part of officers of the state that goes beyond the limits prescribed in the constitution. This is a permanent source of vexation with respect to the activities of subordinate political authorities and the actions of officials. The state is acting illegitimately when it breaks its own rules and exceeds its proper powers. An example concerns the domestic spying operation conducted by the National Security Agency of the Bush administration in 2006. A group of scholars and former US government officials argued that the NSA was violating the Foreign Intelligence Surveillance Act of 1978.[8] This conception of illegitimate state activities is especially conspicuous when states breach the conditions of a charter or Bill of Rights which is entrenched in the constitution of the state with the specific intention of limiting the powers of the state.

In a modern state the remedy for the possibility of a state's acting illegitimately in respect of its own laws is an independent judiciary, but as the Bush 2000 election example shows, claims to genuine independence are more frequently made than conceded. In the background here is an enormously hard philosophical problem which I cannot pursue but which should be stated clearly. The account of legal legitimacy that I have offered so far has been unremittingly *positivist* in the precise sense that the property of legitimacy or legal validity of governments and their activities is a function of the actual (positive) laws of specific jurisdictions. But according to the natural law tradition that we encountered in the last chapter, legal legitimacy or validity cannot be simply a matter of positive legal procedure. Morally bad or unjust laws are like counterfeit pound notes. They are not an unfortunate type of law; they are not genuine laws at all. *Lex injusta non est lex* is the Latin tag – unjust law is not law. Likewise, bad legal decisions, made by a tame or timorous judiciary, that have the effect of 'legitimating' unjust procedures are not properly legal decisions at all. Governments which have their powers ratified by corrupt procedures do not enjoy their power legitimately, and officers of the state whose evil doings are legitimated by the existent legal apparatus cannot defend their activities as legally valid. Crudely, the law cannot be conceptually or normatively isolated from the moral or 'natural' law. That is why, to cut a long story short, some commentators felt able to reject the decision of the Supreme Court in the case of the Bush election as *legally* invalid, although it was enunciated by the highest legal authority with jurisdiction in the case. These claims are plausible but very controversial. There is no need to examine them further here since we shall investigate moral legitimacy in the next section of this chapter.

A final mode of legal legitimacy is an external property of states that are recognized by other states or international agencies in accordance with international law. There are at least two different issues here, and I confess ignorance: I can give no detailed account of how they are settled in law and in practice. The first set of issues concern new (and sometimes, by implication, defunct) states. In our time, the chief mechanism for the formation of new states has been the break-up of empires and federations, both large and small – from the dissolution of the British Empire to the fragmentation of the USSR and modern Yugoslavia. This has resulted in the transformation of colonies and subject peoples into sovereign states, through the granting or seizing of independence in the case of colonies, and through civil war or peaceful secession movements in the other cases. A successful claim to independent statehood will involve the recognition of other states through declarations and treaties, sometimes in the face of opposition from the state claiming hegemony, sometimes with its cooperation. A definitive step in this process according to international law as expressed by the Charter of the United Nations will be the admission of the aspirant state to membership of the United Nations 'by a decision of the General Assembly upon the recommendation of the Security Council'.[9]

A different set of questions concerns the legal recognition by international agencies of specific governments as legitimate state powers. These questions are notoriously fraught during periods of civil war and its aftermath. Long after the dreadful dictator Pol Pot had been chased into the jungles of the Cambodian/Thailand border, his Khmer Rouge representatives were attending meetings of the United Nations in New York as accredited ambassadors – such were the consequences of the machinations of the Great Powers. Similar issues arise with respect to the so-called dysfunctional states, states without effective governments which have generally disintegrated into a cockpit of violent warlords. If there is no effective *de jure* monopoly of power, there can be no successful claim to legitimacy on the part of the government and external recognition will often be a quite arbitrary matter.

Moral legitimacy

We can put to one side the claim of the natural lawyer that there can be no legal legitimacy without moral legitimacy, for we can investigate directly the idea that a state or its government enjoys a moral legitimacy. The point of distinguishing legal and moral legitimacy is expressed by the thought that there are four possibilities here: a state or government or the exercise of power by officials may have:

(a) both legal and moral legitimacy;
(b) neither legal nor moral legitimacy;[10]
(c) legal but not moral legitimacy;
(d) moral but not legal legitimacy.

Obviously, the categories that need explanation if we are to grasp this distinction are (c) and (d). Before we examine further the concept of moral legitimacy, it will help if we can motivate the enquiry by finding examples of cases that plausibly fit into these categories.

It is straightforward to think of cases of governments that are legally legitimate (under at least one of the conceptions of legal legitimacy distinguished above) but not morally legitimate (with respect to at least one familiar criterion of moral legitimacy). Consider this case (which I am assured is legally impeccable, as with all legal advice): the sovereign power of the United Kingdom – the Queen in Parliament, i.e. Houses of Commons and Lords together with the monarch, passes legislation creating the new constitutional position of Great Moral Leader. The incumbent shall have the power of veto over proposed legislation on the basis of his elevated moral conscientiousness. (There is an obvious candidate since the post is created in recognition of the charismatic authority of the Great Moral Leader – it is not expected or provided for that the post will be advertised and continued after the demise of its first incumbent.) I take it that the government that is responsible for this legislation does not exceed its legal powers. I cannot think of constitutional rules which determine that such legislation is *ultra vires* or otherwise legally impermissible. On first inspection, such a constitutional provision does not violate the human rights of citizens. A state that establishes such a constitutional function is odd, to be sure, but it does not seem to violate its own rules (which, to the external observer, are in any case notoriously lax). We must conclude that the rulings of the Great Moral Leader – to permit or reject legislative proposals – are legitimate policy decisions and legally binding on officials and citizens. But suppose that at least one subject of this polity is a democrat who believes that it is a moral criterion of the legitimacy of the rulings of a state that they are the product of representative institutions, and further, that the position and occupant of the post of Great Moral Leader does not have sufficiently democratic credentials. On this basis the government which incorporates such a non-democratic intrusion will be judged to be morally illegitimate. In such a case the properties of legal and moral legitimacy come apart. Nothing hangs on whether or not the reader accepts the criterion of moral legitimacy applied in this case. The detail of the argument could be altered to meet any reasonable alternative criterion that might be put in its place.

Likewise we can describe cases where a government is legally illegitimate but morally legitimate. Suppose a state which enjoys popular support is suddenly faced by a devastating external threat. A neighbouring state is preparing to bomb and blockade the homeland in pursuit of a boundary dispute. Suppose further that the homeland cannot be effectively defended unless the state takes for itself emergency security powers that are strictly unconstitutional. Maybe the constitution should have made provision for legitimate emergency powers which otherwise violate important legal protections – of citizens' rights, for example – but it hasn't done so. And it hasn't time to rush the necessary enabling provisions through the legislature. In such a case, the government or its exercise of power is clearly legally illegitimate – technically, this is a usurpation. But suppose the population consents to these measures. There is no protest because the citizens generally accept that they are a prudent response to the emergency which threatens them all, and understand that a process of legislation can be set in train which will remedy the legal irregularity. The law can catch up later, people believe. This is an example of circumstances wherein there is legal illegitimacy and moral legitimacy (so long as one accepts, for the moment, that the consent of the citizens makes the decision morally legitimate).

In essence we should conclude that a state or government, its laws and the actions of subordinate institutions, is morally legitimate just in case there is an acceptable moral justification for these institutions and their activities. This is the familiar territory of political philosophy. Philosophers have discussed (and in consequence defended or rejected) a wide range of arguments intended to justify the state and particular forms of government constitution. They have investigated the moral probity of the exercise of specific powers by the officers of the state and they have specified limits to claims for legitimacy. Many of these arguments will surface as the central concerns of the chapters to follow.

The right to rule

Earlier, before we distinguished legal and moral legitimacy, we glossed the legitimacy of the state as the right to rule. So we can now make progress by investigating the right to rule. The notion of 'a right to rule' is both dangerous and promising. It is dangerous because the language of rights is philosophically controversial if not downright ambiguous. So these are issues where it is very easy to beg questions, not least because the strategy may well be viewed as one of explicating a reasonably clear concept (legitimacy) in terms of one that is much less clear (rights). Confusion threatens even more ominously since it is reasonable to believe that the paradigm bearer of rights is the individual person. Without denying that social groups or collectives can properly be rights bearers, we should note that assertions of group rights are to be treated with suspicion, not least because the point of postulating them has often been to subvert or to qualify the rights of the individual persons who are group members. And this possibility is barely concealed in the claim that a legitimate state has the right to rule. On the other hand, to speak of a right to rule is promising because rights are linked in well-known ways to duties. One thing that philosophers and jurisprudents have achieved is a range of careful classifications of rights. There is a conceptual apparatus, first articulated by Wesley Hohfeld for the case of legal rights, and expanded and widely used by his successors, which charts a variety of conceptual relations between rights and duties.[11] We should expect Hohfeld's distinctions to be a useful resource in relating the legitimacy of the state – the state's right to rule – to the duties of the citizens.

By implication, it looks as though the legitimate state might have a legal right to rule, a moral right to rule, or both of these. Take the first: to claim that the state has the legal right to rule might amount to some or all of the following:

(a) A Hohfeldian legal *privilege* or *liberty-right* is of this form: A has a legal privilege or liberty-right to ø if and only if A has no duty not to ø. The state has a legal privilege or liberty-right to perform some standard list of state functions. When, for example it makes laws forbidding specific activities and prescribing the (conditional) punishment of citizens it does no wrong. It has no duty not to do these things. On the other hand, nothing is implied concerning the legal duties of the citizens. They may or they may not have a legal duty to submit to the imposition of punishment. This will depend upon other features of the legal system. They would have such a duty if, for example, the law stated that it is legally forbidden to evade or escape duly prescribed punishment, but this is not entailed by the claim that the state has the liberty-right to rule. There are many cases where the exercise of state power bears no obvious relation to the legal duties of the citizen. States declare war and find sources of emergency assistance to foreigners in distress. The only duties in the offing are the contractual duties of officials of the state to administer these policies. *Vis-à-vis* other states the liberty-right to declare war is a legal element of the right to rule.

The claim that the right to rule is nothing more than a liberty-right should be understood as the weakest account of the legitimacy of the state, implying, as it does, no duties on the part of citizens. This minimalist doctrine of the legitimacy of the state has its source, in modern times, in one thread of argument in Thomas Hobbes's work. Hobbes's sovereign enjoys absolute power, an unlimited right to rule – 'he never wanteth Right to do anything . . . And therefore it may, and doth often happen in Common-wealths, that a Subject may be put to death, by the command of the Sovereign Power; and neither doe the other wrong' (Hobbes 1968: 265 [109]). Yet Hobbes insists that 'a Covenant not to defend my selfe from force, by force, is always voyd . . . no man can transferre, or lay down his Right to save himself from Death, Wounds, and Imprisonment' (Hobbes 1968: 199 [70]). It looks as though both parties are right in the contretemps wherein the sovereign orders the death (corporal punishment, imprisonment, etc.) of the citizen, and the citizen resists, rejecting any duty to submit. The implication of this, which Hobbes later spells out, is that the subject is at liberty to disobey the legitimate commands of the sovereign if he judges that his person will be put at risk should he comply.[12]

(b) A Hohfeldian legal *claim-right* is spelled out in terms of both the target and the content of the claim and is of this form: A has a right that B ø if and only if B has a duty (to A) to ø. Claim-rights are rights that others (B, the targets) do or forbear from doing something (ø, the content of the claim); thus they logically entail correlative duties on the part of those targets. It may be asserted that the state has a legal claim-right to rule. In international law this claim-right may be targeted at other states which propose to interfere in its jurisdiction – in which case their duty is one of non-intervention – but the prime focus for us is the case where the target is internal, the body of citizens. In this case, the legal duty that is entailed by the claim-right to rule is the duty of obedience or compliance. The central case is that of the criminal law and the prime duty which states have attributed to their citizens is the legal duty of all citizens to obey the law. I take it (ignoring worries from the camp of natural law) that this claim of the state is entirely non-controversial. This claim-right is expressed by the state's assertion that citizens have the legal duty to obey the prescriptive or proscriptive laws which it enacts, commanding or forbidding actions of some types in accordance with its right to rule. It is of course quite another matter whether or not citizens have a *moral* duty to obey the law, as we noticed in the last chapter.[13]

(c) A Hohfeldian legal power is a second-order right, a right to alter assignments of (other) legal rights and duties. It may be asserted that the state has the legal *power-right* to rule. The prime example of such a right is the power to legislate and thereby grant rights to and impose duties upon citizens. Although there are no correlative citizens' duties beyond those created by the state's subsequent use of its legal powers, citizens will generally have a legal duty not to interfere with or obstruct the state's exercise of its rights.

(d) The final Hohfeldian category of rights is that of the *immunity*, another second-order right bearing on the rights of others. Strictly, a legal immunity is the obverse of a legal power. A party has an immunity with respect to some action, object or status, if some other relevant party – in this context, another state or international agency, or citizen or group of citizens – has no (power) right to alter that party's legal standing in point of rights or duties in the specified respect. There is a wide range of legal immunities that may be invoked in the name of the right to rule. In international law, immunities may be created when states assert powers of derogation, as is permitted, for example, from the European Convention on Human Rights 'in times of war or other public emergency'.[14] Equally familiar examples include the immunities against prosecution granted to representatives (MPs or councillors) and government officials in pursuit of their duties. Such legal immunities may be suspect as potential violations of the rule of law, or regarded as quite proper, as necessary protections for the officers of the state in the rightful pursuit of their duties. In the United Kingdom, some exercises of the royal prerogative, which seems to give the government of the day opportunities for massive and unaccountable discretion, rightly come under suspicion, whereas the immunity from libel proceedings of Members of Parliament speaking in the House, or of persons giving evidence in a court of law, is generally regarded as an acceptable protection against powerful (and wealthy) interests who would otherwise constrain public debate or the administration of justice.

   Specification of this constellation of legal rights and concomitant duties spells out the content of the legal right to rule. To sum up, a state which is legally legitimate, in accordance with some positive criteria of legitimacy, has a legal right to rule, and the content of this legal right to rule can be spelled out in terms of a range of legal privileges, claim-rights, powers and immunities which entail that a concomitantly broad set of legal duties can be properly imputed to citizens. One will find that the detailed content of the right to rule will vary from state to state in accordance with the terms of the municipal legal system, but one can expect some central elements, notably the power-right to legislate for all citizens, and the liberty- or claim-right or power to punish lawbreakers, to be universal.[15]
   I shall take it that exactly the same formal moves may be made with respect to the moral legitimacy of the state. Thus, whatever criteria of moral legitimacy are in play, I think it will follow that the morally legitimate state will have a moral right to rule and that such a moral right can be further articulated in terms of the Hohfeldian schema. It will amount to the state's possession of a structured set of moral liberties, claim-rights, powers and immunities and the citizens' possession of the concomitant duties. To capture the sort of detail involved, consider only that specified legal rights may be described as moral rights if they are recognized as morally justified as well as legally valid. I have dwelt on the detail, albeit in a very sketchy and legally uninformed fashion, in order to prepare readers for the complexity to be encountered when we move on to

consider whether or not states which have a legal right to rule have a moral right to rule, since this latter moral right will invoke, by parity of reasoning, a similar range of moral duties imputed to citizens (as also to other states and international agencies in so far as these can have moral duties – we shall not take up these questions here).

To summarize the argument thus far: if a state or government is legally legitimate, it has the legal right to rule, which is to say that citizens have some set of corresponding legal duties to be specified in accordance with the jurisdiction of the particular municipal (state) powers. Likewise, if the state or government is morally legitimate, it has the moral rule right to rule, which is to say that citizens have some set of moral duties (still to be specified). Many would judge that the most important element of the state's right to rule (both legal and moral) is the power- or claim-right to make coercive laws, laws backed by a legal apparatus that can inflict punishment for non-compliance. Correspondingly, the most important element of the set of citizens' duties (both legal and moral) would be the duty to obey the laws enacted by the state under threat of punishment. I take it that all of the detail concerning the specification of the basis and terms of both legal and moral legitimacy, the detailed content of the state's legal and moral right to rule and the citizens' concomitant duties, will be controversial. But the formal position should be clear. The crucial questions concern the relations between legal legitimacy and moral legitimacy, between the state's legal right to rule and the moral right to rule, between the legal duties incumbent upon citizens as consequences of the state's exercise of its legal rights and the moral duties of citizens – the duties that they are morally obliged to accept.

As I see these matters, there are two directly opposed positions on the conceptual question of whether the state's *legal right* to rule entails that citizens have a set of *moral duties* corresponding to the legal duties which I have claimed (disregarding the worries of the natural lawyer) can be imputed to them. The first account has it that the citizens of a legally legitimate state, a state with the legal right to rule, do have a range of moral duties simply in virtue of that legitimacy. The most important of these is the moral duty to obey the law. The second position denies this. The legal standing of states and citizens is one thing, the pattern of moral governance is quite another.

I have laboured to present this question in its simplest and starkest form, because I believe that thus posed, the answer must be evident. As our previous example of the Great Moral Leader should suggest, the second of the two positions outlined above must be correct. So long as legal legitimacy is a formal matter of the state acting in accordance with its own legal rules or achieving international legal recognition, it must always be possible for the legitimate state, thus construed, to fail to meet substantial standards of moral legitimacy. As soon as one grants that the legal rules *may be* morally defective, that they *may* render legally permissible states of affairs that are morally unjust, it is perfectly possible to envisage circumstances wherein citizens can denounce the state as having no moral right to rule and disavow any imputation that they have moral duties towards it in virtue of its legal standing. Such a denunciation may be quite general, a rejection of the moral standing of the state and all its works, or it may be specific, a rejection of particular duties which the state seeks to impose.

If one accepts this conclusion one is presented with a different agenda for pursuing the philosophical questions that arise concerning the legitimacy of the state and the duties of the citizen. One abstracts altogether from the strictly legal standing of the two parties and investigates directly the moral credentials of the state and the moral duties of the citizen. Of course, if legal legitimacy is conceptually tied to moral legitimacy, as the natural law tradition insists, the possibility of a morally defective yet otherwise legal regime is logically excluded from the start, but the implication of this position is the same as we have reached from our discussion of the claims of positive law, namely that we can confine our investigations to the relationship between the state's moral legitimacy and the citizens' moral duties.

I should emphasize before we move on that nothing in this argument impugns the possibility that a regime with impeccable legal credentials might equally be morally legitimate, having a moral right to rule which is articulated in terms of a set of citizens' duties. Clearly what needs to be established are the grounds for such a judgement of moral probity. In the arguments that follow, readers should take it that when I speak of legitimacy, and of rights and duties, I have in mind moral legitimacy, moral rights and moral duties unless I specify otherwise.

We should also be aware that there are a number of recent philosophers who have severed the connection between questions of state legitimacy and questions of citizens' duty. I confess that I am very suspicious of this manoeuvre if it is formulated in a fashion that begs the question against the state having a claim-right against citizens in virtue of which they have prescribed duties.[16] The arguments I shall examine must be understood as equating the state's moral legitimacy with its moral authority, so that if the state is legitimate it should be understood to have authority, as specified in Chapter 3. And if the state is accepted as a practical authority with respect to the conduct of its citizens, it exercises its authority by prescribing duties to them.

The feeling for legitimacy

It might be thought that my formal and schematic account of the moral legitimacy of states is too 'legalistic' in a wider sense, depending as it does on the applicability and specification of a set of rules ascribing rights and duties to states and citizens. Rather, one may insist, the moral legitimacy of a state is a function of the sensibility of its citizens. This sense of legitimacy 'is meant to designate the beliefs and attitudes that members have toward the society they make up. The society has legitimacy when members so understand and value it that they are willing to assume the disciplines and burdens which membership entails. Legitimacy declines when this willingness flags or fails.'[17] This is a familiar idea. Peter Winch identifies this conception of legitimacy in Rousseau's writings and cites Simone Weil to similar effect:

After 1937, the government [of France] did not merely de facto abandon the forms of legality – that would not matter much, for the British government did the same, and yet there never was a British Prime Minister who was more legitimate than Winston Churchill – but the feeling for legitimacy was gradually extinguished. Practically no Frenchman approved of Daladier's usurpations. Practically no Frenchman became indignant about them. It is the feeling for legitimacy which makes one indignant about usurpations.[18]

So this account of legitimacy has impressive credentials.

Nonetheless, I think it is mistaken. In the first place, this may not be an alternative conception of legitimacy to the rule-based account I have developed – what Charles Taylor describes as 'the seventeenth century use of the term not to describe people's *attitudes*, but as a term for the objective evaluation of regimes' (Taylor 1994: 58). Such attitudes may be cited as evidence of the subjects' consent to the state to which they express their sentiments of loyalty. If so, one is applying perhaps the most familiar standard of legitimacy – the subject's consent – to the particular case. But suppose this is denied. This is not accepted as, at bottom, an argument from consent. Then the most obvious source of error is the conflation of legitimacy as a property of states or their governments with the sense or feeling for legitimacy that a people may exhibit. It certainly does not follow that a state is legitimate (or illegitimate) merely because its citizens believe it to be so, since they may believe wrongly both that an illegitimate state is legitimate and that a legitimate state is illegitimate. One of the lessons of the dismal twentieth century is that no state apparatus can be so awful that it is unable to garner the support of large segments of the population. Just as hostages come to love their captors, so too can subject peoples come to feel loyalty and allegiance to the tyrants that oppress them – the whole familiar, formidable process of engendering support being facilitated by the death, imprisonment or exile of recalcitrant voices and the demonization of alien persons and foreign states, nowadays, most conspicuously, the United States.

For an example, let me cite Suki Kim's account of a visit to North Korea in February 2002. Ms Kim visited Kim Il Sung University. She writes,

> it seemed not so different from most American schools. There was the familiar sight of students rushing about everywhere; girls in groups of three or four, laughing and chatting; boys trailing behind with bundles of books under their arms. Encouraged by the cheerful scene, I turned to Kim ['a third-year student of poetry named Kim Ok Kyung'] and asked what she wanted to do after graduation. With heartbreaking sincerity she answered, "I want to write poems worthy of our Great Leader".
>
> (Kim 2003: 16)

It would be reasonable to conclude from this story that poor benighted Kim Ok Kyung believes that there is a legitimate government in North Korea. If so, I would disagree with her for, amongst other reasons, I believe the regime to be cruel and unjust. The dispute is not to be settled by investigating what many North Koreans happen to (falsely) believe.

It looks as though we have enough conceptual apparatus in place to tackle substantive philosophical questions concerning the grounds on which political duties can be imputed to citizens. Such grounds will specify the conditions of the state's moral legitimacy and the content of its moral right to rule. Unfortunately, if we move on to address these questions directly we shall finesse an important challenge to any account of state legitimacy that arises from the employment of a concept that we have barely mentioned – the concept of political authority.

Chapter 3

Political authority

The peculiar problem of authority

Folks speak indiscriminately of legitimate power, legitimate states, legitimate government and legitimate authority, and so one might think that issues concerning the grounds for judgements of legitimacy are the same in each case. I don't think the folk are wrong in employing these loose equivalences, but they have to be scrutinized and defended since there are many philosophers who mark important distinctions hereabouts. In particular, they argue (or it is a clear implication of their arguments)[1] that there can be, indeed are, legitimate states which do not possess any authority over their subjects. Legitimacy and authority are different normative properties.

One swift way of marking such a distinction is to employ the Hohfeldian apparatus that we outlined in Chapter 2. Thus to say that a state is legitimate but has no authority is to say that its right to rule is a mere *liberty-right*, i.e. it may properly command its subjects to behave in this or that fashion by making laws or by licensing its functionaries to give subjects directives, but this does not imply that subjects have any correlative duties to obey. Of course there may be plenty of reasons why they should comply with the state's commands. Subjects may comply because they believe that what the state commands is, in any case, the right thing to do. Quite generally they may be motivated to comply with the state's directives because otherwise they would be liable to sanctions (to be realistic, we must take it that the legitimate state has the concomitant liberty-right to inflict punishment on those subjects who disobey). But these reasons for obedience do not include the mere fact that the legitimate state has thus commanded them. By contrast, the state that has authority makes *claim-rights* against its subjects, which is to say that subjects have duties to comply with the state's commands in virtue of its right to command them.

We shall examine the possibility that legitimate states may have no authority in Chapter 6 when we discuss philosophical anarchism. For the moment we need to get clearer about authority. To test whether legitimate states are equally bearers of authority we need to analyse the concept of authority with a great deal of care. We shall find that our use of the concept of authority brings with it a whole nest of philosophical difficulties. Some have identified a paradox of authority. As we shall see, there is no paradox here; rather there is a very peculiar problem raised by a (near) universal human proclivity towards obedience which humans are proud to deny.

We can broach these questions by presenting a pair of conflicting observations. We react to claims of authority with both suspicion and deference. With respect to the attitude of suspicion, let us look at a famous argument from Robert Paul Wolff's (1976) In Defense of Anarchism. First there is an account of authority. A state that claims authority claims a right to command understood as a right to obedience from the subjects addressed by the command. These subjects have a

> correlative obligation *to obey the person who issues the command* . . . Obedience is not a matter of doing what someone tells you to do. It is a matter of doing what someone tells you to do *because he tells you to do it*.
>
> (Wolff 1976: 9, emphasis in original)

Second, there is an account of autonomy. The fundamental assumption of moral philosophy is that persons have freewill, and, being rational, are responsible for their actions, which is to say that they are autonomous:

> The autonomous man, insofar as he is autonomous, is not subject to the will of another. He may do what another tells him, but not *because* he has been told to do it. He is therefore, in the political sense of the word, *free*.
>
> (ibid.: 14, emphasis in original)

The conclusion is swift and inevitable: there is an irresolvable conflict between authority and autonomy.

> Insofar as a man fulfils his obligation to make himself the author of his decisions, he will resist the state's claim to have authority over him. That is to say, he will deny that he has a duty to obey the laws of the state *simply because they are the laws*.
>
> (ibid.: 18, emphasis in original)

For the moment I shall put to one side discussion of this elegant argument, because I want to draw attention to an important feature of it. I find Wolff's portrayal of the autonomous agent as freely examining the commands of authority to determine whether or not he will comply deeply attractive. Wolff sternly tells us that the autonomous exercise of the rational will is a duty, but I take his instruction as a compliment, a recognition of my moral capacities. I can't quite say that I hug myself at the prospect of moral athleticism but I find the implication – that I should inspect the credentials and deliverances of authority, challenging it when I smell a rat – strongly appealing. There is a radical, 'Bolshie', side to my nature which this argument quickens. More importantly, I suspect that I am not alone, that many other inheritors of the traditions of liberalism feel likewise. Wolff's powerful argument draws artfully on more than Kant's moral philosophy; I believe it articulates, not to say flatters, a central element of the self-image of modern citizens.

By contrast, however, there is evidence to suggest that this self-image is flawed, that we are not the sturdy moral individuals it portrays. In a famous experiment described in *Obedience to Authority* (1974) Stanley Milgram attempted to test subjects' willingness to obey authority.[2] The 'authorities' were university staff in appropriate uniform ('grey technician's coats') in their natural habitat (a laboratory setting). Milgram briefly describes the experiment in these terms:

> a person comes into a laboratory and, in the context of a learning experiment is told to give increasingly severe electric shocks to another person – who, unknown to the subject is a confederate, and does not actually receive the shocks. This arrangement provided an opportunity to see how far people would go before they refused to follow the experimenter's orders.
>
> (Milgram 1987: 568–9)

The appalling upshot was that many experimental subjects inflicted step by step what they perceived as increasingly serious pain upon the actors who kept making errors. Many did so reluctantly, some did so to their own evident distress. But they continued to inflict the pain because they were told to do so by persons they took to stand in a position of authority and they were disposed to obey the instructions.

Milgram's experiment does surely reveal something that any observant and self-aware reader must suspect – that we are much more ready to obey the commands of authority than it is comfortable for us to concede. The most optimistic conclusion is that most of us are nothing like so disrespectful of authority as we would like ourselves to be, nothing like the potential subversives with whom we smugly identify when we give Wolff's argument an initial sympathetic hearing. The most dire conclusion is that, far from being suspicious of authority, many of us embrace it. We flee from our pretensions of autonomy and radical freedom into the arms of anyone who looks as though they might be in the position of telling us what to do. Milgram concluded that '[T]his research showed that many people do not have the resources to resist authority, even when they are directed to act callously and inhumanely against innocent victims'.[3]

The varieties of authority

One important lesson for philosophers to learn from this portrayal of our conflicted nature is that we need to understand more clearly the authority relation. We can begin by studying the familiar view that there are two radically distinct varieties of authority – which is not to say that philosophers have not been able to elide them or to confuse them or to explain one of them in terms of the other. The first kind of authority is best thought of as *practical authority*. It is the authority of one who commands or gives orders or instructions. Examples abound: the authority of the teacher over the pupil, the parent over the child, the officer over the common soldier, as well as our central interest – the authority of the state and its officials over the citizens. It is dubbed practical authority because the directives generally order subjects to do or omit something, to act or forebear acting in some way or other, although we shall have to be more precise about this. The second kind of authority we should think of as *epistemic authority* or the authority of the expert. An authority of this kind is in command of a field of knowledge or a range of skills. We seek out such authorities for help and advice. If we wish to know what we should believe on a topic of which we are ignorant, or how we should perform a task we are finding difficult, it's good policy to find someone whose response we can take as authoritative. We appeal to authority to display that our beliefs are justified – 'Aristotle hath said it', as they used to say – or that our methods are sound. The nub of this distinction is the difference between commands or orders on the one hand and the giving of information or advice on the other.[4]

It is easy to see how this distinction can be elided. First, we are familiar with, and shall later encounter in some detail, attempts to justify practices of authority which emphasize the need for problems to be solved and decisions to be taken. It is just as well if those who are granted authority in order to solve the problems that co-existence throws up are good at the job, having some sort of expertise. This puts the case at its most general. Authorities don't need to be philosopher-kings of the sort that Plato describes, trained in the highest intellectual skills. But if exercising authority is the kind of thing that can be done better or worse, with more or less competence, it is likely that the finest rulers will display some authority of the epistemic sort as well as the formal standing of being in a position to issue orders to their subjects. In the university this conflation of practical and epistemic authority is most neatly seen when those in positions of practical authority (*Herr Professor & co.*) cite their academic credentials to justify their normative standing to subordinate colleagues and students. It is of course a very controversial matter how far professional political representatives, members of parliament and the like, typically display any of the epistemic authority that should merit the respect of subjects.

Second, it is not as though an authority of the first practical kind simply tells us what to do, whereas the second kind of authority tells us what to believe. Authorities of both kinds tell us what to do and how to do it. The expert bridge player may tell us how to play a hand of cards, the expert carpenter may give us instructions on how to construct a table. The expert on etiquette will tell us which knives and forks to use for which dishes and how to address letters to bishops. I suspect that the expert ethicist employed by the hospital will instruct doctors on how they should treat their patients. Yet these are all epistemic authorities in the wide sense that I gave to this term. To make matters worse, it may be that practical authorities can command belief. This is a puzzling business, as many have seen. On the one hand, there are deep philosophical difficulties in the idea that beliefs are subject to will, the will of the believer or some second party. It has been argued with great plausibility that a subject can't just choose or decide to believe something (Williams 1973). Belief in a proposition that demands reflection somehow emerges from the balance of reasons, taking over its passive subscriber. If so (and even if it isn't; if contrariwise one chooses not to believe what one is told to believe) it makes no sense for an authority to command, or worse, coerce belief, as Hobbes saw: 'because Beleef and Unbeleef never follow mens Commands' (Hobbes 1968: 527 [271]). But on the other hand, the fact that it makes no sense for authorities to do these things has never stopped them trying, and it may be that there are cases where one should judge that they have succeeded, not withstanding the neat philosophical argument sketched above. What is one to think of the instructions given by religious leaders on matters of doctrine? Hobbes insists that those who claim to speak in the word of God have the authority to *teach* but not to *coerce*, but the popes and imams may not see things this way and nor may the faithful whose beliefs they command. And practical authorities may be devious as well as direct. They may induce belief (true or false) by using their authority to manipulate the conditions under which subjects form their beliefs. Minimally they may spin, maximally they may brainwash.

Further, these latter examples should demonstrate that many authorities function in both practical and epistemic roles. The state commands but it also makes information available so that subjects may better decide how to behave. ('Smoking Kills', cigarette packets instruct us.) The state initiates research, publishes reports, and staffs or subsidizes expert institutes to which citizens may resort for the knowledge or skills that they need. And to make matters more confusing, in addition to giving commands and issuing advice the state may authoritatively make requests of citizens and subordinate authorities.[5] Indeed a policy as important and far-reaching as the abolition of the 11 Plus examination and the introduction of comprehensive education in England and Wales was initiated by way of a circular (1965) from the Secretary of State for Education and Science, Anthony Crosland, to Local Education Authorities *requesting* them to submit plans for the reorganization of schooling in their areas and to bid for consequent additional funding. (The *request* was more or less forceful as the education authorities stood in need of extra funds to fulfil their responsibilities. For most this was an offer they could not refuse.) What is true of the state is true of many other structures of authority – parents and teachers inform, instruct and request youngsters as well as commanding or forbidding specific activities and they do these things on the basis of their knowledge and expertise. In the armed forces where raw young officers often command experienced troops I understand this is a grey area.

The nature of practical authority

Notwithstanding this widespread overlap in roles and functions, the authority of the commander is of a different kind from the authority of the expert, although many philosophers have pointed to similarities. To fully understand the core aspect of political authority we should seek a fuller account of practical authority. H.L.A. Hart and Joseph Raz have done most valuable work in this area. Following Hart we should say that the authority of the commander is captured by the formal properties of the reasons for action constituted by his commands. Such commands are binding on those they address, are peremptory and content-independent (Hart 1982: 23–68). To say that the commands or directives of practical authorities are binding on subjects is to say more than that they simply apply to them. It is to echo a Kantian thought, though in a more restricted context. Kant argues that moral laws bind in a categorical fashion, contrasting categorical and hypothetical imperatives. The latter, hypothetical imperatives operate conditionally (and mostly contingently) on the desires or inclinations of the subject. Thus 'Carry an umbrella' is a reason for action only if one wishes to stay dry or look smart. By contrast categorical imperatives apply to the subject willy-nilly – universally and unconditionally. In a similar fashion, the commands of a practical authority are deemed to apply to subjects on the basis of the normative relationship in which the subjects stand to the authority irrespective of whatever desires and inclinations they may have concerning the subject matter of the directives. Authoritative commands cannot be cast off or repudiated as applicable reasons for action simply on the basis of 'I don't want to do that', as all children learn to their cost or benefit sooner or later.[6] (Straightaway this yields a contrast with advice; if one doesn't want to do what one is advised to do, that's that. One doesn't *have to do it*. If the advice is expert one may well be imprudent or silly, but that may be the limit of one's wrong-doing.) To say that the commands of legitimate authorities are binding is to grant that they have some moral force, hence that, other things equal, one does wrong who fails to comply. It is over-ambitious to insist that such commands have absolute moral force in the manner of Kantian moral laws. Many political philosophers have discussed the weaker claim that the laws of the state are binding *prima facie*, i.e. defeasible in principle (though they may still have significant moral force).[7]

The binding quality of authoritative commands is further explained by their peremptory character. They are peremptory in that they cut off 'deliberation, debate or argument' (Hart 1982: 253). A different way of putting this point is to say, with Joseph Raz, that such commands operate as exclusionary or pre-emptive reasons.[8] The essential feature of peremptory commands is the way they feature in the logic of the practical reasoning of the subject. Take the standard background condition as one wherein the subject has reasons for and against performing a given action, say, a soldier contemplating whether or not to advance. A successful advance will eliminate a threat to his own and fellow soldiers' lives. Yet it will expose him to more danger than remaining in the trench. And so on . . . If the officer gives the order to advance, the order does not feature as another reason to weigh in the balance, not even as a decisive reason which will always tip the balance of reasons in favour of compliance. If the order is the directive of an authority, this means that the reasons hitherto assembled as pro and con just do not count.

There will generally be a psychological correlate of this structure of practical reasoning. Suppose a soldier were in fact deliberating on what he should do, assembling and weighing reasons pro and con. Just as soon as an order is given, the reasoning becomes otiose. Deliberation, if there were any, is cut short, debate is misconceived, and argument misses the point. The order, given that it is authoritative, determines how the soldier ought to behave. Of course, the fact that an order has been given can't stop the soldier continuing to deliberate the question of what is the best thing to do if he is so-minded. The point rather is that the order has the effect of making the process of reasoning academic, in the unfortunate sense of that term. It no longer counts as practical reason directed towards action. How the soldier should act has been determined by the order he has been given.

Political authority has the same feature. If directives such as laws or the instructions of properly warranted officials (including army officers as described above) are authoritative, then, of their nature they determine what citizens ought to do, irrespective of whatever reasons they may independently have for or against the course of action they have been commanded to take. If this judgement is thought implausibly severe, remember: nothing in the argument so far has committed us to the conclusion that there *are* any such authorities. To establish this conclusion we would need to outline the sort of argument that might justify a claim to authority thus characterized and, further, show that this argument serves to justify some specific claim to authority. Such a project might fail at either the first or the second stages. As we have seen, Wolff believes that no argument can serve because any such success would compromise the autonomy of citizens. Others might deny this yet believe that no earthly government could satisfy the conditions necessary for citizens to concede its authority.

The final condition that Hart mentions is 'content-independence'. Authoritative commands 'are intended [and should be taken] to function as a reason [for action] independently of the nature or character of the actions to be done' (Hart 1982: 254). Hart contrasts this with standard cases where there is an obvious connection between the reason for action and the action to be done, e.g. the action is a means to some end specified as a reason for performing it. The officer may shout 'Advance' or 'Stay put'; in either case the soldiers' reason for advancing or staying put will be exactly the same: that was what they were ordered to do. Their reason for doing what they do when they obey orders does not bear directly on the content of what they are to do, whatever that happens to be. They must just do what they are told.

Peremptoriness and content-independence, thus construed, may be judged to yield quite unacceptable consequences. If the point of relationships of authority is to get subjects to do what they are told willy-nilly, to adopt operative reasons for action peremptorily, 'independently of the nature or character of the actions to be done', they should be treated with very great suspicion as Wolff saw. 'I was only following orders' is a familiar excuse and is often treated with derision. Yet we are order-following, authority-submissive creatures as Milgram demonstrated, so it behoves us to establish as carefully as we can whether there might be anything other than a dismal pathology underpinning authority relations as we have characterized them. If one accepts that the commands of all authorities are peremptory and content-independent, and understands that to mean that the subjects of authority are required to obey commands *whatever* their content, pre-empting *any* deliberation they might conduct on the substance of the matter, it is quite clear that no rational person will accept that there are practical authorities in any sphere. If content-independence is construed as integral to authority in this totally blank-cheque fashion, it is obvious that no rational subject can regard the commands of authority as peremptory. Thus construed, authoritative directives cry out for deliberative appraisal, and for that deliberation to count as a process of genuine practical reason.

Robert Paul Wolff was challenging the claims of the state to political authority, but we can see, if practical authority is characterized quite generally in terms of the peremptory and content-independent qualities of its binding directives, that the critique of authority cuts much deeper than the challenge of the philosophical anarchist to the state. It suggests that there is something fundamentally irrational in any practice wherein deferment to authority requires subjects to ignore the balance of reasons as this features in processes of practical reason. Of course, deferment to authority is perfectly reasonable in cases (as with children) where ignorance or impaired rationality preclude the subject's own rational deliberation and determination. But in all other cases authority seems to usurp the claims of fully rational agency.

Faced with this challenge, the justification of authority is a stiff task and there are plenty of philosophers who believe that it cannot be accomplished successfully in the particular case of the authority of the state. My intention in the rest of this chapter is to prepare the ground for a defence of practical authority, and in particular the authority of the state, by demonstrating that the related properties of peremptoriness and content-independence of authoritative directives are not as threatening as they first appear.

The domain of authority

The thesis of content-independence becomes less alarming if it is qualified, if we reflect that authority relationships are always features of identifiable social practices[9] and circumscribed within some specifiable domain. Let me explain the notion of a domain. I take it that all authority relations are triadic, holding between an authority, a subject or group of subjects, and a domain, and articulated by a schema of the form:

a has authority over *b* with respect to [some domain] *c*.[10]

Thus for example an army officer (*a*) may order the soldiers (*b*) to advance or retreat (*c*) – advancing and retreating are activities which are within the domain of the instructing officer.

I claim that the proper domain of any authority is limited. I can't claim this as a conceptual point since I can easily imagine a religious enthusiast popping up to tell me that the authority of God is unlimited. He has the authority to order me to do things which are [otherwise?] immoral or just plain silly, to command me to slaughter my first-born son or to forbid my eating cabbages. Such a claim to unrestricted authority doesn't strike me as conceptually flawed, though I believe it would be very hard to defend. So let us say that all earthly authorities operate within a circumscribed domain, a domain restricted by conditions that establish boundaries intended to determine the propriety of orders as *intra-* or *ultra vires*.

This idea should be very familiar to members of the armed services and those who observe them. John Locke gives us a good example:

> [Y]et we see, that neither the Serjeant, that could command a Souldier to march up to the mouth of a Cannon, or stand in a Breach, where he is almost sure to perish, can command that soldier to give him one penny of his Money.
>
> (Locke 1960: Ch. XI, §139)

The rules of war tell us that army officers who command their soldiers to kill innocent civilians do so without authority and the soldiers have no duty to comply. Schoolteachers in a secular educational system who instruct their pupils to say their prayers before they go to sleep every night exceed their authority. Parents find that as soon as their children come to understand that all claims to authority come with boundary conditions attached the battle to establish and subvert those conditions is engaged. Parents do or do not have the right to tell their children what they should wear, what they should eat, what time they should come home or go to bed, depending on the children's age and maturity, and if one thing is certain it is that there are no agreed rules hereabouts until permissions are granted and the rules are regarded as otiose by both parties.

The specification of *intra/ultra vires* conditions to authority is a parochial exercise which varies from authority to authority as religions, armed forces, schools and families vary in the content and stringency of their rules. In each case the specification of what matters are within and what matters outwith the domain of a particular authority is of crucial importance. Rules are sometimes clear, often not; sometimes explicit, often not. I daresay, for example, that Locke's case of the *ultra vires* command to the soldier to hand over money to his commanding officer is just about universal amongst armed services yet is nowhere specified as one of the things that officers cannot do. No doubt such conduct on the part of a commanding officer would be found to violate some catch-all rule proscribing conduct which is unbecoming to an officer, or conduct not designed to promote the furtherance of Her Majesty's purposes. These things are surely true of orders given by the office-holders who claim political authority, and we shall have more to say on this topic later.

If it is correct that all earthly authorities operate within the fixed boundaries of some specifiable domain, it follows that the peremptory and content-independent character of authoritative commands has to be understood differently. Directives have a peremptory character only when it is clear that they are *intra vires*. If it is obvious that they are not, or if the issue of whether the commander is acting within his proper authority is raised as moot, then the directives cannot have peremptory force. Similarly, the thesis of content-independence should be understood to operate only within an accepted domain. If it is obvious that the content of a directive does not respect the proper domain within which authority should be exercised, or if the issue is thought to be controversial, the matter of appropriate content should be examined.

Domain-limiting principles

Are there any principles which limit *all* claims to authority, which circumscribe *all* putative domains? I can think of several principles which might operate in this way.

Immorality

The most obvious principle is that:

> commands which require subjects to violate moral principles or otherwise to act immorally are void.[11]

Such a command could have none of the binding force that the directives of authority essentially carry. This looks self-evident in the case of moral authorities (if there be any) or political authority (in so far as this is a type of moral authority). Let us accept the presumption that acting in accordance with authority is the right thing to do, or at least is morally defensible. We should remember that 'I was following orders' *is* a satisfactory defence in standard cases. But since orders are void if they require subjects to act in ways that are morally wrong for independent reasons, in these circumstances 'I was only following orders' fails to exculpate the obedient subject from the charge of wrong-doing, though it will also certainly implicate the authoritative superior who delivered the orders in the crime that was committed. It cannot be right (in virtue of an authority relation) to perform an action that is otherwise wrong. This is exactly where the subjects in Milgram's experiment went astray. They forgot, or failed to understand, that their compliance with the university authorities should cease just as soon as it is clear that what they are doing is morally wrong. Likewise, it is always morally wrong for the soldiers to shoot the prisoners, notwithstanding the order of their superior officer. In this way authority works like promise-giving and unlike consent. Promises are (generally, if not always) void if they are promises to do wrong, or if doing wrong is the only way to fulfil them, whereas consent (as we shall see later) can transform what is otherwise morally wrong (e.g. punching a fellow in the face) into something which is morally permissible (boxing).

This is a clear enough view but it invites an objection. Grant that it is wrong to break down a door and invade someone's private property. What are we to say of cases where a duly authorized police officer forcibly enters someone's house in order to release a hostage? This certainly looks like a case of a person doing something that is otherwise wrong but which is vindicated by the fact that the person was commanded (or authorized) to do so by a legitimate authority acting within its proper domain. To make this clear let us suppose that the officer had a legal warrant. I suggest that we view matters in a different way: moral principles are rarely simple and generally subject to qualifying clauses. So we should expect the legal rules governing the ownership of private property to encode complex moral judgements which assert the legitimacy of invading private property in specifiable circumstances. Thus it is not the fact that the police officer has been commanded to forcibly enter the property or is in possession of a legal warrant that converts what is otherwise wrong into an action that is permissible. The police officer is authorized to do so because releasing the hostage is the right thing for him to do, all things considered. We should expect the law of private property to recognize derogations from citizens' rights which permit forcible entry by legal warrant or otherwise *in extremis*, in just the way that fire officers break down doors without permission in order to save lives.

It should be obvious that here we have entered a very tricky area of applied ethics, and one might expect many grey areas and controversial decisions. My discussion of these contrasting examples demonstrates that a full account of the concept of authority would need to follow Hobbes in chapter 16 of *Leviathan* and study the related concept of authorization. More specifically, it demonstrates the importance for an investigation of political authority and the modes in which this is transmitted to subordinate agencies of spelling out the detailed boundary conditions of that authority's proper domain.

Harm to self

We should consider a second putatively universal boundary condition, not least because it has a curious (and celebrated) pedigree. Thomas Hobbes, as we have seen, argues that subjects are not obliged to comply with authorities' commands to the point of putting themselves at risk of death or serious harm. This implies (although the attribution of the implication to Hobbes is mistaken) that:

> *authorities may not legitimately direct their subjects to put life and limb at risk.*[12]

Citizens may properly resist such a command or, in the case of conscription, substitute another to take their place. G.W.F. Hegel rejects this.

> The substantial essence [of the modern state] does not consist unconditionally in the protection and safeguarding of the lives and property of individuals as such. The state is rather that higher instance which may even itself lay claim to the lives and property of individuals and require their sacrifice [in time of war].
>
> (Hegel 1991: §100R; also §§ 70, 323–6)

But, Hegel insists, the state is the *only* authority that can require a subject's self-sacrifice.

I am willing to concede that it is illegitimate for an authority to command subjects to destroy themselves. Socrates famously was ordered to put himself to death by drinking the hemlock potion. But I suspect that the reason why I believe this is that I don't accept that any political authority has the right to kill its subjects as punishment for their wrong-doing. If, by contrast, one were to grant that capital punishment were legitimate, the oddity of a practice of requiring subjects to kill themselves lies in the sanction for non-compliance. This would have to be at least as bad as the alternative, and would presumably take the form of the state doing the job for those who were unwilling to do it for themselves. Maybe there is a point to the strange practice of self-administered punishment. Perhaps it is a mercy or a sign of respect to offer such unfortunates the choice of administering the poison to themselves. But I am happy to leave discussion of the pros and cons of the matter to those who fantasize over possible regimes of capital punishment – of whom there have been sadly many.

More to the point, we should recognize that the Hobbesian restriction is curiously limiting in the modern world, given our familiarity with the practice of authorities requiring their subjects to accept the risk of death and (the certainty of) serious harm. No state would restrain itself from claiming the power to conscript citizens into the armed services in time of war, thus hazarding their lives. Military authorities, whilst not actually commanding their troops to die, will order them into the breach or over the top in circumstances where the chances of survival are extremely low. All states seriously harm those citizens whom they punish severely, and many citizens regard the imposition of high taxation or the implementation of planning decisions as seriously harmful to them. I suspect that if one were to propose that the state or subordinate authorities must accept that a strong possibility of death or serious harm operates as a universal restriction on their authority, one would be left with political authorities that are unrecognizable in the modern world. (Of course this would not faze the classical anarchist who emphasizes the harmfulness of the state institution.)

Since I endorse (but do not here argue for) Hegel's point that the state is the only institution which can plausibly claim the authority to oblige citizens to engage in activities which carry the risk of death or serious harm, the question of whether there is a universal domain restriction in play here cannot be settled independently of reviewing the substantial arguments in favour of citizens' acceptance of a sovereign authority. If it turns out that there may be good reasons why the rational subject should endorse an authority which possesses such fearsome powers – so be it. Thus if, for example, it transpires that the best way to preserve one's life is to put that life at risk in particular circumstances – to accept a liability to capital punishment or conscription – one would reject such a restriction on the domain of political authority.[13]

Absurdity

There is a third possible universal boundary condition limiting all authorities' claims to obedience:

subjects need not obey any commands that are palpably absurd, pointless or trivial.[14]

The remit of any authority runs no further than is recognized by common sense. This condition can be put to good work in defence of the claim that authoritative commands are peremptory and content-independent, since it is an obvious objection to this thesis that whether or not a command is absurd or pointless is surely relevant to whether a subject should comply. Sensible citizens, it is claimed, do not recognize a moral duty of any substantial weight not to run a stop sign at two o'clock in the morning, although the state requires them not to do so.[15] And if the absurdity or pointlessness of the content of the directive is relevant to the issue of whether a subject should comply, this compromises the claim that the commands of authority are peremptory and content-independent, since the apparent absurdity or pointlessness of a command calls for the subject to reflect on the matter of whether the command should be complied with on the basis of its content.

It is possible that this challenge can be met in much the same way as the challenge that folk should always investigate the content of putatively authoritative directives whenever compliance appears to require conduct that is palpably immoral. Just as we argued that commands to perform immoral actions were *ultra vires*, so we could claim that absurd or pointless directives are so, too. This is a difficult route to take. Of course the commands of a Mad King George or a Red Queen will be inspected with very great care, but then none of their commands is likely to carry authority.

First we need to distinguish a straightforwardly absurd or pointless directive from a directive that is absurd or pointless only in the specific circumstances of a particular case. For straightforwardly absurd directives, I refer readers to Suetonius' *Lives of the Caesars*, particularly his accounts of the regimes of Caligula and Nero. Here you will find many non-controversial examples of genuine idiocy – which is not to deny that plenty of prudent citizens readily complied with the lunatic commands. I shall assume that such cases are straightforwardly *ultra vires*.

The sort of cases that have figured in the literature concern rules wherewith compliance is sensible for the most part but not universally, for example, rules designed to achieve the safety of pedestrians that have little point between two and six o'clock in the morning, as mentioned above. But readers can work out for themselves why crude and simple directives may often be better than flexible instruments in this area of human activity. Really stupid or pointless directives from otherwise respectable regimes tend to be rules that are applied mistakenly or are out of date. Imagine that the road works have been completed, yet the traffic speed notices have not been altered. Drivers are still required to drive at 30 mph on the (now clear) motorway. I suspect that as soon as drivers realize that there is an error in the signage, they will ignore it and it's not obvious that they are wrong to do so. In similar fashion, had it been immediately obvious that 'someone had blunder'd', as Tennyson put it, then the command to charge the enemy guns should not have had peremptory force and the Charge of the Light Brigade would have been called off.

We have not yet solved the problem, however, since we are left with a couple of conflicting intuitions: first we have a general claim that the directives of authority are peremptory and content-independent only within the bounds of evident reasonableness, and that absurd or pointless commands are outside the domain of any authority. Yet surely it must be one of the main aims of employing a regime of authoritative directives precisely to exclude deliberation (and consequent self-directed exemption) on those grounds. There is a spectrum of cases between the absurd and the sensible, and an authority that is considerate of the lives and well-being of its citizens will gold-plate rules of the road and many other regulations in accordance with a precautionary principle which protects them from unreliable fellows who have devised cunning plans. But in the second place, and by contrast, one feels that if it is blindingly obvious that the commander has blundered, then a review of the directive is called for and its content must be carefully examined. A problem of similar structure may be raised concerning the 'immorality' domain restriction. Can we resolve this tension?

In the background here is a more general problem that we can usefully bring into the open. What looks to be a problem for authoritative directives has long been recognized to be a difficulty with almost any set of rules.[16] This shouldn't be surprising since many authoritative directives themselves constitute the imposition of rules – the practice of legislation, notably. There is a very limited set of rules which are absolutely mandatory in the sense that compliance is so integral to the activity they regulate that they just cannot be permissibly broken. You can't move a pawn backwards at chess and still be playing the same game. If such moves were permissible, you would be playing a different game. For the rest, we can easily recall or imagine circumstances wherein it is prudent or right to break a rule. Sometimes difficulties of this sort will have been anticipated and the rule itself qualified, but it is unrealistic to attempt to protect the integrity of a rule by introducing qualifications intended to anticipate every conceivable circumstance in which a violation might be judged legitimate. And there is surely a limit to the degree of complexity that can be introduced into the statement of a rule if it is to operate peremptorily in the psychological sense, finessing deliberation. Rules cannot operate as effective substitutes for onerous exercises of practical reason if successfully following them requires much careful thought on the part of those who are subject to them.

If this is true, it looks as though the subject of any regime of rules must be reflectively schizophrenic – acting as the rules dictate without further reflection yet being alert to circumstances in which breaking the rules is the right thing to do. Does this fact suggest a deep philosophical incoherence, contradiction or paradox in the very concept of an authoritative command or rule, or does it represent an uncomfortable feature of a world that is meant to try us, a real practical difficulty, but one we can live with? I suggest that the latter is the truth of the matter, because it is not *always* difficult for an otherwise committed rule follower to identify an occasion when breaking the rule is opportune and correct. Sometimes it is obvious that the right thing to do is to break the rule and that one can permissibly do this without the force of the rule being significantly weakened.[17] There must be countless examples. Here is one I recall because incredibly and shockingly, as reported, rules of public decency as voiced by a troupe of Afrikaaner matrons on a South African beach triumphed over common sense and the poor casualty died: touching a woman's breasts without her consent is ruled an impermissible assault, but if she is unconscious and requires urgent resuscitation the rescuer should just get on with the business of pressing down hard on her chest. Doubtless there are also countless cases where the matter is quite unclear. These are the cases that are meant to try us. But the fact that there are clear cases suggests that committed rule-following need not entail general moral obtuseness. One can perfectly well go through life following the rules dictated by an appropriate authority and yet be brought to a sharp stop when the moral or prudential alarm bells ring. I take it that this is a fact of our moral experience. This gives us no reason at all to believe that the alarm bells are going to go off so frequently that the rule becomes useless, or that there might not on occasion be a false alarm.

In the same manner that one can respect a rule yet violate it if the circumstances dictate that it would be absurd to follow it in the present case, so too one can respect an authority even though it would be absurd in the circumstances to comply with its instructions. In neither case does one deny or subvert practical authority quite generally. Despite the difficulties of the position, I am inclined to judge that it is a universal boundary condition on authoritative directives that they not be absurd or pointless, that it not be manifestly unreasonable to follow them in the circumstances. I conclude, in respect of all authorities, that they are circumscribed by general boundary conditions which restrict their proper domains to exclude directives which prescribe immoral or absurd actions.

Unlimited authority?

If all authorities are limited by the domain restrictions which proscribe immoral and absurd or clearly unreasonable commands, so too are political authorities. They will be constrained by the universal restrictions we have discussed above as well as by specific restrictions judged proper for the specifically political domain. This claim appears to be more controversial than it ought to be. There is a common belief to the effect that many political authorities claim unlimited authority, so we need to demonstrate either that this belief is false or, should political authorities indeed claim unlimited authority, that their claim is unfounded .

Joseph Raz states that 'in most contemporary societies the law is the only human institution claiming unlimited authority'.[18] His evidence is that English constitutional theory has it that Parliament 'can make or unmake law, on any matter, and to any effect whatsoever'. And even where, as in the United States, there is a Constitution which limits the legislative power of the Congress and the agency of the executive, the Constitution itself is open to change. These matters of fact cannot be challenged but they do not yield the conclusion that Raz wants.

They do not amount to a judgement that law claims for itself unlimited authority, 'that there is an obligation to obey it whatever its content may be' (Raz 1986: 77). Matters would be different if one were able to identify the voice of the law making such a claim explicit, but the law itself does not speak to matters of theory of this generality. We have to look elsewhere.

We should distinguish what constitutional theorists say *about* the law and what politicians or judges (or citizens) claim *on behalf of* the law, attesting its self-understanding in their own persons. It is true that politicians make these sorts of claim, instructing potential rebels that it is always wrong to break the law, whenever there appears to be a prospect of widespread disobedience to some particular item of legislation. Indeed I remember hearing such voices at the time of the Poll Tax protests in the United Kingdom in 1990. But one can insist (truly or falsely) that citizens must obey the law as it stands whilst denying that Parliament *can* legislate any law to any effect. What does 'can' mean in this context? It means that either there are no determinate constitutional limits to what laws Parliament can enact or, if there be limits, that these limits themselves may be legitimately rescinded. But this is not to say that Parliament claims the authority to command citizens to perform immoral acts or stupid acts as it so wishes, as if it were a modern day Caligula. If politicians or judges had relied on such a principle to make their polemical point they would have been laughed out of court.

That said, there is in the literature one famous argument due to Thomas Hobbes which insists that the authority of the sovereign must be absolute and unlimited – 'as great, as possibly men can be imagined to make it' (Hobbes 1968: 260, Ch. 21 [107]). The argument for this is simple: rational persons are taken to grant (authorize) the sovereign just such powers as are necessary for the sovereign to accomplish the citizens' purposes of securing their own lives and the conditions of their commodious living. If any limits were set to the sovereign's power, then there would need to be some higher authority with the remit to judge whether or not the sovereign had exceeded the proper limits, whether or not his actions were *ultra vires*. But if there were such a higher authority, that authority would be the true (and absolute, unlimited) sovereign.[19] If, by contrast, there were no higher authority to adjudicate the conflicting claims, the dispute would be irresolvable and the parties would stand to each other as in a state of nature, a condition of incipient war. *Ex hypothesi*, such folk would work out that they stand in need of an absolute sovereign.

Hobbes's argument is elegant but unsound. Amongst the faults that critics have detected two stand out. In the first place, and this is an *ad hominem* criticism, Hobbes contradicts himself by placing a limit on the authority of the sovereign power which we have already noticed. The authority of the sovereign rests upon the rational choice of citizens to invest him with an unlimited range of powers in virtue of their judgement that nothing less can secure their self-preservation. But suppose the sovereign threatens their life. What are they to do?

> If the Sovraign command a man (though justly condemned,) to kill, wound, or mayme himselfe; or not to resist those that assault him; or to abstain from

the use of food, ayre, medicine, or any other thing, without which he cannot live; yet hath that man the liberty to disobey.

(Hobbes 1968: 268–9; Ch. 21 [111–12])

Hobbes clearly cedes the (conditional) right to disobey to subjects of a sovereign that has an (unconditional) right to their obedience. Even if these rights may conflict without contradiction, which is implausible but possible if they are both liberty-rights, there remains a serious difficulty concerning how practical conflicts might be adjudicated. The implications of this passage and its dialectical context for the soundness of the major thesis of *Leviathan* concerning the absolute range of sovereign authority are devastating.[20] Hobbes's moral geometry is fallacious. But second, the substantive point is in any case a serious error. It may well have been the case in Hobbes's day, in the aftermath of Civil War, that England needed a sovereign with pretensions to absolute, unlimited power. Maybe the assertion of absolute, unlimited secular power is necessary to contain the destructive ambitions of contending clerics, as Hobbes believed. Then as now the curse of religious war made a strong case for illiberal tyranny. Nonetheless it is just false to claim that limited governments must be unstable and self-destructive, liable to degenerate into an anarchic state of nature.

There is a very strong tradition of political philosophy which emphasizes, against Hobbes, the limitations of legitimate authority. John Locke in the *Second Treatise of Government* (published in 1690 and taking Hobbes as one of its philosophical targets) insists that the authority of the sovereign is limited to the execution of those purposes for which we must presume that authority was first instituted – the public good, the preservation of the lives and property of the citizens, the protection and prosecution of their natural rights (Locke 1960: Chs XI, XVIII–XIX). Sovereign power which violates these limiting conditions is illegitimate. If the commands of the sovereign compromise the pursuit of these goods, or if they exceed this very broad remit, they are *ultra vires*. And the people have no duty to comply with the commands of a sovereign – a tyrant – whose actions are *ultra vires*. By implication, and Locke makes the inference crystal clear, the people have a right to rebel. The form of this argument is particularly interesting since it suggests that claims to political authority may be intrinsically self-limiting. If such claims are advanced on the basis that political authority is necessary for the achievement of specific goods, the argument that succeeds in justifying political authority extends no further than the secured domain. It is not as though we first have an argument that grounds absolute authority, which authority then finds its horns drawn in as further independent values are brought into play. On the contrary, we should recognize that arguments which establish the legitimacy of authority in the political (as in other) spheres may bring with them their own domain restrictions.

Finally we should set out what looks to be an example of the alternative dialectic. In *On Liberty* John Stuart Mill takes it for granted that political authority is justified, and further, he takes it that the philosophical case has been made out in favour of a constitutional settlement in which 'the rulers should be identified with the people; that their interest and will should be the interest and will of the nation' which is to say, roughly (and incredibly: *On Liberty* was first published in 1859) 'We are all democrats now'. His novel question was this: regardless of the necessity and constitutional form of sovereign authority, is there any 'recognised principle by which the propriety or impropriety of government interference is customarily tested'? His answer is that

> The object of this Essay is to assert one very simple principle as designed to govern absolutely the dealings of society with the individual in the way of compulsion and control, whether the means used be physical force in the form of legal penalties, or the moral coercion of public opinion.

That (not, as it turns out) 'very simple principle' is encapsulated in Mill's Harm Principle: 'That the only purpose for which power can be rightfully exercised over any member of a civilised community, against his will, is to prevent harm to others.'[21]

It applies to the sovereign power of government (democratic sovereigns notably) as well as to society more generally. Sovereigns who reach beyond this specified purpose, attempting, for example, to promote the citizens' own good by preventing them from harming themselves, are acting *ultra vires*, failing to respect the boundary conditions on the legitimate exercise of their authority.

Clearly we cannot resolve these massively complex and controversial problems here. I mention these well-known positions only to emphasize that some of the implausibility that might otherwise attach to the conceptual claim that the directives of political authority are peremptory and content-independent is disarmed as soon as we recognize that there are strong arguments to the effect that political authority is, or always ought to be, limited in respect of its domain. Hence its voice is peremptory and its commands content-independent only when it sticks to its proper limits.

Chapter 4

Questions of justification

The dialectic of state and citizen

In the first chapter, we set up the ancient problem of political obligation as framed by a clear tension and a strong possibility of conflict between two claims – the claim of the state to allegiance, authority and obedience, and the claim of the citizen to autonomy, to moral self-governance. There is no problem of political obligation, no question of citizens recognizing any duties to the state, if there is no legitimate state. And a 'state' that does not command allegiance, assert its authority or demand obedience is not a state. Likewise, there is no problem of citizens' obligations or duties if citizens make no claim to autonomous judgement concerning how they shall behave. But if the state claims a right to govern and the citizen claims a right of autonomous agency, a very real problem is raised, since the state might require the citizen to act in a way that conflicts with his judgement of what is best for him to do. We saw in Chapter 3 that this conflict threatens the thought that a state can have authority over the citizen, but it does not generate a paradox. It does not make it logically impossible or impossibly difficult to justify the authority of the state since the authority will be limited to some specified domain and it is open to argument whether or not an autonomous agent may reasonably endorse the claims of a state to authority within some delimited domain. Nonetheless, the state still requires to be justified, and this task of justification is best conceived as an effort by the state to make a plausible case to independently minded citizens in support of its authority.

Thinking of matters in this way, we distinguish two countervailing parties – state and citizen – and their respective claims. We distinguish them in a fashion that identifies each as prospective protagonists in real disputes in the way that Socrates took himself to confront his city state, personified as the Laws of Athens, in Plato's *Crito*. And again, there are some who believe this dialectical scenario to be a hopelessly misleading fiction. There are those (classical anarchists) who believe that the state is an evil thing which has no moral standing, and to be specific, can make no valid moral claims on its citizens. There are those (philosophical anarchists) who believe that claims made by the state have no moral force at the point where they conflict with the best judgements of autonomous citizens on how they should behave. Contrariwise, there are those (communitarians, for want of a better term) who maintain that the autonomous agent who detaches himself from the political ties that bind him in order to investigate their moral credentials is an impossible creature, a mythical beast created by philosophers' imaginings and never to be encountered in a well-ordered polity. We shall look more closely at these opposing positions in following chapters. For the moment we shall proceed as though there are no challengers to this portrayal of the problem as a confrontation (or, nicer: a dialogue) between contending parties. And we shall investigate the dialectical contours of the real dispute that we mentioned above, as described by Plato.

Socrates has been sentenced to death. He has been commanded to take poison as punishment for being a menace to society and corrupting the minds of young Athenians. He is visited by Crito and other friends and admirers. They tell him that they can fix his escape – the gaoler is beholden to them, they can buy off informers, and he will be perfectly safe in exile in Thessaly. It is evident to Socrates that if he makes good his escape he will be failing to fulfil the duties incumbent on him as a citizen of Athens. Should he or shouldn't he take up Crito's invitation? Should he do what the city requires of him – stay and drink the fatal potion – or should he disobey, flee and live in exile? Socrates deliberates these questions in a very straightforward fashion. Speaking in the voice of the Laws and Constitution of Athens, he argues in favour of obeying the state and accepting the decreed punishment. He puts forward the strongest argument he can on the part of the state and declares himself convinced by it. The potential conflict between the claim of the state to obedience and the judgement of the autonomous citizen has been resolved, since it has been shown that Socrates' best judgement, which he commends to the friends who would rescue him, is that he should comply with the deadly demands of the state.

This drama gives us the template: the state proposes, the citizen disposes; the state puts forward arguments to support its demands for compliance, the citizen reviews these arguments and reaches a conclusion as to their success. If the independent-minded citizen is convinced by the arguments as put, he accepts the conclusion concerning how he should behave. In the case of Socrates, he should take the hemlock.

This portrayal of the dialectic of the *Crito* conceals a crucial ambiguity which we should bring out into the open. First of all, the circumstances of the case require the state to command the citizen to act (or forbear) in a specific fashion and the citizen to raise the question of whether or not he should comply with this command. Socrates, we should notice, raises two very different types of question which are conflated by the circumstances of his predicament. The first of these is the issue of what types of reason might be offered by the Laws of Athens as grounds for Socrates' obedience. I shan't investigate the dialogue in the scrupulous detail that scholarly interpretation requires, but roughly, the state as personified by the Laws claims that those who have consented to the authority of the regime have a duty to comply with its commands. There is a further argument based on the citizens' receipt of benefits from the state, and to my mind it is obscure whether this is an argument based on tacit consent or convention, on reciprocity or appropriate gratitude, or some combination of these. Clearly there is a lot of philosophical work to be done investigating the cogency of these arguments, and we shall go over this ground ourselves in very great detail in what follows. This is the first, philosophical, task – to work out which philosophical principles might serve to ground citizens' duties. The second issue concerns the *applicability* to Socrates' particular circumstances of putative principles which pass the philosophical tests of cogency or plausibility. Thus, the citizen's consent may well ground a duty to obey, but has Socrates actually consented? The receipt of benefits may well be judged to imply that the citizen tacitly accepts the attribution of a duty to obey the sovereign, but has Socrates actually received the touted benefits? Are they benefits enough to ground the duty?

These considerations are linked in an obvious way whenever the duties of a specific citizen are under review. This linkage will be evident if we portray the reasoning of the parties as articulated in the following sequence. First, the sovereign commands the citizen and the citizen deliberates the question of whether citizens generally have a duty to do what they are told. One way of characterizing this process of deliberation is for the citizen to imagine that the sovereign advances an argument which purports to answer the general question. Suppose the sovereign comes up with an argument of this form: if the citizen has consented to obey the lawful commands of the sovereign, then she has a duty to do what the sovereign commands her to do.[1] Next suppose that the citizen accepts this argument. We now have a philosophical agreement between sovereign and citizen on the grounds that may in principle be adduced as sufficient to attribute duties to the citizen. What we don't yet have is agreement on the fact of the matter concerning the citizen's duty in the specific circumstances of the actual command. So suppose the state goes further and claims that the citizen has in fact consented to its exercise of sovereign authority. Again, the citizen reviews this claim, and we can imagine that she accepts it. Agreeing that her giving consent would compel her acceptance of the duties of citizenship, she accepts the sovereign's further claim that she has so consented, just as a matter of fact. In which case, the citizen will go on to accept that she has a duty to do what she is told.

The structure of the linkage is familiar: there is a major premise of conditional form, if P then Q, which represents the agreed conclusion of the philosophical debate on the putative grounds for citizens' obedience. In this case:

1   If the citizen consents to obey the sovereign, the citizen has a duty so to do.

Next there is a minor premise, attesting the facts of the matter:

2   The citizen consents to obey the sovereign.

The conclusion is straightforwardly drawn:

3   The citizen has a duty to obey the sovereign.

The argument is of the simple *modus ponens* form: if P then Q, (and) P, therefore Q.

The debate concerning the truth of the major premise is properly philosophical. If there is any debate concerning the truth of the minor premise, it is debate about a matter of fact. Either the citizen has consented or she has not, and the facts will decide which of these propositions is true. Suppose she has not consented. In this case we cannot deduce that the citizen has a duty to obey the sovereign. Thus, from:

1   If the citizen consents to obey the sovereign, the citizen has a duty so to do.
2   The citizen does not consent to obey the sovereign.

nothing follows concerning the duties of the citizen. The incomplete argument has the form: if P then Q, and not P. . . . Notice that 'not Q' – 'it is not the case that the citizen has a duty to obey the sovereign' or 'the citizen has no duty to obey the sovereign' – does not follow. It may well turn out that the citizen *has* a duty to obey the sovereign, but if she has, it is not to be imputed on the grounds of her consent.

In the discussion that follows I shall say that issues concerning the major premise, the sorts of principle or argument that may serve to ground the citizens' duties, constitute the Philosophical Problem. Issues concerning the minor premise, considerations bearing on the question of whether or not principles or arguments are applicable in specific circumstances, are part of the Political Problem. It will be an important feature of my developing argument that these problems are kept distinct. Throughout the rest of this book I shall keep reminding readers that the prime focus of the philosopher should be the Philosophical Problem. The philosopher *qua* philosopher has nothing distinctive to say about the practical Political Problem as this might be encountered by any citizen of any state.

The distinction between the Philosophical Problem and the Political Problem is important for another reason, too. There are many reasons why citizens may reject the attribution of duties to them. They may reject duties wholesale or retail. They may be anarchists of one stripe or another (and we shall briefly survey the varieties later). Or they may reject some particular duty or range of duties that are charged to them by the state. They may be conscientious objectors or engage in civil disobedience, repudiating the authority of the state quite generally or some specific claims it makes upon them. The sensitive state, which, we should remember, possesses very severe coercive powers, will wish to know the reason why the citizen takes the recalcitrant position she does since this will (in part) determine the state's response to overt disobedience. The philosopher, too, will take note of the variety of reasons for the citizen's rejection of her obligations as a citizen.

If these reasons are philosophical, bearing on the cogency of the major premise as this is advanced in an argument for the attribution of duties to citizens, the philosopher can contribute to the dialectic. Suppose the state argues that the citizen must accept the duties attributed to her on the grounds that she ought to be grateful to the state for the benefits it has conferred upon her, and that her acceptance of such duties as the state imposes is the appropriate response of one who is properly grateful. If the citizen rejects the cogency of this form of argument (and we shall examine it in detail later in Chapter 9), arguing perhaps that an institution such as the state is not a proper object of gratitude – we can be grateful to persons but not to institutions – then we have a philosophical dispute, and everyone can get involved. But suppose one accepted the philosophical credentials of the argument from gratitude, and believed that citizens who have accepted significant benefits from the state should be grateful for them and should express their gratitude by taking on the duties of the citizen. It is possible that a citizen who accepts this form of argument denies in her own particular case that she herself has received any benefits, or claims that she has received small benefits insufficient to ground a duty of gratitude. It will then be a matter of fact, and not a matter to be settled by philosophical disputation, whether the duties of citizenship can be attributed to her.

The good reasons thesis

To summarize and recapitulate my understanding of the dialectic of state and citizen: the state proposes; the citizen disposes. This is to say that we interpret arguments for the attribution of duties to citizens as positions advanced by the state and reviewed by its citizens. The claim to authority made by the state is couched in terms of good reasons why the citizen should accept the duties imputed to her. All goes well when the state advances *good reasons* which the citizen endorses. We can make this point another way: political power is legitimate, claims to authority are valid if and only if citizens can find *good reasons* to support it. This is the good reasons thesis.

I should explain, too, that when I speak of 'good reasons' I have in mind good *moral* reasons. Citizens may have all sorts of reasons for obeying the state, in particular cases and in general. Often they will have strongly prudential reasons for fulfilling the duties that the state has ascribed to them. They may simply fear the consequences of disobedience or, less likely, they may be actively seeking some rewards which compliance may bring. Their motivation in these cases may be entirely self-interested. This is easy to see in particular cases, but it is also possible that citizens may engage in a systematic, exceptionless, policy of compliance with the law on the grounds that this is most likely to lead to a secure and prosperous life for themselves. Now I accept that it is a matter of philosophical controversy whether reasons for action that concern solely the self-interest of the agent can be considered as moral reasons, but I want to side-step this dispute. I take a Kantian view and deny that reasons of self-interest are moral reasons, but whether they are moral reasons or not I want to state that these are not the sort of reason we shall be examining in this book. They don't count as 'good reasons' as I employ that term in the 'good reasons' thesis. The reason why I want to insist on this is that I don't believe that one's having a strong prudential reason to obey a command or otherwise support a commander can legitimize the agency that delivers the commands. If this were so, the Mafia boss would have genuine authority over both the gangsters who believe they can make a good career out of following his instructions and the tradesmen who pay up to secure their own protection.

The good reasons account of political authority is a liberal position since it gives to the citizen a decisive say on the attribution of authority and the distribution of duties. One might say that this dialectic securely fastens the burden of proof on to the state which advances the putative good reasons, but I prefer not to put matters in this way since the aim is to characterize the circumstances of agreement (or disagreement). One might just as well say that, since the state is putting arguments for citizens' compliance on the table, the burden of proof is on the citizen to refute them. And I see no grounds on which any disputation on this matter of the burden of proof might be resolved. The state has to make good its claim, but equally the citizen has to make good her claim, should she decide to reject the state's advances.

This latter point is important because it implies that the citizen cannot reject her imputed obligations arbitrarily. It is not a matter of plumping, of simply choosing one way or the other whether to accept the authority of the state. An argument has been put forward for the citizen to appraise, and this argument must be treated on its merits. We have seen the form that the complete argument must take. In respect of the Philosophical Problem, the state must establish, on philosophical grounds, a principle that serves as a major premise, and, in respect of the Political Problem, it must establish, on factual grounds, that the principle applies to the citizen who is reviewing her duties. It follows that the citizen who would reject the duties imputed to her by the state must be able to challenge successfully either the philosophical arguments that purport to establish a principle or the factual claims that secure the application of the principle to her case.

We should say more about these 'good reasons', not least since the nature of reasons is a very controversial matter amongst contemporary philosophers. It is usual nowadays to distinguish (at least) two different kinds of reason. Bernard Williams pointed out that, if we say 'A has a reason to ϕ' or 'There is a reason for A to ϕ', these sentences bear two different interpretations (Williams 1981). On the first reading, to say that A has a reason to ϕ is to attribute some motivation to A which will be served by his ϕ-ing. The sentence is false if there is nothing in A's subjective motivational set[2] that will be advanced or satisfied by his ϕ-ing; most likely there is nothing that he seeks or desires to which ϕ-ing is an effective means. On the second reading (more conspicuously perhaps with 'There is a reason for A to ϕ'), the reason statement is not falsified by the absence of an appropriate motivation. Thus we can say that there is a reason for someone to do something irrespective of what they believe or how they feel on the matter. Suppose we learn that Albert is going hiking. We can say that there is a good reason for him (or he has a good reason) to take a map and compass, and this will not turn out to be false if it is shown that taking these things has never occurred to Albert. This is a much-simplified version of Williams's distinction, but the point should be sufficiently clear. The first kind of reason is dubbed an 'internal' reason; it concerns the agent's state of mind. The second kind of reason is an 'external' reason; it is a fact about the world. It might mean simply that Albert is more likely to have a successful trip if he is carrying a map and compass, and, by implication, can use them should he have difficulty in route finding.

My claim is that the *good reasons* which determine whether or not the citizen has the duties imputed to her by the state are external reasons in the rough-and-ready sense described above. This should seem surprising, given my insistence that the citizen disposes. If the citizen 'disposes', that is to say, appraises the argument which has been put forward and accepts or rejects it on the basis of that appraisal, is not the reason which issues an *internal* reason, a reason which reports an appropriate linkage between the argument as given and the citizen's subjective motivational set? Clearly, I need to explain things further.

One way of squaring matters is to insist that whatever reason there is for the citizen to accept the duties that follow from the state's making out its case is an external reason because there is no requirement that the argument put by the state should appeal to or be rendered applicable by any element of the subjective motivational set of the citizen, such as a specific desire or inclination or personal project. This would be to deny the so-called 'Humean' thesis, that *all* reasons for action engage some conative feature of the agent's motivational set, a desire or something like that. This would be a useful strategy since it evidently opens up the field to a wider range of dialectical resources than are otherwise available; the Humean thesis operates as a severe constraint on the applicability of arguments. I do not want to go down this road because I think we should be able to characterize the reasoning of the citizen without taking a stand on this issue.

A second way of eliminating the puzzle (or worse, the threat of self-contradiction) is to point out that the character of the reason as 'internal' or 'external' cannot be a feature of the state of mind of the citizen since no 'actual' citizen is involved in the dialectic. The argument as presented is engaged by personifications, idealizations rather than real persons. And since we are not dealing with real persons, there are no agents whose subjective motivational sets are engaged or otherwise. This will readily be conceded as far as the state is concerned. There can be no answer (for the moment) to the question of which state is putting forward the argument.[3] We are doing so, as philosophers, not as the advocates of any particular state. But this is not so obvious with respect to the citizen. It is a pertinent question: Who does the voice of the citizen in the dialectic represent? It could be all citizens or most citizens or just some citizens or even one particular citizen – she who is conducting the argument perhaps, or she who is portrayed as being addressed by the state. It could be the 'normal', the 'typical', or the 'average' citizen, or an arbitrarily selected citizen. Thus far there is nothing to tell us which, if any, of these is the correct characterization of the citizen as she features in the argument. In which case we cannot conclude that we are not reviewing the reflections of real persons. So this way of dismissing the problem is too swift.

Rather what I have in mind, in describing the 'good reasons' that the citizen might recognize as external reasons, is that they are reasons that, in the first place, will follow from a philosophical examination of their credentials. In speaking of good reasons, I focus on the major premise (as explained above) and on the arguments that establish the conditional statements that purport to solve the Philosophical Problem. I don't insist that the validity of these putative reasons will be a matter of strict logical or conceptual necessity. That would be to set the bar of philosophical probity too high for this domain of investigation. It will be enough that the arguments display that quality of *a priori* credibility that philosophers have typically sought, whatever premium they have officially placed on the deductive (or geometric) provenance of their efforts. (Obviously, at this point I have in mind the pretensions of Thomas Hobbes to deliver a science of subjects' duties.) The first task of the citizen who 'disposes' of the arguments of the state is to conduct a philosophical audit, to seek out fallacies, unexamined assumptions or presuppositions as well as simple blunders, looking for suspect items from the long catalogue of philosophical failures – and any philosopher can do that. The second task, of course, is to establish that whatever reasons survive this philosophical examination apply in some specified circumstances – and this is the point at which 'the state' and 'the citizen' cease to serve as abstractions or personifications.

'Good reasons', in other words, will be reasons that pass philosophical muster. This might seem so obvious as not to merit saying. The task – of conducting a philosophical investigation – might seem so politically disengaged ('unencumbered' one might say, borrowing the term from Michael Sandel (1984), not to say professionally self-serving on the part of philosophers, that it fails to denominate any distinctive position, still less a position that identifies itself as recognizably liberal. But it would be a serious error to believe these things. At this point, I can do little more than gesture towards Kant and Hegel to mark out a distinguishing feature of modern ethics. The story can be told as follows: once upon a time, folk who were unsure how they should behave or, more generally, what principles they should employ to guide their conduct, would seek out an authority who would instruct them what to do. The favoured authorities, the most typical claimants, were princes and priests. The law – of properly established political sovereigns, or of God as communicated by his appointed representatives on earth, or of the former as the earthly voices of the latter – dictated the content of social norms. But it became evident (to a significant number of serious thinkers on these matters in the sixteenth century) that rulers can be wicked and enact unjust laws, and that there are competing and conflicting claimants to the role of interpreter and promulgator of God's word. The conclusion – of wars and rebellions as much as political, religious and recognizably philosophical reflection – was Kant's attribution to each competent person of a rational will that enables her to determine (to test and if necessary to generate) the moral rules that fix all persons' duties and motivate them to comply.

This critical capacity is distinctive of the modern 'enlightened' temperament; it is the ability 'to make use of one's own understanding without direction from another', the 'freedom to make *public* use of one's reason in all matters' (Kant 1996b: 17–18 [8: 35–6]).[4] To see its importance one does not need to take on board Kant's heavyweight apparatus of the 'rational will'. All that is necessary is a dose of curiosity or scepticism (which may, in the outcome, be dispelled) concerning the ethical credentials of established institutions. In the Preface to the first edition of the *Critique of Pure Reason*, Kant spells out the implications of this thought:

> Our age is the genuine age of criticism, to which everything must submit. Religion through its holiness and legislation through its majesty commonly seek to exempt themselves from it. But in this way they excite a just suspicion against themselves, and cannot lay claim to that unfeigned respect that reason grants only to that which has been able to withstand its free and public examination.
>
> (Kant 1998: 100–1 [4: A xi])

On my reading, Hegel makes exactly the same point when he emphasizes 'the *right of the subjective will* . . . that whatever it is to recognize as valid should be perceived by it as good', and continues: 'The right to recognize nothing that I do not perceive as rational is the highest right of the subject' (Hegel 1991: §132 & R).[5]

There are important differences between Kant's and Hegel's accounts when these are spelled out in full detail, and as the reader might suspect, the differences largely concern the nature and function of reason or rationality as this is employed by the moral subject. But these differences do not occlude the crucial point of agreement between them which concerns the attribution to subjects of the capacity to discern the validity of claims to, and exercises of, authority in the prescription of rules of conduct. I repeat: we do not see this thought as radical or striking, still less revolutionary, but that is because we are all Kant's children in this regard. Moral, and more broadly intellectual, self-governance or autonomy is mother's milk to us. It is because of the central place of moral self-governance in the account I give of good reasons that I dub my position a *liberal* position. Now some may judge that this is a meagre sense of 'liberal', and that the version of liberalism attested by the good reasons thesis is a barely identifiable component of the rich and various liberal tradition. I understand this complaint. But I don't want to engage in a defence of this terminology, since the employment of it is not mandatory. If the reader wishes to employ another term to characterize this position – 'individualist' or 'atomist' perhaps – so be it. But these terms carry their own philosophical baggage.

At this point I expect the reader to be (just a little) puzzled by what the 'good reasons' might amount to. What sort of reasons do I have in mind as candidates? I don't want to hold readers in suspense if they are anxious for full disclosure. Suffice it to say at this point that I will discuss theories which cite, for a range of examples: citizens' consent, actual (express and tacit) and (very differently) hypothetical, their receipt of benefits and the appropriateness of sentiments of gratitude, considerations of utility, arguments from fairness, and a natural duty to comply with the demands of just institutions – variants of all these positions and more besides. These 'good reasons' are not exclusive. There may be many such. And so far as the citizen is concerned, when he addresses the Political Problem and examines which of these 'good reasons' apply to him as governing his ethical relations with his state, he may find that all or several do, and that his political obligations are morally over-determined.

I regard each of these as substantive arguments which merit careful examination, but the 'good reasons' thesis itself should not be regarded as just another theory – as if it were a competitor – on a par with these others. I advance this thesis as working at a higher, more abstract, level. This is not to say that the thesis might not be confused with the subordinate candidate theories, or that there might not be competing or complementary 'meta-theories' on the table. There are both. We shall have to sort out confusions and confound contrary competitors. Let us begin this task by distinguishing the 'good reasons' thesis from a familiar doctrine with which it has been frequently confused – the doctrine of *voluntarism*.

Voluntarism

Voluntarism in political philosophy is the thesis that 'political power over me can be created only as a consequence of my voluntary acts. Another person can have political power over me only if I have granted them that power' (Wolff 1996: 42).[6] This is not intended as a definition so much as a sketch or summary of a complex position. The crucial idea is that a person or social entity such as a church, a company or a state has authority, which is to say legitimate power, over an individual only if that individual *has willed it* that the putative authority has legitimate power, and has expressed that will in some recognizable voluntary act. Thus theories that claim that a citizen's actual consent is a necessary and sufficient condition on the legitimacy of political authority are 'voluntarist' theories. So, too, are theories that derive legitimacy from the phenomenon of a social contract amongst citizens, a contract either between citizens to authorize a sovereign or a contract between the body of citizens and a sovereign whom they thereby legitimate. If citizens are deemed to have agreed with each other, or with a sovereign power, this attests the sort of voluntary act that converts the exercise of power into legitimate authority, and the same is true if citizens are held to have made promises thereto. Acts of consent and contract, agreement and promise-making, vows, oaths and other acts of allegiance – all these and more performances of free, voluntary, willing acceptance – are the stuff of voluntarism. (We should also make it clear that theories which derive citizens' duties from their willing acceptance of benefits and a consequent duty of fair play, as discussed in Chapter 9, should also be considered voluntarist accounts in some measure.)[7]

Voluntarism is the most familiar philosophical thesis concerning the authority of the state advanced in modern times. It is perhaps the most plausible as well as the most attractive theory. It is presented in a variety of forms that need to be distinguished with care, but in one or other of its garbs it can be identified in the writings of the founding fathers of modern liberalism – Hobbes, Locke and Rousseau. We shall examine voluntarism as a substantial principle purporting to solve the Philosophical Problem in later chapters. For the moment, I want to draw readers' attention to the way in which the thesis of voluntarism might very easily be (and indeed has been) confused with the 'good reasons' thesis as this has been stated above.

Let me set up the discussion by quoting an argument put forward by Thomas Hobbes. To orientate readers to the issue of controversy, each of the great contract theorists mentioned above, Hobbes, Locke and Rousseau, found that they had to refute the claim that the authority of the state over the subject was natural, established somehow in the order of things. I put matters in this vague way because the standard arguments to this conclusion were arguments from analogy: the sovereign stands, in point of his authority over the people, in the same or a similar natural relation as the father does to his children.[8] And for many, the point or relevance of this analogy was established by the fact that God had ordained the authority of the father over his children. Hobbes denies this assertion of natural authority. What is Hobbes's explanation of the paternal authority of the parent (mother or father, for Hobbes, subversively) over the child?

> The right of Dominion by Generation, is that, which the Parent hath over his Children; and is called PATERNALL. And is not so derived from the Generation, as if therefore the Parent had Dominion over his Child because he begat him; but from the Childs Consent, either expresse, or by other sufficient arguments declared.
>
> (Hobbes 1968: 253; Part II, Ch. XX [102])

We should be well aware how striking this argument is. I guess there are few folks nowadays, in times even when the rights of children against their parents are frequently invoked at home and in law, who would explain whatever rights parents can legitimately claim against their children as founded in the consent of the children. So what exactly is Hobbes arguing for?[9] This is my reconstruction of a recognizable argument in this vicinity, if not quite a respectable interpretation of Hobbes: mothers and fathers have authority over their children if their children consent to the parents' exercise of this authority. Such consent as is given will be valid just in cases where the children are competent, well-informed (but not necessarily uncoerced)[10] adults. What of children who are not able to give valid consent, generally because they are too immature and ignorant? What is the source of the authority that their parents may rightfully claim in these familiar circumstances? In such cases we must suppose that there are 'other sufficient arguments declared', as Hobbes puts it, to attest the child's consent. What might these arguments amount to?

They must be arguments of this sort: if the incompetent and ignorant children were, contrary to the facts of the matter, rational, well-informed and uncoerced, they would consent to the dominion of their parents. How might we reach this hypothetical conclusion? It can only be established by a philosophical demonstration that there are good reasons why such children should accept parental authority quite independent of the actual consent which, *ex hypothesi*, they do not give.

We can see now that Hobbes in this very brief passage conflates actual consent and hypothetical consent. This is easy to do since actual consent may be explicit (or 'expresse' as Hobbes recognizes), or implicit (or tacit) in the way that Locke was later to describe, and it is a simple error to identify tacit and hypothetical consent on the grounds that neither kind of consent is expressed directly. We shall return to these important issues later. But for the moment we should notice that arguments which purport to establish good reasons for accepting claims to authority on the basis of *hypothetical* consent are not characteristically voluntarist arguments. Though such arguments are put up for all to reflect upon when they consider the authority of the power that attributes duties to them, the soundness of these arguments does not depend on consent, or any other act of will, on the part of those to whom they are addressed. As we shall see later, the structures of actual and hypothetical consent arguments are strikingly different.

We can make the same general point by using a different candidate for a relevant 'good reason'. Thus, suppose for example that a utilitarian argues that a form of government is legitimate on the grounds that the welfare of (the aggregate of) citizens is most likely to be secured if they fulfil the duties it prescribes to them, and suppose further that utilitarianism is the correct normative theory for judging actions, rules and institutions. It would then follow that citizens should fulfil their duties whether or not they consent to the government that prescribes them. Utilitarian theory would have established that this is what citizens ought to do, since it has stated the good reasons for the authority of the state. The utilitarian argument advances a putative good reason, but it is not a voluntarist argument.

We should notice, too, that voluntarist or consent theories are even more likely to be confused with the good reasons account since voluntarist theories themselves are an attempt (and often a successful attempt) to provide the good reasons that might underpin claims to authority. It is a plausible claim, and one which, to repeat, we shall examine in very great detail later, that the fact of the citizen's consent is itself a good reason why that citizen should accept the sovereign she has thereby authorized. Of course, if it were demonstrated that the actual consent of the citizen is the only grounds on which the authority of the state rests, the only reason good enough to fasten duties on to the citizen, then the good reasons theory and this version of voluntarism would coincide in the specific sense that voluntarism has been successfully defended as articulating the only good reason there might be. But we can't reach this conclusion without examining both voluntarist theories and the many rival non-voluntarist theories on their merits as offering good reasons.

Joseph Raz: the dependence and normal justification theses

The argument so far has distinguished arguments at two levels: at the level of higher generality we advanced the good reasons thesis as establishing the form of argument which should be put forward to ground the validity of claims to authority; at the level of greater specificity we adduced with examples but no detail the sort of good reasons that have been advanced by philosophers who tackle the problem of citizens' duties. In distinguishing the 'good reasons' thesis from voluntarism I demonstrated how this distinction of levels may be transgressed. We shall now consider a different account of the form that the putative good reasons should take. This is the well-known argument of Joseph Raz for his 'dependence thesis'. If correct, this position, as I understand it, would entail that investigation of the credentials of candidate good reasons – consent and so forth – would be redundant.

This is the dependence thesis:

> All authoritative directives should be based on reasons which already independently apply to the subjects of the directives and are relevant to their action in the circumstances covered by the directive.
>
> (Raz 1986: 47)

At this stage in his argument Raz is reviewing the nature and justification of authority quite generally. We are to take this thesis as applying to the authority of parents over their children, of schoolteachers over their pupils, of officers over the soldiers under their command, as well as the authority of the state over its subjects. The dependence thesis is advanced as 'a moral thesis about the way authorities should use their powers' (Raz 1986: 53). This thesis can be taken as a constraint on the deliberations of authorities as they formulate their directives or, whatever the deliberative route to directives, it can indicate the only way in which authoritative directives can be defended. Authorities must be prepared to demonstrate that their activities conform to reasons which apply independently to their subjects and that subjects can, in principle, recognize that their ends will be promoted or their interests protected by the authority which directs them. Notice though, and this is a point we shall take up later, there is nothing in the dependence thesis, as stated, which determines the level of generality at which this thesis is supposed to operate. Is it a thesis which applies to each directive taken singly and to each subject in turn, or might it be employed in wholesale fashion, say to the institution of parental authority and to dependent children taken generally, or to a government and its relation to political subjects? Would it do, for example, for a government to defend its claim to authority and to the consequent validity of its directives by pointing to its overall mission to protect and promote the rights and interests of subjects generally, granted that the subjects themselves believe that the protection of their rights and interests constitute reasons for action? Raz's subsequent discussion suggests that he intends the thesis to apply with maximum specificity, to each directive and on each occasion to which it may be relevant.

This dependence thesis is related to a further thesis concerning the form to be taken by arguments which are aimed at justifying or legitimating an authority. This is dubbed the normal justification thesis. It claims that *the normal way to establish that a person has authority over another person involves showing that the alleged subject is likely better to comply with reasons which apply to him (other than the alleged authoritative directives) if he accepts the directives of the alleged authority as authoritatively binding and tries to follow them, rather than by trying to follow the reasons which apply to him directly.*

(Raz 1986: 53, italics in original)

(Notice that it is unclear once again whether this thesis should be understood generally, as concerned with the justification of an authority relation and hence with the directives of that authority (wholesale), or whether it is concerned with the justification of each exercise of authority (retail). The latter is the reading of Raz's statement which best captures the spirit of Raz's discussion but I shall argue that it is an implausible construal of the task of justifying authority. But if we read Raz in the former way, the dependence thesis and the normal justification thesis are at odds. It looks as though one might justify an authority by application of the normal justification thesis yet find that each directive of the authority has to be defended individually, in piecemeal, retail fashion. If this is so, one should ask: what is the point of justifying an authority if all of its directives (and, we might suppose, all of its other activities) stand in need of individual justification?)

The normal justification thesis supposes that the subject has some goal or purpose, some subjective good, which dictates what counts as reasons for him to act in one way rather than another. In the simplest case, we can think of the goal as the end to be pursued and the reasons to perform some specific act as determining the most effective means to that end. It follows that we can establish the legitimacy of a putative authority if we can show that the subject is more likely to pursue effective means to given ends if he complies with the directives of the authority than if he determines for himself how best to accomplish his goals.

This thesis bears a superficial similarity to the 'good reasons' account that I sketched above. Recall: the claim to authority made by the state is couched in terms of good reasons why the citizen should accept the duties imputed to her. It looks as though we can rewrite this condition in terms compatible with Raz's 'normal justification thesis', for the good reasons which the state puts to the citizen as grounds for its authority are *ex hypothesi* reasons which the subject should share. Thus it might well be thought that the subject is irrational if he rejects what he accepts is the most effective means to a goal he acknowledges. If it is in the nature of authority to better secure the success of goals that the subject pursues for independent reasons, then he should accept the claim to authority.

Notice, too, that the reasons which apply to the subject, and which would be better complied with were he to follow the directives of authority, may well be external reasons in the sense in which I introduced that term above (though this is not clear from Raz's discussion; as I read the two theses, this is more comfortably inferred from the statement of the dependence thesis than the normal justification thesis). The credentials of the putative good reasons are those of being the most effective way to attain the subject's goals, and these credentials are valid whether or not the subject understands them to hold. The subject may not be aware of this independently – indeed in many cases he will not be. It is wise of parents to drill their children in how to cross a road safely. They should just tell them to look right, look left, and look right again before they cross the road. The parents should not wait until the child has the intellectual capacity to fully understand the rationale behind the drill before they are thus instructed. If, unlike the child, the subject were fully aware that (and why) in every case the directives of the authority represent the best way to secure his goals, he would gain no benefit from being subject to authority. He would already be in the optimal position for determining for himself how he should act. But if the good reasons which should direct the authority and the subject alike are external reasons, we should expect the presentation of them to invite controversy. I have characterized these reasons as representing efficient means to agreed ends, and this is the simplest case. But there is no reason why the statement of the good reasons which the authoritative direction advances as applying independently to the subjects should not be complex, prescribing ends or values as well as appropriate means to satisfy them. If this is right, philosophers can expect to have a lot to say about what sort of reasons subjects should look to authorities to advance on their behalf.

I should say at this point that I suspect that the attractiveness of Raz's proposal may well rest on the (unstated) implication that the dependent reasons on which the authority acts are in fact internal reasons which independently motivate the subject. In these circumstances, the dependence thesis may be taken to articulate the insight behind the different forms of voluntarism, all of which assume the rationality of whatever acts of will authorize the sovereign agency. Typically, the rationality in question will be displayed by showing how subscription to authority advances the subjects' ends, and this may imply that there are constraints on the activities of the authority which derive from its restricted license to promote these ends – and these ends alone. Again, this cast of argument is familiar from the work of the great contract theorists, John Locke in particular. We should not presume that acceptance of Raz's dependence and normal justification theses precludes the investigation of all traditional strategies for justifying the authority of the state.

These things said, we should notice the differences between these two approaches. In the first place it seems to me just false that the normal justification thesis is the normal way to establish that a person, or group, or institution has authority. For a start we must take it that when Raz speaks of a 'way to establish that a person has authority over another', this phrase is not being used in its normal signification. The normal way to establish a person's authority is to examine their credentials, to ask for a warrant card or otherwise to investigate whether they actually enjoy the normative status advertised by their uniform or social circumstances, whether they are properly authorized agents of an authoritative institution. What Raz has in mind here is very different; presumably it is a *philosophically grounded* investigation of the alleged authority of a person or the institution they represent.

Suppose then that I regularly seek a person's advice: to use Raz's examples, it may be Ruth, a broker whom I consult for financial advice, or John, who gives me instructions on how to cook Chinese meals (Raz 1986: 64). Suppose next that one of these characters begins to give me orders – Ruth 'phoning me with directions to put all my assets in cash, or more absurdly, John commanding me to marinade the chicken. When I demur, they claim in reply what is patently absurd – practical authority in their particular domains. If Raz were correct, this claim could be checked by employing the normal justification thesis. So suppose finally that my sole goal in my financial affairs is to maximize my savings, my sole aim in the kitchen is to cook the finest Chinese meals of which I am capable. I think the normal justification thesis would have it that John and Ruth *do* stand in positions of authority over me, since it is easily shown that I am likely better to comply with reasons that apply to me independently if I accept the directives of these self-appointed authorities rather than try independently to maximize my savings and cook excellent Chinese meals. And to repeat, this conclusion would be absurd for all that it falls out of the testing procedure prescribed for claims to authority. A further implication of this argument is that the normal justification thesis justifies too much if it can be used by paternalistic authorities to validate compulsory interventions in citizens' lives designed to make these lives go better by securing goods that the citizens would otherwise pursue for themselves.

It is of general importance that we should be able to distinguish advice from authoritative directives and this cannot be achieved merely by attending to the language of advisors and authorities. The use of the imperative mood: 'Do this! Don't do that!' cannot capture the difference, since consultants are as likely to use it as commanders. Some otherwise stern authorities phrase their commands in the courtliest of fashions: 'I'd gather some sticks before you attempt to light the fire'. I've known some (particularly annoying) employers who prefaced every instruction with the question: 'How would you like to . . . ?' (I guess this was annoying since frequently the answer at the tip of one's tongue was 'Not very much'.) Of course, whether or not the utterance is the prescription of an authority or the advice of a consultant is in practice settled by examining the context. And here the normal justification thesis is of no help at all. It will not permit us to distinguish wise advice from legitimate authority since in both cases, *ex hypothesi*, we have good reason to do as we are told.

A second difference between the role of reasons in my 'good reasons' account and Raz's normal justification thesis concerns the type or scope of the reasons adduced. As I read Raz's account, the reasons he adduces are specifically related to persons, themselves related as authority and subject, and to the content of the particular directive. This is paraded as a virtue of the account: 'it allows for a very discriminating approach to the question' [of the authoritative credentials of the directive, presumably]. Thus '[A]n expert pharmacologist may not be subject to the authority of the government in matters of the safety of drugs' (Raz 1986: 74) since following the directives of the government is not likely to improve the pharmacologist's conformity with reason. I can't see why the applicability of reasons must be pitched at this level of specificity, with respect to both persons and the content of the directive. Why not cast the question in terms of persons accepting the authority of specific institutions and then regarding as authoritative the directions addressed by officers of that institution quite generally? In respect of the example of drugs we should consider patients finding that they are generally better able to look after their health if they comply wholesale with those directives of the state which constitute the institution of a health service. If the question of conformity with reason has to be addressed directly to each person in respect of each directive, this will preclude any systematic administrative response to the provision of goods such as health care. If, as in the case Raz mentions, pharmacologists are permitted to prepare and distribute dangerous drugs on the strength of their professional expertise, without, e.g. authorized prescription or official records being kept, an otherwise efficient system of drug production, distribution and use may become a regulatory nightmare – and whatever expertise pharmacologists may have with respect to the constitution and properties of drugs, that expertise does not translate smoothly into an expertise in the management of bureaucratic systems.

A final worry with Raz's normal justification thesis follows from this last point concerning the specificity of the reasons adduced and their appropriateness for the acceptance of authority. We saw in Chapter 3 that to grant the status of authority to exercisers of *de facto* power is to accept that their directives have some measure of peremptory force, that they should be accepted, not universally but in the general run of things, independently of an assessment of their specific content. This point has been stressed with particular force by Hart and by Raz himself. If it transpires that the normal justification thesis must be applied with maximum specificity to license an investigation of the credentials of each allegedly authoritative directive taken singly as it is issued to subjects, it looks as though the point of having authoritative institutions is undermined by the strategy employed to justify their directives as expressed by the normal justification thesis. This requires in each case of authoritative prescription that subjects establish the reasons which should guide their conduct in the domain governed by the directive and enquire whether or not these reasons are motivating the authority which directs them. Suppose again that the domain is health policy. How can I check that a particular government decision concerning the licensing of a drug is motivated by a concern for citizens' health rather than by a desire to make economies in the health service, other than by working out for myself whether or not the decision not to license the drug is likely to promote my health? What then remains of the peremptory status of the reasons for action adduced by authoritative directives?

I am conscious that this critical study of the role of reasons in the application of Raz's dependence and normal justification theses is inconclusive, but we should move on. I need to explain how the good reasons thesis works. So we should state it again:

> Claims to authority are valid, political power is legitimate, if citizens can find *good reasons* to support it.

Chapter 5

The scope and limits of justificatory arguments

The scope of 'good reasons'

We saw earlier that a statement of good reasons, as advanced by the political authority and accepted by the citizens to whom it is addressed, will have the form of an argument. The conclusion of the argument can be more or less ambitious. The most ambitious argument will conclude that all citizens of all states – *de facto* political powers – should accept all the duties imputed to them by the sovereign authority. The least ambitious argument will seek to establish that some citizens of some states should accept some of the duties ascribed to them. In between these extremes there will be a range of claims, differing in the scope of the different elements identified in the arguments: all, most or some states; all, most or some citizens; all, most or some of the duties that states may impute. These offer a range of permutations and we shall review these possibilities in a schematic fashion.

There is a different way of putting the issues that are at stake here. We could state them as conditions that have to be met by a satisfactory theory of citizens' duties (or political obligation, widely construed). If we think of matters in this way, it makes sense to review the possibilities in order of the strength of the conditions, discussing first the strongest set of conditions as those which the most ambitious argument aspires to meet and then weakening the conditions in a way that makes less ambitious arguments plausible. We shall see that it is an open question as to what is a theory of citizens' duties. I should state in advance that I take a very relaxed view of the conditions that a useful theory should meet.

First, we should look at the most ambitious argument, stating the most stringent conditions, to the effect that a theory of citizens' duties should be able to explain why

1   *All* citizens of *all* states should accept *all* the duties prescribed to them.

This claim seems, at first sight, quite absurd, but there is an argument to this conclusion which has a distinguished provenance in the work of Thomas Hobbes. As we saw in Chapter 4, the reason why one may conclude that all states have unlimited authority is that limited authority will lead inexorably to anarchy, the state of nature in which 'the life of man [is] solitary, poore, nasty, brutish, and short' (Hobbes 1968: 186; Part 1, Ch. XIII [62]). The obvious objection to Hobbes's defence of the state is that rational persons should not endorse a political apparatus with such fearsome, absolute, powers as Hobbes attributes to the only kind of stable state. In such a state, one might think, 'the Condition of Subjects is very miserable; as obnoxious to [i.e. liable to suffer from the exercise of] the lusts, and other irregular passions of him, or them that have so unlimited a power in their hands' (238; Part 1, Ch. XVIII [94]). Hobbes concedes that times might be difficult: 'the estate of Man can never be without some incommodity or another' (ibid.), but no state is so bad as the state of nature. The worst that could possibly happen under any form of government 'is scarce sensible, in respect of the miseries that accompany a Civill Warre; or that dissolute condition of masterless men, without subjection to Lawes, and a coërcive Power to tye their hands from rapine, and revenge' (ibid.). In other words, the worst state is far better than the no-state condition, the state of nature. And Hobbes believes that even the worst state would not be so bad as short-sighted worriers tell us since the most self-interested and personally ambitious of sovereigns would soon recognize the obvious truth that he needs a vigorous and prosperous citizenry to fund his pursuit of strength and glory (ibid.). We have the advantage of Hobbes, since he was 'scarce sensible' of the hideous examples that the twentieth century has yielded of truly awful states. Nothing is as bad as life in the worst state – select your own candidate – where the powers of the state are employed with deadly efficiency and irresistible force to persecute in random or systematic fashion very large numbers of its own citizens. So we should conclude that Hobbes was mistaken.

Notice an important implication of this swift rejection of the most ambitious claim on behalf of the state. Following Hobbes's failure we should recognize that no plausible argument can hope to demonstrate the legitimate authority of the state quite generally. This does not mean that we should embrace anarchism or scepticism on the basis that 'The State' cannot be justified. The advocate of the state must draw in his horns and the constraints on a satisfactory theory should be relaxed. The arguments put forward must speak to the legitimacy of certain sorts of state only: broadly, just and democratic states. So I shall suppose in what follows that the arguments to hand, which purport to attribute duties to citizens, are *always* conditional on the fact that the state which puts them forward meets specified constraints (which we shall discuss). It is therefore no objection to any of these arguments that they are not fully general. They are not intended to be. It is not a weakness of any of the arguments put forward in what follows that they do not apply across the board to all states.

Faced with these formidable difficulties, a less ambitious argument will conclude that

2   *All* citizens of *some* states should accept *all* the duties that may be prescribed to them.

Modern jargon has it that such a claim is *universal* in respect of its application to all citizens (Simmons 1979: 35–6; Smith 1999: 76–7).[1] If some or all citizens have *all* the duties that may be prescribed to them, I shall say that they have a *complete* set of duties. So we can rewrite (2) above as stating that the duties of the citizens of some state are universal and complete. Again, this claim on the part of the state – a state which has not disqualified itself by failing to meet some minimum standards of propriety – is very ambitious. Whether or not it is true will depend on the force of the arguments which the state is using to establish this conclusion.

As we shall see in the upshot, several of the arguments in the traditional repertory of the state are conditional. There are familiar arguments which rely on the citizens meeting some condition. Since it may well be true that some citizens meet this condition, whereas others do not, such an argument will not meet the universality condition. An argument that works in this way is the argument from express consent. A citizen who expressly consents to assume all the duties of citizenship has a correspondingly complete set of duties, but the citizen who does not expressly consent has not assumed any duties on this basis. (Of course duties may be ascribed to them on some other basis.) In respect of citizens who do expressly consent we may conclude that

3   *Some* citizens (of *some* state) should accept *all* the duties of citizenship.

A different sort of conditionality concerns the content of citizens' duties. A familiar group of arguments which the state may use (e.g. from fairness and gratitude) stress the benefits of citizenship and conclude that the proper response to the citizens' receipt of benefits is the citizens' acceptance of (all or) some subset of duties. For example, the arguments from fairness and gratitude will emphasize the citizens' willing receipt of the state's protection of their rights through the forces of law and order. One might judge that a minimum response on the part of all citizens who are thus benefited should be an acceptance on their part of legal duties not to violate others' rights, as well as the further duty to help fund these services through the payment of taxes. We shall have more to say later about the detail of this argument, but we should notice the possibility of hypothecation, of arguments which assign some set of duties to some group of citizens on the basis of the specific services the citizens have received from the state. I use the term 'hypothecation' as a generalization of its common usage in respect of public finances raised to fund specific services, denoting any linkage effected by argument of citizens' duties to the accomplishment of state functions. Thus the state may make a weaker claim than that of completeness of duties. It may conclude that

4   *All* citizens (of *some* state) should accept *some* of the duties of citizenship.[2]

The weakest claim of all on the part of the state will be based on arguments that establish that

5   *Some* citizens (of *some* state) should accept *some* of the duties of citizenship.

It is possible, in cases of successful arguments which yield both (4) and (5), that different duties are attributed to different groups of citizens. As the different arguments are worked out in the specific circumstances of application to a particular state it is possible that we might find a variegated pattern of duties distributed across different groups of citizen. This is to reject as a constraint on a satisfactory theory of political obligation what Jonathan Wolff has termed the assumption of uniformity: that 'all citizens have the same type or level of political obligations', 'that the content of each citizen's political obligation is the same' (Wolff 2000: 182, 187). Wolff is happy to reject this assumption and this must be the correct position. Of course, life is made easier for a government if it can successfully attribute the same list of duties to its citizens, and we should notice that it might turn out that all citizens, or at least all those who have duties to the state, have the same set of duties. Everything will depend upon whether and how both the philosophical and the political questions are settled. Only then can we come to a judgement of what a particular state is due from which of its citizens.

We should notice a further implication of the range of possibilities that I have canvassed. Readers will have gathered that there is a variety of arguments which purport to establish duties on the part of citizens, and as I have suggested, some of these will be more ambitious than others. None of these has yet been investigated with a view to demonstrating their philosophical cogency. However, we should be prepared even at this early stage to find that a number of these arguments are philosophically acceptable and we should not be surprised to find that several of these find application within the circumstances of some particular regime. It may be that different arguments yield exactly the same conclusion: that all citizens have some specific duty – say the duty to obey the law. This will be a happy result from the point of view of the state. Philosophically, one of these arguments will be redundant, but that is not a defect. Further, it may turn out that arguments overlap in their successful attribution of duties: Argument 1 may attribute duties a and b to all citizens, Argument 2 may attribute duties b and c, and so on. In this way, a cluster of arguments, severally incomplete in their scope may yield a complete set of attributable duties. In similar fashion, universality might be the product of a number of arguments working together: Argument 3 might attribute the duties of citizenship to group A, Argument 4 may capture group B, and so on until all citizens have been included as they have been found to be members of one or other applicable groups. In fact arguments of all these types, differing as they do in respect of the scope of citizens captured and the duties they may successfully attribute, may be combined so long as they do not contradict each other in respect of their premises and construction.

I cannot see any reason why there should be only one argument or principle to justify all obligations of all citizens. This condition has been dubbed 'singularity in ground' and rejected by A.J. Simmons (Simmons 1979: 35). It is discussed and rejected by Jonathan Wolff (Wolff 2000: 184–5). Other theorists accept that a number of different justificatory principles might be combined, either to secure universality or completeness, or simply because they are philosophically acceptable and practically applicable although they might be redundant in their application. Thus George Klosko argues that a theory that is universal and complete requires both an argument from fairness and an argument from natural justice (Klosko 1992: 4 and 2005). Of the six main justifications that he identifies as aiming to justify the duty to obey the law, Chaim Gans argues that two are flawed – which leaves four satisfactory arguments in the field (Gans 1992: 42–94). John Rawls believes that there are two sound arguments in play: the argument from fairness applies specifically to office holders; the argument from a natural duty to support just institutions applies quite generally to citizens of a just state (Rawls 1972: 333–50).

We shall see which arguments survive examination in what follows. In the meanwhile, we should permit the state to be profligate in its assembly and presentation of arguments. It wants to capture as many citizens as it can and attribute to them as wide a range of duties as it believes to be necessary for it to function successfully. The state is not fazed if it is revealed that several of its arguments lead to the same conclusion, if some of them turn out to be redundant, if there is over-determination of the grounds of compliance.[3]

A methodological interlude

I believe that my account of the dialectic which governs arguments concerning the authority of the state and the duties of citizens – the state proposes, the citizen disposes – is elegant and accurate as a portrayal of how philosophical disputations in this area should be conducted. But then 'he would, wouldn't he?' . . . as she said. There is a different account of how a philosophical theory should work in this domain of applied ethics, and we should review it, not because it speaks as the voice of a competitor, but because it gives a different verdict on the cogency of specific arguments.

George Klosko argues that the task of a theory of political obligation, as an element of moral theory quite generally, is to explicate the rationale of the common belief of most citizens that they have an obligation to obey the law.[4] Klosko takes it as given that

> most people feel strongly that they are somehow bound to obey the laws of their societies [and that] a theory of obligation should address these feelings . . . the main task of a theory of obligation is to explain the obligations that we owe to governments.
>
> (Klosko 1992: 5)

Klosko believes that it is the task of a philosophical theory in this domain to cohere with, or to explain, the settled belief of most people – most citizens of liberal democracies – that they have political obligations, notably an obligation to obey the law.

I believe this is a mistake. In the first place, this methodology begs the question against the anarchist.[5] Even if it were demonstrated, as a matter of fact, that most citizens of existing societies do believe that they have an obligation to obey the law, the anarchist argues that this belief is mistaken. We shall discuss the anarchist position later, but roughly the anarchist claims that no good reasons have been given why citizens should recognize political obligations. Either this is a matter of argument failure (and hence the case for political obligation goes by default as successive attempts at justification are shown to be fallacious or inconclusive – this is A.J. Simmons' sceptical view), or it is demonstrated that no argument *could* serve to justify political obligations. A philosophical anarchist such as R.P. Wolff argues that any claim to political authority and consequent citizens' obligations will conflict with persons' autonomy. A classical anarchist will argue that the state is such an evil institution that it cannot be justified. These positions cannot be dismissed by taking the task of political philosophy to be the articulation of a contrary view. This illustrates a more general point to the effect that it is not the job of moral theories to *explain* in some quasi-scientific sense beliefs that may well be erroneous. Rather, the task of the philosopher is to seek a *justification* for such beliefs, a justification that will hold firm regardless of the number of folk who in fact believe it.

Second, this methodology assumes that arguments which cannot establish the universality or generality of political obligations – that they apply to *all* or *most* citizens – must fail. Thus Klosko states that arguments from actual consent must be rejected. Since it is taken as a matter of fact that most citizens of existing societies have not actually consented to the imposition of the political obligations that are attributed to them, an argument from actual consent cannot explain the political obligations that most citizens believe themselves to have. This is true, but it is only a defect of consent theory if consent theory takes itself to be a justification for the political obligations acknowledged by all or most citizens (as against simply those citizens who in fact consent) or if the consent theorist claims that the argument from consent is the only argument that can in principle justify political obligations. I have suggested that there is no reason why we should accept either of these assumptions. Obviously a theory that meets the conditions of universality and singularity of ground is more powerful than a theory which does not, but it doesn't follow from this that a less powerful theory should be abandoned.

We should stick to our task of reviewing the philosophical cogency of any argument that the state puts to any number of citizens as a possible ground for some or all of their political obligations.

The justice constraint

We argued above that it is unrealistic of the state to attempt to demonstrate that citizens of all states have political obligations. Some states have been, indeed are, so dreadful that they have no moral claim on their citizens. Against Hobbes we argued that it is not always rational for a person to submit to the state rather than accept life in a state of nature. I suspect that we don't really know how bad life for folks like us would be in a state of nature. The thought experiment is too hard to construct, the evidence base is too flimsy for us to be confident about the soundness of our speculations. On the other hand, we do know, or can easily find out, how awful life can be in some states. Everyone should be able to recite a list of horrors, of states that have imprisoned and murdered millions of their subjects.[6]

So we should conclude that only some states have the moral standing to put forward a case for their own authority and their citizens' obligations. What are these moral credentials that a state must establish?[7] I say that the state must be *just* in the broadest sense of the term as employed by Plato and in recent times by John Rawls to denote the characteristic virtue of a state.[8] The just state is the good state and there are a variety of dimensions to this quality of goodness. Clearly I need to give a broad-brush account of a just state.

In the first place, the just state will be a democratic state. By this I mean that there should be some opportunity for citizens to participate meaningfully in decision-making processes. Minimally, this amounts to an elected legislature with representative institutions such as Parliament and local government which are not so distanced and diluted that citizens are unable to identify with the decisions taken by their representatives. Decision-makers must be recognizably accountable to the electorate for their law-making and public administration. Second, a just state will promote the public good by protecting the rights and liberties of all citizens. Clearly there are many different specifications of what this might involve, from charters of rights to articulations of an operative harm principle. And again, all the details will be controversial. But if it were agreed that a state did not effectively protect citizens' rights and liberties, particularly if it were shown that the state itself was a violator of rights, then such a state could not claim authority over its citizens or justifiably attribute duties to them. Third, the just state will prosecute violations of persons' rights and other breaches of the law by the use of due process of law. Those accused will be treated as innocent until proven guilty, will be able to make out a case in their own defence in a public trial, and so on. Fourth, and more controversially, the just state will secure a measure of distributive justice in the allocation of benefits and burdens to citizens. There is no uncontroversial way of spelling out what this principle requires; it might be further articulated in terms of equality or justified inequality, as provision for basic needs or the receipt of specified entitlements. But again, if a case has been successfully made out that a particular regime is unjust in respect of the distribution of goods, one consequence of this is that the citizens will be in a position to repudiate duties that are imputed to them. Finally, if the state is unjust in its dealings with other states, if it conducts unjust wars or exploits other states, particularly the poorest, in its trade policies or other economic dealings, its own citizens may justifiably reject its authority as they denounce the evils which are done in their name.

Readers will be aware that the above portrayal of the just state is sketchy in the extreme and that all elements of it are controversial. The point of this account is to establish the broad condition that must operate on the applicability of arguments for the authority of states and the duties of the citizen, a constraint to the effect that unless the state which claims authority to impose duties on its citizen is just, as thus conceived, none of the arguments that might otherwise vindicate its claims will apply in the specific circumstances of any claim.

This is not uncontroversial. For example, one might argue that citizens who have explicitly consented to a specific regime of duties are bound to accept these duties as political obligations. Or one might argue that if citizens identify in an unqualified fashion with the political institutions of their state, a state that they feel to be legitimate on the basis of an established tradition of authority and allegiance, then they are duty bound to accept just such duties as the state imposes, whatever its constitution might be. In neither case is it suggested that there are further, independent constraints that must be met. If the citizens consent to, or feel allegiance towards, an unjust state, so be it – one might think. So long as their consent is valid (and there will be more on this later) or their allegiance is not evidently irrational, they must accept the consequences, even if these consequences include the imposition upon them of unjust laws. This is the position that I challenge.

I believe, on the contrary, that in circumstances of demonstrable injustice, a state's claim to authority is void and its imposition of duties on citizens is invalid. Citizens of an unjust state have no duty to comply with its commands, whatever they might believe. It matters not that they have consented to undertake the duties of citizenship or feel allegiance towards the state with which they identify as citizens. They have no duties as citizens and the state has no authority over them if the justice condition is not met. I produce this minimal account of the just state solely in order to demonstrate that one of the things at stake in a debate about whether or not a particular state is just or unjust in any of these central respects will be the authority of that state. That said, these certainties conceal a difficulty concerning the strength or scope of this condition which is hard to resolve.

A verdict that a particular state is unjust can cover a multitude of sins. One might be attesting the existence of particular unjust laws in an otherwise reasonably just state or one might be claiming that the regime as a whole is unjust.[9] The worst of states is a tyranny, governed by a dictatorship which violates some of the rights of all citizens and all of the rights of some, prosecuting and punishing citizens arbitrarily, distributing benefits to a small group of favourites and burdens to the great oppressed majority, whom it enlists to fight unjust aggressive wars. This state is unjust on every count I have mentioned and probably more besides. We should conclude that it is illegitimate, that it has no authority over its citizens, and that the citizens have no duties towards it, no duties of obedience or aught else. But what if the state violates the canons of justice in small measure? Is all authority stripped away? Are all commands void and no duties left in place? That would be a harsh view, but maybe it is correct.

This is an alternative. We might deem duties to the state as somehow proportional to the justice of the state's constitution and its dealings with citizens. Suppose some number of citizens judge that a war is unjust. In these circumstances they are likely to review the political duties ascribed to them and redress the account. If they are conscripted, as happened in the United States during the Vietnam War, they may evade the draft, rejecting the specific duty to enlist by fleeing into exile, Canada, Scandinavia or elsewhere. Whilst abroad they may comply with other duties that are assigned to them. They vote if they receive a ballot paper and complete an income tax form, paying up whatever is due. Other citizens who object to a war but who don't face conscription may seek to withhold some portion of their taxes, a specific proportion which they judge to be funding the war effort. They willingly pay the balance. Readers will have come across dozens of cases of citizens who seek to adjust the balance of their obligations in the face of what they see as injustice, from pensioners who refuse to pay increases in local taxes to demonstrators who continue to protest despite a ban on their activities. In all other respects these are compliant and dutiful citizens. These are all examples of folk who act in a specific way that they believe appropriate given the degree and kind of injustice to which they are subject.

There is another response which makes the same point in a less obvious way. Citizens who would otherwise obey the law willingly will cease to do so over a greater or lesser range of their activities if they regard themselves as the victims of injustice. They will recognize no, or a limited set of, obligations and hence will comply unwillingly, grudgingly on the basis of self-interest in the face of compulsion and the threat of punishment. If they could disobey with impunity, they would do so with no bad conscience and a sense that they are recouping what they are due, but they may never find the occasion to do so. We should recognize such examples as having the same ethical profile as disobedience. Dutiful citizens have been transformed into amoral opportunists within a domain of erstwhile duties that they have reassigned as burdens to be avoided whenever possible. I suspect that political arithmetic of this kind is familiar. Disenchantment, alienation and the loss of an active sense of moral engagement in the affairs of the state are a natural consequence of perceived injustice.

For the sake of argument, let's agree that it is unjust for a government to give massive tax breaks to the very rich, calculating that this will be an effective method (by way of rewards and incentives) to fund future election campaigns and that on balance this fiscal policy will increase its chances of re-election. (This is not the appalling tyranny I sketched above. In many ways this society is just. In fact it might remind readers of the first George W. Bush administration in the United States.) What should be the response of the citizen who believes that such a government is acting unjustly because it is subverting the democratic process ('the curse of money') and it is placing an undue fiscal burden on the poor and middle-income earners? Should she repudiate all her political obligations, disowning the state on the basis of the policies of the government and acting opportunistically across the board? Or should she repudiate just some?

I confess that I cannot find an argument to challenge the more radical response. If faced with an example such as this, of specific but limited, but not minor or trivial, injustice (as we have agreed, for purposes of argument), a fair-minded billionaire were to say, 'That's it. I'm leaving. I'll emigrate and transfer all my assets to a country in which I can live in good conscience as the citizen of a just polity', has she done wrong? I think not, but concede that the issue is moot. But if we change the scenario at little, and suppose that our fair-minded billionaire says, 'That's it. This government has just shown that it has no concern for justice. In consequence, I disavow all my political obligations and shall henceforth seek and follow all legal and not-so-legal advice as to how I might best avoid and evade all taxes and other levies that may be imposed, living as an outlaw but in effective impunity from legal penalties' – as though she regards herself as living in a Hobbesian state of nature in relation to the state, a condition in which morality (in the form of citizens' duties) is no restraint – I suspect that her responsive is excessive. And supposing that my suspicion is widely shared this would surely suggest a deeper suspicion: that her recalcitrance is self-serving. But the law of suspicion doesn't operate here: suspects aren't thereby guilty. (Imagine that the outlaw billionaire is a Robin Hood who donates her financial gains, legal and illegal, to the suffering poor.)

I can find one line of argument that might justify a limited response to limited injustice. Earlier I mentioned the possibility of hypothecation, of arguments that serve to justify the imputation of some specific set of duties to a subset of citizens on the basis of some particular feature of their circumstances. Suppose that an argument from gratitude can successfully ground some citizens' duties (we shall examine the soundness of this argument later). The basis of the feeling of gratitude and the fair attribution of an obligation (to pay income taxes as demanded, say) is the citizen's receipt of benefits from the state. Now imagine in a particular case that a group of citizens are denied a benefit in circumstances where the officers of the state can exercise some discretion. And suppose these citizens are right to believe that this discretion has been exercised capriciously to their loss. In circumstances like these they are likely to judge that they have been treated unfairly, that they are the victims of a clear injustice. One consequence of this state of affairs is that the citizens concerned do not have the reasons that other more fortunate citizens have for accepting the duty to pay all taxes demanded from them. They have no reason to be grateful since, unjustly, they have been arbitrarily denied a benefit that a reasonable person would consider that they are due. If we assume finally that the particularly appropriate response of the grateful citizen for the receipt of benefits is the acceptance of a duty to pay taxes, then we should conclude that the properly ungrateful citizen does no wrong if she evades some taxation or pays up grudgingly under conditions of *force majeure*. Such a citizen may well have other duties – to participate in the democratic process, for example. There is no exact science here which fixes a precise measure of duty to be subtracted from the full regime, but plausible claims can be put forward and they should be carefully heeded by a state which detects measured recalcitrance.

The justice constraint, as first stated, serving to void all obligations if it is not met, looks to be a very blunt instrument. Perhaps it can be sharpened so that it operates less indiscriminately and with more finesse. But even an unsophisticated employment of it by the citizen who believes herself to be the victim of injustice, however potentially self-serving such a use may be, should cause the state to be alert to the consequences of casual but limited oppression. The moral legitimacy of the state, its standing as an authority over its citizens, is a precious asset which it should be careful not to squander carelessly. If a citizen believes herself to belong to a group whose liberties have been infringed, the state should not lightly claim that this is at worst a small violation and that the citizen's response is excessive. I doubt that one can be oversensitive to injustice.

On the other hand, the citizen should not be too quick to claim that a particular law is unjust. A number of philosophers caution us that 'citizens will have a hard time drawing a line between just and unjust laws, and if they perceive their duty to obey as reaching only just laws, they will end up disobeying many laws they think are unjust' (Greenawalt 1989: 186). This is fair. For obvious reasons the judgement that a particular law or a policy in the name of which laws are framed is unjust will often be controversial. Caution surely is due before the citizen rejects a particular duty or denies the authority of the state on the grounds of injustice. But it remains a fact that the reflective citizen who is convinced of injustice will not recognize a duty to comply. They may comply perforce, but their obedience will not be dutiful.

The publicity constraint

The publicity constraint operates on the terms in which the various good reasons which the state offers to citizens as grounding for its authority are couched. The state which proposes and the citizen who disposes are personifications which assist in the articulation of a philosophical dialectic. From one point of view, the account given by the state can be as sophisticated a piece of philosophy as one likes. It can employ whatever terminology and instruments are the order of the day for the philosophical audience to whom the arguments are addressed. But from another point of view the problem of political obligation is raised whenever actual living citizens question the basis of the duties which the state ascribes to them, and it would be a rhetorical weakness of the account of good reasons which the state gives that it is inaccessible to the enquiring citizen, being a technical exercise in philosophy incomprehensible to untrained minds.

This philosophical point is raised in the work of Plato and Hobbes; it has resurfaced in recent times in the work of John Rawls. When Plato is discussing the institution of the Just City in Book III of the *Republic*, he assumes that members of the constituent classes will find it difficult to hold to a conviction 'that what they think the interest of the State is to be the rule of their lives' (Plato *Republic*: 413c). It is not clear (at least at this stage of the argument) whether the source of the problem is epistemological or motivational, whether, that is, members of each of the classes of guardians, auxiliaries and workers are unable to fathom the philosophical reasoning that Socrates has adduced or whether they will find the philosophical account insufficiently motivating, unlikely to produce the unstinting allegiance required in citizens of a stable state. I suspect that Plato believes that it is a mixture of both, but for the purposes of this argument I shall assume that the difficulty is primarily epistemological.

Plato's solution to the problem is the 'noble lie', 'the old Phoenician tale' of the metals, communicated 'gradually, first to the rulers, then to the soldiers, and lastly to the people' (414c–d). The essence of the 'noble lie' is a metallurgical-cum-biological nonsense concerning the fundamental natures of members of the different classes as consisting of gold, silver or bronze. Notice that the noble lie is to be told by Socrates to all classes. It is not told by the rulers to gain the compliance of the ruled. It is not government propaganda, as many have believed. What Plato is offering here is a sharp distinction between a proper philosophical vindication of the constitution of the Just City and the actual account, here a lie, a myth or a fiction, of how the citizens are to understand themselves and the relations in which they stand to the state and their fellow citizens.

We should notice the implications of Plato's doctrine for an account of citizens' duties. Presumably the differential duties ascribable to members of the different classes are vindicated by the claim that the constitution which determines them is just, and this claim in turn is backed up by a theory of justice which is itself vindicated as the product of sound reason. The just state is the rational state. It is unfortunate that the citizens cannot perceive this, but the philosopher's task is accomplished when the philosophical demonstration is complete. Suppose Plato is right: the philosophical grounding of the just state is not accessible to (most) citizens. Assume further that stable institutions grounded in firm allegiance are a universal good. What exactly is wrong with Legislators (to use Rousseau's term for nation-builders and constitution-framers) treating their citizens in this fashion?

A first and obvious answer is that Socrates is telling a lie. Indeed he acknowledges as he tells it that he finds it hard to look his listeners in the face. But the obvious reply to this is that some lies are fine, and this is a needful falsehood. I stress: it is not the philosopher-rulers of the ideal city-state of the Republic who are telling the lie, it is Socrates the philosophical constitution drafter and ethos creator who fashions a lie with sufficient plausibility to cascade down to all citizens.

We find a very different answer to this question in Thomas Hobbes. Hobbes was well aware of the tradition of *arcana imperii*, the noble lie, but he rejected this approach to the art of ruling. He did not reject it because it is straightforwardly immoral; he rejected it because it was foolish and unnecessary.[10] It is foolish because the project of securing stability is undermined if the method employed is vulnerable to being exposed as a falsehood – and that's the trouble with myth and allegory. Their proponents may get found out and then the normative edifice collapses. Folk don't need to be able to work out the whole truth in order to smell a rat, and as soon as they do, the motivation which deception was designed to induce will vanish. These are empirical claims, and I guess they have some plausibility. More importantly though, Hobbes thought the noble lie was unnecessary because he thought, unlike Plato, that the truth of the matter concerning the grounding of citizens' duties was not arcane. It could be spelled out demonstratively on the basis of premises evident to everyman. Careful argument is needed; the terrain is not uncontroversial since competing doctrines are in play. But Hobbes was sure, not only that it is of the utmost practical importance that correct doctrines are established and widely understood – being a matter of war and peace, life and death – but also that *he* had established the groundings of citizens' rights and duties in a style that is publicly demonstrable.

Following Hobbes, we can now state what I introduced earlier as the 'publicity constraint'. Negatively, the constraint prohibits any account purporting to ground citizens' duties that is based on lies, myths, allegories, or falsehoods generally. Positively, it requires that the account which is given be comprehensible to fair-minded, decently educated citizens generally. Since publicity in this sense is a constraint, it cannot establish that such an account is available for promulgation. That remains to be seen.

In recent times, John Rawls has drawn attention to the centrality of a principle of publicity in the liberal tradition. Rawls's discussion of what he calls the publicity condition is not easy to unravel because publicity operates in his writings both as a basic standard of ethical reasoning, a 'formal constraint of the concept of right' with Kantian credentials (Rawls 1972: 130–3), and as a natural implication of reasoning from a contractarian standpoint which seeks to model the principles of justice that regulate a well-ordered society as the terms of a hypothetical agreement amongst all reflective citizens.[11] It is clear, though, that Rawls's publicity condition has the negative and positive features that we distinguished in Hobbes's theory. Negatively,

> such devices as Plato's Noble Lie in the *Republic*, bk. III, 414–415, are ruled out, as well as the advocacy of religion (when not believed) to buttress a social system that could not otherwise survive, as by the Grand Inquisitor in Dostoyevsky's *The Brothers Karamazov*.
>
> (Rawls 1972: 454, footnote 1)

Elsewhere he insists 'that a well-ordered society in which the full publicity condition is satisfied . . . is a society without ideology (understood in Marx's sense of false consciousness)' (Rawls 2001: 121). Positively, the account that is given of the principles of justice, and derivatively of the legitimacy of the well-ordered society, must respect the standing of citizens as moral persons, with 'the capacity for a sense of justice: the capacity to understand, to apply, and to act from (and not merely in accordance with) the principles of political justice that specify the fair terms of social cooperation' (Rawls: 18–19). Though Rawls, like Hobbes, believes that public recognition of the just state contributes to the stability of the social system, it is arguable that the Kantian echoes in this positive account mark an advance on Hobbes, whose aim might be characterized as strategic.[12] Publicity, Rawls believes, enhances self-respect and, derivatively, mutual recognition amongst persons who claim, and are worthy of, the respect of others. An important element of the natural duty of mutual respect which requires that citizens deal with each other civilly is that they 'be willing to explain the grounds of their actions, especially when the claims of others are overruled' (Rawls 1972: 179).

Thus far we have described the alternative positions pro and con the publicity condition. I should state my own view. I think that no amount of philosophical argument can refute Plato's epistemological claim. It just might turn out that the best and deepest account of the good reasons which ground citizens' duties and command acceptance of the authority of the state is too difficult, too technically demanding for the run of decently educated, well-motivated citizens to comprehend. The soundest philosophy in this domain may be as hard as rocket science. This will be a factual matter. But Plato is surely ethically mistaken in judging that a noble lie is called for in these unhappy circumstances. A bowdlerized version of the best account is called for – political philosophy for kids – if the full story is epistemically inaccessible. (I suspect that this is Hegel's solution to the problem: his treatment of the rationale of hereditary monarchy sharply distinguishes the kosher account delivered by philosophical science from the common-sense story concerning heredity as a source of stability in the modern state.)[13]

But equally, Hobbes and Rawls may turn out to be right. It is better, from the point of view of state and citizen alike, if the best account of citizens' duties is epistemologically accessible to the citizens who insist that the duties imputed to them be well-grounded. Not only will this contribute to the stability of the state but it will satisfy the ethical demands or philosophical curiosity of the fair-minded, enquiring citizen. Furthermore, as Rawls sees clearly (although it is a nice question whether his practice belies his methodological strictures) only such an account is fully respectful of the equal moral standing of citizens of the modern state. (Plato's hypothesized reply would be obvious: citizens do not enjoy equal moral standing or merit the respect which pays tribute to that equality.) I shall regard the rest of this book as an attempt to demonstrate that Plato and Hegel are mistaken. I aim to satisfy the publicity constraint in the arguments which follow and leave to readers the judgement of whether or not I have been successful in this rhetorical task.

Thus far we have been concerned to establish the philosophical apparatus that is required to tackle directly the question of whether there might be philosophical arguments which are good enough for the state to employ in its attempt to ascribe duties to citizens, and concomitantly, good enough for citizens to recognize that they are not mistaken or self-deceiving when they take these arguments to apply to them, serving as the basis for their acknowledgement of a regime of duties. Nothing that we have said so far should be taken to entail the existence of any such duties. In fact, there are strong and well-known claims to the effect that no such arguments are successful. These are the claims advanced within the anarchist tradition. Before we tackle the substantive arguments that address the Philosophical Problem we should look briefly at the anarchist claim that the task of justifying a regime of citizens' duties is a lost cause.

Part II

The arguments: ancient and modern, for and against

Chapter 6

The anarchist challenge

If the anarchist is right, readers might as well stop here. The anarchist denies that citizens have any duties in virtue of their citizenship. There are no political obligations. Anarchism comes in different varieties and, in fact, this denial of duties to the state represents the common core of anarchist views. I shall demonstrate that the main arguments in support of the anarchist rejection of the state, and with it any regime of citizens' duties, are either mistaken or inconclusive. The latter, weak, conclusion is all that we need to give point to the project of examining arguments that might solve the Philosophical Problem as that was explained in Chapter 4. We need to examine the major anarchist doctrines in turn, but we shall have to do so briskly – so the anarchist may justly complain.[1] Following recent practice I distinguish political and philosophical anarchism, and deal with political anarchism first.

Political anarchism

Political anarchism holds that the state is an evil institution. It is in the nature of the state to harm citizens and to violate their rights. Recall that it is a defining feature of the state that it has a monopoly of violence within a society. It may be that other agencies and individual persons are permitted to employ coercive measures against their fellows, but they do so on licence, as agents of the state or because the state judges that its interests are furthered by permitting a measure of private violence. This capacity to enact permissible violence is the source of most of the evils that ensue. These were memorably summarized by Proudhon:

> To be GOVERNED is to be at every operation, at every transaction, noted, registered, enrolled, taxed, stamped, measured, numbered, assessed, licensed, authorized, admonished, forbidden, reformed, corrected, punished. It is, under pretext of public utility, and in the name of the general interest, to be placed under contribution, trained, ransomed, exploited, monopolized, extorted, squeezed, mystified, robbed; then, at the slightest resistance, the first word of complaint, to be repressed, fined, despised, harassed, tracked, abused, clubbed, disarmed, choked, imprisoned, judged, condemned, shot, deported, sacrificed, sold, betrayed; and, to crown all, mocked, ridiculed, outraged, dishonoured. That is government; that is its justice; that is its morality.[2]

As David Miller notes, this suggests that the state is excessively coercive, cruelly punitive, widely exploitative (and supportive of exploiters), and, when it engages in war, destructive of citizens' lives. This is a thick and heavy debit column.

The anarchist position is the obverse of the Hobbesian argument for the state. Just as Hobbes believes that he has demonstrated that no condition could be worse than the stateless state of nature, which is a state of war, and hence that any functioning state is better than the no-state alternative, so the political anarchist claims that no condition can be worse than that of those who live under a state. Typical state structures compromise some or all of a list of widely accepted human goods. The lives of citizens are put at risk and their well-being is severely constrained. Their freedom is limited and their standing as moral equals is denied. Their individual autonomy is violated on a daily basis by the institutions of the state, and their capacity for genuine solidarity and fellowship with other human beings is frustrated. The details of the critical account of the state will differ from anarchist to anarchist, but the heart of the story is the same. The state makes the good life impossible.

This conclusion is especially pertinent if one believes, as we shall see that some philosophers do, that the ground of political obligation is furnished by the citizens' receipt of conspicuous benefits from the state. If one argues quite generally, as a utilitarian might, that citizens are better off as a result of living under a state, and that this beneficial condition will only be stable and permanent if citizens recognize a duty to support state institutions, or if one argues that considerations of fairness require those who have accepted benefits from the state to support the state that has provided them, or if one argues that gratitude to the state for its provision of benefits should prompt a recognition on the part of citizens that they ought to comply with a duty to support the state, one's argument is in each case vulnerable to the charge that the citizens do not in fact benefit from the state, or that the benefits are small and outweighed by the very great costs.[3]

What we have here is a straightforward dispute about the respective benefits, as computed by some specific measures of the good, to be attained in the state and no-state conditions respectively. On the side of the state, proponents argue that the state is necessary for defence against external aggression. The anarchist opponents argue that the state (and the international order of independent nation states) is itself the cause of war and has been responsible for the deaths and hardship of millions. On the side of the state, proponents argue that the state is a necessary resource for the many vulnerable persons who need protection against aggression from hostile neighbours. It is a mutual protection agency writ large.[4] The anarchist opponent argues that it is the state itself that is responsible for creating the disastrous moral environment wherein aggression and hostility are commonplace. It announces laws backed by sanctions, ordering citizens upon pain of punishment to act in ways that a moment's moral reflection would tell them to act in anyway. Thereby it causes their moral sensitivity to shrivel through lack of use. Citizens of the state typically ask themselves, not 'What is the right thing to do?' but 'What does the state command me to do?' and, consequent to this loss of moral sensibility, 'Can I get away with not doing what I am told? Is the game worth the candle?'

We can continue to articulate the dialectic between defenders of the state and their anarchist opponents, as the defenders cite clear benefits and the opponents deny them. How might the issue be resolved? One major difficulty which plagues both the Hobbesian argument for the state and the anarchist rejection of it concerns the characterization of the stateless condition – the state of nature. Both Hobbes and the anarchist address the hypothetical question: what would life be like for persons like us if there were no state? Famously, Hobbes tells us that mankind would live in a state of war, 'where every man is Enemy to every man'. Life in such circumstances would be 'solitary, poore, nasty, brutish, and short' (Hobbes 1968: 186; Part 1, Ch. 13 [62]). No doubt Hobbes's experience of civil war was in the back of his mind, but the chief argument to this conclusion is carefully deductive, grounded in a clear account of human nature.[5] But the detail of Hobbes's account of individual and social psychology, his study of the individual man and 'men in multitudes', which emphasizes psychological egoism, is very controversial. So, too, must be his description of the state of nature.

The anarchist faces the problem of convincing us that life in conditions of anarchy would be better than life in the best, realistically attainable, state. After all, we may agree with Proudhon that life under government is truly awful in many of the ways that he describes, yet also believe that life in the state of nature would be worse still. The only way that we could have any assurance that an anarchic life would be an improvement on life in the state would be to subscribe to truly generous beliefs about human nature. It is easy to see how this anarchist strategy works. Obviously the sceptic about anarchy will point to folks' vulnerability if there are no laws, police and prisons. The anarchist replies that ordinary, decent, people will respect each others' rights. That most persons respect each other and regard each others' rights as inviolable, that they care for each other because they have a genuine concern for other folk's interests: some anarchists adduce these points as facts about daily life under the state – which could not function if it relied upon coercion alone to ensure compliance. But if we were to take seriously, foster and reward the respectful and altruistic dispositions that are attested by humanity at large, we should find that even potential villains would conform to the basic rules for fear of exclusion from a society that they enjoy. Basically, the anarchist instructs us that we are much better creatures than we generally take ourselves to be. If we were to trust ourselves and our fellows to be concerned with each other's welfare, we should find that trust rewarded by the generous and compassionate responses of our fellows.

This is a noble vision that stands as a counterpoint to Hobbes's dismal picture. But this account, too, is controversial. Some say that the only place where real, die-hard villains do not predate on their fellows is Cloud-Cuckoo Land. Sensible folk take guard against them – don't we all lock our doors and cupboards, Hobbes asks (Hobbes 1968: 186–7; Part 1, Ch. 13 [62]). The only defensive strategy that works is to employ a greater coercive force than the villains can muster – that is, the state. The political anarchist has an easy task in describing the horrors of life in the state but a much harder task in persuading listeners that life without the state would be tolerable. The suspicious reader of the anarchist literature will note that the evils committed by the state are all of them put into effect by persons in its employ and it is obvious that many of the servants of the state take very great pleasure in dishing out the hard treatment. The anarchist then performs a conjuring trick. Along with the coercive state apparatus that they serve with such enthusiasm, these rogues and villains somehow disappear from the picture of life in the stateless condition.

I regard it as an open question whether the state is on balance an evil. We know that some states are, just as some states have been, hideous afflictions on the lives of the poor souls who are or have been subject to them. But not all states are or have been anything like as bad as the worst – even the anarchist must accept that there are degrees of awfulness. The issue is at bottom a factual one and I have no idea how it might be settled one way or another. That is why I conclude that the case made against the state by the political anarchist is inconclusive.

A *priori* philosophical anarchism

We should move on to consider the varieties of philosophical anarchism, and treat of *a priori* philosophical anarchism first. The *a priori* philosophical anarchist does not consider that the state is an unremitting evil (though of course she may be a political anarchist as well – the doctrines are not inconsistent). The key element is the identification of a necessary property of statehood as logically inconsistent with some deep value that individuals pursue. It might seem as though the obvious characteristic of the state for the anarchist to target is its exercise of coercive power, threatening and inflicting hard treatment such as imprisonment and worse on its citizens, but this does not reveal any necessary inconsistency. Suppose it is true that coercion is an evil; it may also be true that overall coercion against persons is reduced by the state's having coercive powers at its disposal. It is possible, indeed many have thought it plausible, that coercion is minimized by the activities of the coercive state.

The clearest argument for *a priori* philosophical anarchism is Kantian in form, though Kant would not endorse it, and as we shall see, versions of it have been advanced by writers who were most definitely not Kantians in respect of the general orientation of their ethics. In what follows we shall state and examine the forms of *a priori* philosophical anarchism to be found in the writings of William Godwin, Max Stirner and Robert Paul Wolff. Each in his own way seeks to demonstrate that a fundamental aspect of personhood concerned with the power of persons to decide what they ought to do (broadly: the autonomy of persons) is inconsistent with an essential property of the state which claims authority over its citizens (broadly: the right of the state to determine through laws how citizens should conduct themselves).[6]

An early variant of this form of argument was advanced by William Godwin. Although broadly a utilitarian, Godwin insists in his *Enquiry Concerning Political Justice* of 1793 that each individual has a 'right of private judgement':

> Every man is bound to the exertion of his faculties in the discovery of right, and to the carrying into effect all the right with which he is acquainted. . . . [T]he conviction of a man's individual understanding, is the only legitimate principle, imposing on him the duty of adopting any species of conduct.
>
> (Godwin 1971: 96)

In the case where the state commands a citizen to act in a given way upon threat of punishment, the state takes away that private judgement of what is the right thing for the citizen to do and replaces it with a judgement of what the self-interest of the citizen dictates. Suppose the state (a 'positive institution') forbids murder upon pain of capital punishment or a sentence of life imprisonment.

> This immediately changes the nature of the action [abstaining from murder]. Before, I preferred it for its intrinsic excellence. Now, so far as the positive institution operates, I prefer it, because some person has arbitrarily annexed to it a great weight of self-interest. But virtue, considered as the quality of an intelligent being, depends upon the disposition with which the action is accompanied. Under a positive institution then, this very action, which is intrinsically virtuous, may, so far as relates to the agent, become vicious.
>
> (Godwin 1971: 91).

It follows that it is always morally wrong, vicious because it is necessarily self-interested, for the citizen to obey the commands of the state. So we must assume that it is always wrong for a state to enact laws backed by sanctions because that converts otherwise intrinsically virtuous action into vice. It follows directly that no state can be justifiable since, of its nature, it compromises a right of private judgement and thereby eliminates the possibility of virtue.

This is an extravagant argument. It has an element of truth which has already been rehearsed in the political anarchist's claim that individuals' powers of moral judgement will shrivel when citizens deliberate their conduct in light of one question only: What does the state require me to do? Matters would be much worse if this question in turn were construed as asking what conduct will I be rewarded or punished by the state for doing. But there is no reason to think that submission to the coercive institutions of the state must eliminate all independent moral deliberation. That it does not was one lesson which we learned from our study of authority in Chapter 3. Citizens may properly exercise their judgement concerning the limits of state authority and, within those limits, they may be called to judge whether or not there might be more urgent moral considerations which require that their duty to obey the law be over-ridden. Godwin makes this mistake because he takes an erroneous view of the nature of authority and obedience, identifying the authority which government claims as a demand for respect for the force at its disposal (Godwin 1971: 120–2).

In any case it looks to be just false that the enactment of coercive law commanding citizens to behave in a certain ways robs them of their right of private judgement. All of us will have encountered situations where the state commands us to perform actions we believe to be wrong, or more likely forbids our doing actions we believe to be morally innocent or even praiseworthy. We may then do as we are commanded to do for fear of sanctions, and no doubt there is a story to be told of how our freedom is diminished. But it does not follow from the fact that we grudgingly comply that our right of private judgement has been violated. As noted above, our capacity to apply private judgement may shrink through lack of exercise but that's an entirely contingent matter. We can imagine the opposing happening in particular cases: fresh legislation, if it is onerous, may provoke us to examine with very great care whether what the government commands us to do is what we ought to be doing.

Altogether we would need to know a lot more about the right of private judgement, and in particular about the mechanisms and logical moves whereby that right is violated by sovereign commands before we accept Godwin's argument. Since this does not look a promising agenda, we should move on.

As a philosopher, Max Stirner is even more curious than William Godwin. He is one of the very few ethical egoists, although his egoism employs a highly original account of a person's self-interest. The true egoist does not value whatever he wants for himself – after all, he may value something silly like fast cars. If his desires are inauthentic, formed, for example, in a constricted bourgeois environment, he ought not to pursue their satisfaction. What is right is the expression of pure self-will.[7] By contrast, the law of the state is an expression of the will of an authority which effectively usurps the *own will* of the citizen. In *The Ego and His Own* Stirner argues that 'The State cannot forbear the claim to determine the individual's will . . . [F]or the State it is indispensable that nobody have an *own will*'. He continues, 'The own will of Me is the State's destroyer' (Stirner 1915: 254–6). Stirner here elaborates a straightforward contradiction: he says persons ought to act as their own will dictates; the state says persons ought to act as dictated by the will of the state. There would be no contradiction here if it were possible for the authentic own will of persons to will to act as the state dictates but that would be a self-destroying will on Stirner's account, since subjects of the state are in effect slaves. 'State, religion, conscience, these despots, make me a slave, and their liberty is my slavery' (Stirner 1915: 139–40). In outline, the argument that Stirner is using is familiar from Rousseau's discussion of slavery. One cannot rationally alienate one's humanity and become a slave, Rousseau insists. 'To renounce liberty is to renounce being a man, to surrender the rights of humanity . . . Such a renunciation is incompatible with man's nature; to remove all liberty from his will is to remove all morality from his acts' (Rousseau 1973: 186; *The Social Contract*, Book 1, Ch. 4).

In Stirner's hands, this is another extravagant argument. We shall not pick it apart and examine it in detail because its foundations in an egoistic conception of self-mastery, unadorned self-will, are so unattractive. Shorn of its trappings, it is clear that the egoist philosopher must deny that citizens have a moral duty to obey and otherwise support the state because they have no moral duties at all. (This is one great difference between Stirner and Rousseau: for Stirner, but most definitely not Rousseau, conscience, too, is a despot.)

The idea that a person's autonomy is in fundamental conflict with the state's claim to authority is present but poorly articulated in the anarchist writings of Godwin and Stirner. The argument has been put much more clearly in modern times by Robert Paul Wolff, as intimated above. It runs as follows: it is an essential feature of the state that it claims authority over its citizens: they should obey the commands of the state simply because they have been so commanded. But to obey a command simply because one has been commanded by a sovereign authority, without subjecting that command to inspection or challenge, is to abdicate one's powers of independent reason – one's autonomy. And one has a moral duty to act autonomously. It follows that citizens should not obey the commands of the state simply because the state commands them. Despite its claims to the contrary, the state has no authority over the citizens.

Despite its elegance and simplicity, Wolff's argument has not gained many supporters. There appear to be clear weaknesses. The first concerns the moral duty to act autonomously. Many philosophers accept that autonomy is a value to be protected and promoted. What is not clear is why acceptance of the worth of autonomy requires that one reject all structures of authority. There seem to be many circumstances wherein autonomous persons can rationally concede to others the powers of decision-making which govern how they ought to act. In taking on a job under the condition that employees act under the instructions of a boss or supervisor, the worker one gives up the autonomous power of deciding what she should be doing during the working day. Today you weed the flower-beds; tomorrow you mow the lawns. Of course this may be irksome, but it may also be welcome. In certain domains of one's life she may judge that things go better if she is just given simple instructions. I don't compromise my autonomy if I ask my head of department to tell me when and where to turn up to give a course of lectures. In similar fashion, it is a feature of the family life of couples who don't want to be arguing all the time that responsibilities which involve a measure of authority may be shared out. You organize the holidays, telling me which weeks to book off work; I'll organize the housework, giving you deadlines for doing the ironing and washing the windows. Both of these examples suggest that a person may sensibly abdicate *some* responsibility without abdicating *all* responsibility.[8]

We can follow Rousseau and many others in judging that it would be quite irrational to alienate one's whole freedom, to yield to another all of one's powers of autonomous decision-making (as the defenders of slavery were wont to describe the conquered slave as having done). But the argument to this conclusion does not imply that partial alienation of one's autonomy is impermissible. It may be perfectly sensible. So, if there are circumstances wherein it is sensible to give up some of one's autonomous powers to govern his own conduct, it cannot be illogical or somehow self-contradictory to give up some of his decision-making powers to the state and submit to its sovereign authority. This is just the point at which we should recall the lesson of Chapter 3 – that the domain of political authority (like the authority of the employer or the spouse) is always limited. Wolff argues as though submission to authority and the consequent concession of autonomy is an all-or-nothing affair. This is a mistake. A person can enjoy more or less autonomy in some or other domains of decision-making and action, and although autonomy is a value of great importance, it is but one value amongst others. There may be overall gains consequent upon the surrender of some measure of it. The crucial questions then, with respect to submission to the state (and any other authority relationship) concern how much autonomy one should yield over which specifiable domains.

A second point of criticism against Wolff's argument is directed at the consistency of his position with respect to the state. Simmons points out that Wolff's statement that

> "a contractual democracy is legitimate, to be sure, for it is founded upon the citizens' promise to obey its commands. Indeed any state is legitimate which is founded upon such a promise" [Wolff 1976: 69] directly contradicts his earlier *a priori* claim that "the concept of a de jure legitimate state would appear to be vacuous" [Wolff 1976: 19].
>
> (Simmons 2001: 111, n. 15)

Maybe Wolff can defend himself against this charge since he uses the term 'would appear' [to be vacuous], as against the more straightforward 'is vacuous' – and a careful discussion ensues. But Wolff does have a real difficulty hereabouts. He accepts that some states may be legitimate, yet denies that citizens have a duty to support them.

If we take the example that Wolff gives of a legitimate state – a direct democracy governed by a rule of unanimity which each citizen has promised to obey – we can see that it would be very difficult to deny that individual citizens have an obligation to comply with any rule that they agreed with at the decision-making stage. The only grounds on which such a denial might be founded would be a rejection of the rationality of promise-making and promise-keeping, and a defence of the propriety of changing one's mind after a decision has been taken in a particular case. Within reason, the latter is acceptable, but the former, the rejection of promises, is an extreme position. This view on the irrationality of promises was taken by Godwin and Stirner both, but Wolff does not accept it. In which case one might ask: if one is bound by rules established by unanimous decision, why is it irrational to bind oneself to rules set up by majority decision?

We can see the sense of deciding issues by majority decision in small-scale examples. Suppose Tom, Dick and Harry each prefer to go on holiday together rather than go to the holiday resort of their own choice if that differs from their friends'. How are they to settle where to go? Here are two ways: first, they could decide to take it in turn to choose where to go; second, they could decide to take it in turn to propose where to go, then go to the first resort that at least two of them agree to be suitable. In both cases they put themselves in a position where they may be bound to accept an outcome that they would not have autonomously chosen had the decision been their own to take. But given that their priority is to go somewhere together, that is a sensible chance to take. We would not think that they have compromised their own autonomy by agreeing to a decision procedure of each taking a turn to be decision-maker. Equally it is hard to see why a decision in favour of the rule of the majority compromises their autonomy. It is an attractive solution to the problem of what to do when any number of people unanimously agree that they should all act in the same way but differ in the respect of what that way might be. I can think of no plausible reason for believing that one has failed to fulfil a moral duty to act autonomously in these examples. But if this is true of the small-scale cases, why is it not equally true of the large-scale political case, of democratic states governed by majority rule?

It may well be that there are other features of such states that are unattractive, or that such states must be very rare in practice, or whatever. But we should remember that it is *a priori* philosophical anarchism that we are discussing. What we have to respond to is the view that it is not logically possible that there be a state with the right to command its citizens which does not violate their autonomy.[9] And we have shown that it is not irrational for citizens who have a moral duty to act autonomously to autonomously institute such a state.[10]

A *posteriori* philosophical anarchism

The term '*a posteriori* philosophical anarchism' was coined by A.J. Simmons as a term of art to label the position he and a good few other political philosophers espouse.[11] In contrast to the *a priori* philosophical anarchist,

> a posteriori anarchism . . . maintains that while all existing states are illegitimate, this is not because it is impossible for there to be a legitimate state. Nothing in the definition of the state precludes its legitimacy; rather, existing states are condemned as illegitimate by virtue of their contingent characters.
>
> (Simmons 2001: 105)

This is anarchism by default, as Horton sees (Horton 1992: 131). The default position is exposed by two kinds of argument. In the first place, arguments are canvassed against the traditional solutions to the Philosophical Problem – few survive the testing examination to which they are put by the anarchist. The arguments that do survive – a suitably qualified version of the argument from express consent is extremely hard to fault on philosophical grounds, as we shall see – are then reviewed as answers to the Political Problem, and subsequently dismissed. For example, the phenomenon of express consent which might in principle justify the attribution of sovereign authority is claimed to be generally inapplicable. Since there are no present states in which most (rational, well-informed, uncoerced, etc.) folks have given their express consent, the Political Problem has not been solved. In consequence, philosophical anarchism falls out, by default, of the failure of theorists who attempt to solve both the Philosophical and the Political Problem. Thus Simmons feels able to conclude that 'no existing states are legitimate' (Simmons 2001: 156).[12]

Again we should judge that this is an extravagant conclusion. Simmons has been so cautious in the elaboration of his 'a posteriori philosophical anarchist' position that the state, his philosophical opponent, may be sanguine in the face of his challenge. Most importantly Simmons insists that he is not advocating rebellion. One can be a philosophical anarchist and yet recognize no duty to undermine the state. Philosophical anarchism, as against most varieties of political anarchism, is practically inert. Philosophical anarchists can be as practically docile as their flag-waving loyalist neighbours. The *weak* philosophical anarchist (as against the *strong*, political, anarchist who fights under the black flag to demolish the state) simply takes a view on how he should act given all the non-political reasons that bear on his conduct. Given the attractions of conformity, for independent moral as well as prudential reasons, it is unlikely that the fastidious philosophical anarchist can be distinguished from his cap-doffing fellow citizen. Both will abstain from murder, pay their taxes and take their children to school – as the state demands. The only difference is that the philosophical anarchist will likely hug himself in the privacy of his own home as he maintains the purity of his conscience and secures the best interests of himself and his family.

Some have derided this kind of anarchism as toothless, a pale shadow of the real article; others have suggested that it is not really anarchism at all, believing with some justification that there is something comical about the stance of the armchair, self-proclaimed anarchist who receives his pay from the state and pays his taxes to it, and never risks, still less solicits, the penalties of disobedience. To many, 'a posteriori philosophical anarchism' carries the same whiff of the oxymoron as 'champagne socialism' or (remember where you first came across the term) 'New Conservative'. Given the noble tradition of independence and sacrifice, struggle and rebellion, it is too easy and too cosy. But this is not a philosophical complaint and it's not my business in this book to establish the credentials of anarchism and make a judgement as to who shall claim them.

What I do insist is that the distinction between the Philosophical Problem and the Political Problem, as this was drawn in Chapter 4, should make us very suspicious of the identification of a posteriori philosophical anarchism as a properly *philosophical* position at all. Of course, if no putative solution to the Philosophical Position is judged to pass the test of philosophical plausibility or reasonable cogency, then anarchism is established as the default position. But let us suppose, in advance of careful examination of candidate arguments, that this is not the case. There are some (I will later defend a good few) philosophical survivors. Whether or not the arguments that survive the philosophical test apply to you, I, our fellow citizens, or citizens of other regimes in our actual concrete circumstances is a matter of current affairs and the judgement of knowledgeable citizens given the information at their disposal. How do things stand in my, your, or their polities? I claim no expertise in respect of the facts of the matter as these pertain to all jurisdictions except mine own. I must say that when Simmons tells us that 'no existing states are legitimate', I do not feel in need of the advice of an American philosopher to make a judgement on the legitimacy of the present government of the United Kingdom in so far as his judgement is based on the facts of the matter as he sees them.[13] Insofar as the *a posteriori* philosophical anarchist takes a position on current affairs, as Simmons clearly does, philosophers *qua* philosophers should think: so what? He may be right. He may be wrong. But we have no more reason to accept the views of a philosopher on the facts of the modern political world than we have to accept his opinions on modern ballet.

We should conclude that the credentials of *a posteriori* philosophical anarchism are no better than the quality of the best objections that can be raised against the philosophical groundings that are offered in support of the duties of the citizen. We can put the different varieties of anarchism to one side in good conscience. In what follows we shall examine the cogency of a range of arguments that purport to solve the Philosophical Problem of establishing the grounds of the duties of the citizen to the state. We shall begin our investigation by looking at the most familiar modern theory of political obligation – the theory of consent.

Chapter 7

Consent and contract

It is arguable that philosophers have employed the notion of consent in arguments to vindicate citizens' duties and sovereigns' claims to authority at least since Socrates voiced the opinion of the Laws of Athens in Plato's *Crito*. In modern times, which is to say from the middle of the sixteenth century to the present day, consent arguments have been prominent amongst the answers that philosophers have given to the problem of justifying a regime of citizens' duties. It is easy to see why consent arguments serve as an attractive solution to the Philosophical Problem. If citizens consent to assume such duties, one is tempted to conclude straight away that that's that: they've assumed them voluntarily so they've got them – though we shall have more to say about this very simple conclusion later. For the moment, we need to get clear about the variety of arguments that come under the consent rubric. There are important differences that need to be established. I shall outline the salient distinctions in a schematic fashion and elaborate the differences in the course of our discussion.

First, we should distinguish consent arguments from social contract arguments. I shall discuss social contract arguments in this chapter because social contract arguments may be thought of as a sub-class of consent arguments. They always include two or more parties to the contract. The contracts most frequently invoked have been contracts established between the citizens severally with each other – the citizens may then hand over or entrust sovereign authority to a third-party state – and contracts established by citizens (individually or collectively) with the state directly. (By contrast, although acts of consent always imply two parties – the agent who consents and the party to whom consent is given – the giving of consent is something that is done by one person.) I say that contract arguments may be thought of as a sub-class of consent arguments because contracts may be represented, as they are by Hobbes, as acts of mutual consent – a 'mutual transferring of Right' – whereby each party consents to the acquisition of a right against them by the other party (Hobbes 1968: 192; Ch. 14 [66]).

Second, we should note two very different types of contract argument, actual and hypothetical, referring to actual and hypothetical contracts respectively. Arguments from both actual and hypothetical contract have been used to justify the attribution of duties to citizens, but we shall explain the workings of a hypothetical contract argument in a separate chapter since, as Ronald Dworkin famously (and correctly) stated, 'A hypothetical contract is not simply a pale form of an actual contract; it is no contract at all' (Dworkin 1975: 18). Philosophers have also distinguished actual and hypothetical consent arguments. As I explain them, hypothetical consent arguments have a completely different form from hypothetical contract arguments – to the point that I shall claim that hypothetical consent has no part to play in the philosophical arguments which may in principle justify the state's claim to authority.

Third, we should distinguish amongst the arguments from actual consent those that appeal to express or explicit consent, and those that appeal to tacit or implicit consent. It has been suggested that there are actual consent arguments which are neither express or tacit. Philosophers have discussed indirect consent and quasi consent. We shall discuss whether these terms denote distinct phenomena. But first let us establish in general terms the credentials of consent arguments.

The meaning of consent

The thought that the government which cannot attest the consent of its citizens has no right to demand their compliance, support and allegiance emerged as a feature of popular political rhetoric in Britain during, and in the aftermath of, the Civil Wars in the seventeenth century. In the great Army Debate at Putney of October 1647, Colonel Thomas Rainborough insisted,

> For really I think that the poorest he that is in England hath a life to live, as the greatest he; and therefore truly, sir, I think it's clear, that every man that is to live under a government ought first by his own consent to put himself under that government; and I do think that the poorest man in England is not at all bound in a strict sense to that government that he hath not had a voice to put himself under.
>
> (Woodhouse 1938: 53)[1]

Later in the same debate, John Wildman intervenes,

> I conceive that's the undeniable maxim of government: that all government is in the free consent of the people. If [so], then upon that account there is no person that is under a just government, or hath justly his own, unless he by his own free consent be put under that government.
>
> (Woodhouse 1938: 66)

These are men speaking out freely in debates of huge political import and, as it happens, of important philosophical principle. They are not philosophers in the first instance; they are good and decent (if, at the time, radical) citizens putting an argument, advancing a position on the affairs of the day. The practical, immediately political, relevance of consent arguments to debates about citizens' duties in the United Kingdom, and I am sure elsewhere, has been a constant of our political experience – whatever their cogency. 'Not in my name' the banners read, and we should take this as stated, as an explicit avowal that citizens do *not* consent to the war that their government wages. So we should remember this about consent arguments: they are philosophers' devices, but they are also common coinage in actual political debates concerning the proper attribution of duties to citizens as the Political Problem is addressed.

Now that we have a firm grip on the practical, political import of discussions of consent we can move on to (less gripping) issues of analysis. What is the meaning of consent? What is the structure of speech acts of consent? More prosaically, what does consent do?

At bottom, to give consent is to give permission (and maybe more, to invite intervention), so we should ask: what does that presuppose? It presupposes a state of affairs with this rough normative structure: it is wrong for y to ø, or, just as likely and more perspicuously, x has a right that y does not ø. Consent can now work its moral magic and be morally transformative:[2] if x consents to y's ø-ing, then what was hitherto wrong, being perhaps a violation of x's rights, becomes permissible. This is the dialectical apparatus that distinguishes hiking from trespass, love-making from rape, and boxing from assault and battery. In some ways astonishingly, consent has become central to the ethics of medical practice. *Ceteris paribus*, medical intervention without the consent of the patient who stands to benefit is deemed an assault, however necessary the treatment might be to the patient's good health.[3] As it happens, x consents to y's walking across her ground, to y's making love to her, and to y's thumping her in a boxing ring. The patient consents to the operation. So what was hitherto impermissible and morally wrong is now fine – permissible, innocent, maybe admirable, maybe required even, in the case of the medical treatment.[4]

Rainborough and Wildman understood (and exploited) the fact that consent arguments are congenial to citizens. Now we can see why consent arguments are attractive to the state that wishes to justify the relation in which it stands to its citizens. From one viewpoint, as we saw in our study of anarchism, the state has a very nasty face: it coerces its citizens. It regulates the conduct of citizens by the imposition of laws carrying sanctions for non-compliance. It punishes lawbreakers, imprisoning and fining them, and at a sad extreme, taking their lives in grubby acts of capital punishment. It conscripts them to fight in wars, to risk their lives and perhaps even, to die. It marshals an army of police and prison officers, judges, soldiers, Inspectors of Taxes and intrusive bureaucrats. Small wonder that apologists for the state have loved consent arguments since, if successful, they transform a body that is ugly and threatening into an agency that citizens welcome as being of their own choosing. However awful the state may appear at first glance, if the citizens consent to its authority and to the instruments of its rule, the very hard task of justification looks to be accomplished at a stroke.

Some philosophers have sought to explain this moral magic as a kind of promising.[5] But this is a mistake. Consent is similar to promising in that both kinds of speech act (granted that both can be tacit) alter the moral landscape.[6] I have no duty to deliver the coal to your door, but if I promise to do so then

I do acquire a duty to deliver it – one that I have created for myself in making the promise. In the same fashion – but this would be an arsy-versy way to describe the moral transaction – one who consents to another's acting in some fashion has forgone the right they might otherwise claim to forbid that action or seek remedy for its occurrence. Of course one can give consent by making a promise, thus: 'I promise not to prosecute or otherwise charge you with wrong-doing if you walk across my ground' is an act of giving consent, but consent does not generally take this form. The instruction 'Go ahead' would do the job more directly. Acts of promising commit the *promiser* to a course of action; acts of consent permit, and often invite, a second party to act, should they so wish.

It is intrinsic to acts of consent that they permit or legitimate. But it is important to note that there are limits to be placed on the moral miracle. In one sense, as soon as someone says, 'I consent', they have consented. However, it does not follow from mere utterance of the words or any other such sign that the consent is valid.[7] Other conditions must be met. This point is of the greatest importance. Standard conditions on valid consent are as follows.

Competence

The person who gives consent must be rational, not suffering from a disabling mental condition or clearly immature. If someone were fool enough to argue that being born a citizen is sufficient to attest consent on the part of the child, the application of this condition of competence would render the consent invalid. It must be said that Hobbes comes very close to imputing valid consent to children, however young.[8] In the context of consent as a possible source of citizens' duties it follows that if persons who are immature or otherwise incapable of forming rational beliefs or taking rational action are deemed to have duties as citizens, these duties cannot derive from their consent – whatever they say or do. If they do have such duties – think of a child or an adult with crippling mental disabilities who has a duty to pay tax on their private income – such duties must derive from a source other than consent. Suppose that morally incompetent citizens do have such duties, albeit with other persons or agencies assigned responsibility for their compliance, both this competence condition and the condition of full knowledge which follows establish that consent cannot be a necessary condition on their political obligation to comply with the (just) tax regime.

Full knowledge

For consent to be valid, a person must have full knowledge of what it is to which they are deemed to give consent. The most familiar examples here come from medicine and the requirement that patients give fully informed consent to any medical intervention. Should a surgeon operate without gaining the fully informed consent of the patient (in circumstances where fully informed consent could perfectly well have been given) the operation will be judged an assault. One difficulty which arises in this context concerns how much information it is necessary to give (and for the patient to understand) in order for the consent to be fully informed. Should patients be told of all possible side-effects of the intervention or just the most likely? A further serious difficulty arises where the process of seeking fully informed consent is likely to be very onerous to the person whose consent is being solicited. Should such a person be enabled to give short-form consent, if they so wish, accepting as a consequence that the consent that they have given is not fully informed?[9] This condition also has obvious relevance in respect of sexual consent. Take the case of the person who knows himself to be HIV positive: if he does not disclose his condition to a sexual partner, can he excuse his infecting her on the grounds that she consented to the act of intercourse which was its cause? I say not, because she was not fully informed. Happily, the law agrees.

My intention in raising these mostly unhappy issues has been to alert readers to clear examples of the operation of this condition. In respect of political life and specifically the duties of the citizen, the condition of full knowledge has all sorts of implications. This is one very obvious example. Assume in the first place that citizens who vote in an election consent to the government of the party which wins.[10] Next, suppose that the party which forms the government after a particular election lied in its election manifesto: it promised to legalize some conduct but had no intention of doing so and doesn't repeal the specific statute, as promised. It follows that those citizens who voted for the government didn't (and couldn't) know what they would be presumed to consent *to*, having justifiably false beliefs concerning what their duties would be under the new regime. So do citizens who voted in this election have a continuing duty to obey the law as kept in place and enforced by the elected government notwithstanding the described deception and the voters' consequent ignorance of the obligations that would be imputed to them and enforced against them? I say not. Their consent was not valid – at the very least in respect of the continuing operation of this particular proscription.

Needless to say there are many variations that can be played on this theme. What are we to make of governments that systematically lie to their electorate? You must not think this question is entirely hypothetical. As I write, I have to hand the following avowal of Ferenc Gyurcsany, the Prime Minister of Hungary and by many reports a decent man, secretly recorded in a speech to party officials in May 2006 and as stated in the *Times* (19 September 2006):

> Obviously we lied throughout the past one and a half, two years. It was completely obvious that what we said was not true. . . I almost died of having to pretend for the past year that we were actually governing. Instead we lied day, night and evening.

Some citizens revolted in the streets of Budapest when this was made known. Were they failing to fulfil their political obligations? This is an example of the Political Problem as described in Chapter 4, so I leave readers to find an answer for themselves. So far as the Philosophical Problem of political obligation goes, we can say this: if citizens' valid consent is a good reason for them to accept the duties imputed them as citizens, and if, as suggested, this consent must be fully informed to be valid, citizens cannot be deemed to have duties in virtue of their consent to a lying prospectus, or to policies which are defended on the basis of lies about the facts of the matter, or to a policy of whose real justification they are kept in ignorance.

This full-knowledge condition can be taken further. One might very plausibly argue, against the background assumption of consent through voting (which is still to be defended) that the decisions of voters can legitimate the rule of an elected government only if those citizens are kept fully informed – which is to say that citizens must have full information about the processes and deliberations of government. In political terms, though I leave the details to be specified, there must be full freedom of information, which is to say access to all the facts and values on which policies are based.[11] How much information does this condition require? Formally: as much information as is necessary for citizens to recognize that the consent which is the basis of their obligations is valid, that they are not kept conveniently ignorant or duped. This is not to say that the rational citizen would wish or rationally requires to know everything a government intends to do and why. To use a famous example the (true, patriotic!) citizen does not want to know and should not ask whether the government intends to devalue the currency.

Coercion or duress

The old example is that of the bridegroom who walks up the aisle, closely followed by the bride's father – who is carrying a shotgun. Does the shivering wreck consent to marry her when he stutters 'I do'? Of course not, as every philosopher and careful thinker on these matters since Aristotle has decided. If a government required citizens to swear a vow of allegiance or else . . . and the advertised consequences of recalcitrance were dire, citizens should not have to cross their fingers under the table in order to disavow their explicit consent. Whatever they (are forced to) say, their consent is invalid. There are many clear cases; we pity and understand and partly excuse those poor citizens of the Third Reich who unwillingly saluted 'Heil Hitler!' These are clear cases, but we all know that there is a great grey area between the rabidly patriotic idiot at one extreme and the thoroughly ashamed and intimidated weakling who submits perforce. Philosophers can and should delineate very carefully the excusing conditions, but they are in no better position than anyone else to make judicial decisions in circumstances of inevitable complexity. The only things that can stated with certainty are that acts of consent which are straightforwardly coerced are invalid and that acts of consent which are subject to duress short of outright coercion are tainted with guilt but otherwise excusable by decent souls who admit that 'there but for the grace of God go I'.

Immorality

Some believe that consent cannot legitimate acts which are immoral in all circumstances. In English Law (and according to the morality of many citizens) acts of voluntary euthanasia and extreme sadism are proscribed notwithstanding the fully informed consent of the victim. Does the consent of the citizens legitimate the authority of the immoral state? We broached this issue in Chapter 3 where I suggested the following universal domain-limiting principle: *commands which require subjects to violate moral principles or otherwise to act immorally are void.* And in Chapter 5 I introduced the justice constraint which limited our task to that of charting the ethical relations between citizens and the just state.

As a rule, consent arguments have been used to ground the authority of a par-ticular state and by implication citizens' duties considered across the board. Consent to the state seems to legitimate the whole regime, in the terminology of Chapter 5 the complete set of citizens' duties. However we can characterize a state as immoral or unjust in respect of both form and content, that is, its insti-tutional structure on the one hand, and, on the other, its deeds, notably its direc-tives to officials and the laws it prescribes to citizens. We can give examples of governments which are evil on both counts, as '[I]n Africa, where gangs of armed men grab power – that is to say, annex the national treasury and the mechanisms of taxing the population – do away with their rivals, and proclaim Year One' (Coetzee 2007: 20).[12]

This sort of government is an institutional evil – a gang of robbers despite its political trappings – and we can suppose that it makes evil laws, issues immoral instructions, and enacts evil policies. Notwithstanding the limitation of our enterprise to the study of citizens duties in the just state, I suggest that the citi-zens' consent cannot legitimize an evil regime: this is most perspicuous when those who dissent have been eliminated, as suggested by J.M. Coetzee in the quo-tation above. An evil state (unconstitutional, arbitrary, an exercise of brute power) cannot possess moral authority, notwithstanding the consent of the gov-erned. We argued for this conclusion in Chapter 2. If this is correct, the impli-cation is that consent to the state as an institution, embracing the whole powers of the regime, is not to be considered to be sufficient condition of its legitimate authority. Generally, as in the pathetic case of the poor benighted Kim Ok Kyung (discussed above at p. 29), such consent will be based on ignorance. But it may be self-serving, based on venality – the consenter is a member of the ruling class or the dominant tribe. I shall conclude that however much consent the evil state can muster, its exercise of power is never legitimate. It cannot claim moral authority for its prescriptions.

But suppose a state which is constitutionally just and generally decent in its dealings with citizens gets things wrong in a particular set of cases. Under very great pressure, nowadays most clearly evidenced in the response states make to terrorism, the state requires or permits officials (or citizens generally) to act in ways that are clearly unjust. Suppose further – a likely occurrence in the modern world – a very large majority of citizens consent to the violation of basic rights, which is the upshot of these knee-jerk reactions.[13] Can consent (or explicit sup-port) of this magnitude legitimate the immoral acts of state officials? I claim not.

We are left with this conclusion: it is reasonable to believe that acts of con-sent undertaken by citizens can legitimate sovereign authority both generally and in particular, but only when that consent is competent, well-informed and uncoerced, and when the state acts within its proper domain, notably when it is not itself evil nor prescribing and permitting immoral actions. We should move on to consider the types of consent that may be attested.

The varieties of consent

Actual (historical) contracts

I have already stated that we should distinguish sharply between arguments which adduce actual, generally historical, contracts and arguments which employ the device of a hypothetical contract. As will become clear, there is a massive difference in the logic of these argument types, not least because, as we stated above, hypothetical contracts are not contracts at all. Arguments which ground political obligation in some actual contract often concluded in the dim and distant past promise to be little more than a historical curiosity. There was a view, common apparently in England in the sixteenth century, that legitimate government had its source in an original contract. This was taken to be a contract between King and people. It is sufficient evidence of the common knowledge of this 'theory' that when, following the flight of King James II of England in 1688, Parliament resolved that 'having endeavoured to subvert the constitution of the Kingdom, by breaking the original contract between King and people . . .' James II had *de facto* 'abdicated the Government'.[14] Locating the original contract and specifying its content (Magna Carta was a favoured candidate) was a cottage industry amongst the students of the 'Ancient Constitution'. The quest was hopeless for other than polemical purposes. In point of the great political philosophers in the 'Social Contract Tradition' the methodological status of the social contract is a vexed interpretative issue. I can do little more here than state my position in a dogmatic fashion.[15]

I claim that the core argument in Hobbes's *Leviathan* does not adduce any historical contract. The famous two-stage *covenant* (Hobbes's term) whereby all persons agree with each other that they shall accept as sovereign whoever the majority shall determine, which persons then determine by majority vote a specific candidate for sovereign who is not party to the covenant (Hobbes 1968: Chs XVII–XVIII), is primarily hypothetical on my reading. It is what rational persons would do were they, hypothetically, to be in a state of nature. This pattern of reasoning would also be followed by citizens who found themselves subject to a sovereign who has acquired his dominion by force (Hobbes 1968: Ch. XX) – a sovereign by acquisition. The upshot of the argument is that one has good reason to accept a sovereign with the powers ascribed by Hobbes whether or not one already has one, and, if one already has a sovereign, whether or not that sovereign was instituted by the people in an original contract. No doubt Hobbes would agree that if citizens had in fact instituted a sovereign authority according to the procedure he describes, the rules governing the making of covenants described in chapters 14 and 15 of *Leviathan* would bind them to obedience.

In such a case, having made an actual historically attested covenant, they would have taken on a concomitant obligation: they should 'performe their covenants made' (Hobbes 1968: 201; Part 1, Ch. XV [71]). But Hobbes wants to cast his net much wider than this. Such people (and he attests no actual cases) would have a further reason to accept an obligation beyond that prudential reason which applies to mankind quite universally. We shall return to hypothetical contract arguments at the end of this chapter.

I believe that in Locke matters are much more confused and confusing. Locke speaks of 'the original Compact' when he is describing the first incorporation into a 'Society'[16] of men who are by nature free and independent. Those who have incorporated themselves as members of society then entrust the protection of their natural rights to the specific government that they subsequently create by majority vote. At this second stage, together with subsequent acts of affirming allegiance by members of successor generations, citizens are deemed to have *consented* to the authority of the sovereign.[17] (This two-stage act of political institution is very similar to that described by Hobbes.) Locke subsequently explains the mechanics of consent, famously distinguishing express and tacit consent – and we shall discuss these arguments later. Concerning ourselves with the first compact (contract) to establish a society, we should notice that Locke writes of this as an historical occurrence. Specifically, he defends himself against the objection that

> there are no Instances to be found in Story of a Company of Men independent and equal one amongst another, that met together, and in this way began and set up a Government [sc. 'society', as I am using that term].
>
> (Locke 1960: §100)

by telling us some Just-So stories: where history fails (but he also suggests that there is some factual evidence from ancient Persia, Sparta and Brazilian Indians!) speculative or conjectural history should be persuasive. If this reading of Locke is correct, his position should be sharply differentiated from that of Hobbes. That said, it is an open (interpretative) question whether there might not also be a hypothetical contract argument employed hereabouts from within Locke's rhetorical repertoire.[18]

We should note this fresh field of academic study – conjectural or speculative history – not least because it explains one of the strangest elements of Rousseau's political philosophy. In Part Two of the *Discourse on the Origin of Equality*, Rousseau offers us a mesmerizing History of the World in thirty pages. At a late but still lawless stage in world history a gang of rich men desperate to preserve their holdings conned the poor into a mutual agreement to establish society and law: 'All ran headlong into their chains, in hopes of securing their liberty; for they had just wit enough to perceive the advantages of political institutions, without experience enough to enable them to foresee the dangers' (Rousseau 1973: 99). Rousseau conjectures that things must have happened this way, since he is explaining the origins of government which is a moral and rightful relation.

There may well have been prior episodes of conquest and subjugation but such relations (being the product of violence) could not have generated 'a real society or body politic, or any law other than that of the strongest' (Rousseau 1973: 100). This is conjectural history akin to that we found in Locke in all respects except for the crucial and clear-mindedly cynical twist which transforms what for Locke is the means of preserving one's liberty into Rousseau's account of its irrecoverable loss.[19] I should say that historical contracts play no part whatsoever in Rousseau's book *The Social Contract*.

So we see that the great philosophers as well as their contemporaries, philosophical under-labourers and political polemicists, used the idea of the historical social contract or covenant or compact to describe, speculatively, an historical episode wherein a people moved from a state of nature to a condition of political society. To my knowledge no political philosopher of any repute has articulated in detail an argument which suggests that all citizens of any present state have an obligation to obey that state (in a wide sense that includes all putative duties) on the basis of such an historical contract. That is why I suggested that this argument may be an historical curiosity. But we are philosophers. The historical oddity of this line of argument should not prevent us from taking a view on whether it might solve the Philosophical Problem. So let us suppose that we take a particular case in which this suggestion is made. Suppose that at Runneymede in 1215 the whole people of England (instead of a gang of revolting barons) had come to an agreement with Bad King John concerning their respective rights and duties: would this historical contract bind you or me to the government of the United Kingdom? Notice, before we rush to answer 'No' that this question brings the Political Problem into focus rather than the Philosophical Problem. But we don't need to belabour the Philosophical Problem: had we been there, competent etc., of course we would have imposed on ourselves the full duties of citizenship if those were the terms of the agreement we made. I've no doubt that the actual contract argument, whether the contract adduced is one between all citizens with each other or between citizens and the sovereign, is a very strong argument. But as many commentators have pointed out it is of very restricted application. Few will reach for it when they address the Political Problem of whether they in fact have an obligation to obey their sovereign.

The reason for this is well-known. It is conspicuous if the actual contract which is adduced was made in the distant past. How could the contract which my ancestors made bind me, now, to duties imposed by my present government? Surely I am not to be bound by a contract to which I was not a party. That said, we should notice that actual contract arguments may have a wider applicability than many have believed. It is a familiar aspect of modern political practice that new constitutions or striking constitutional innovations may be put to a vote of the people in a referendum so that the ensuing settlement can be recognized as legitimate. De Gaulle's Fifth Republic in France was instituted by referendum in 1958 and modified, again by referendum, in 1962. Following the downfall of the Communist regimes, referendums proposing draft constitutions were held throughout Eastern Europe. Britain's membership of the EEC was endorsed by a referendum in 1975 and a devolved Scottish parliament was established following a referendum in 1998.

Such modern constitutional settlements differ from the sketchy accounts found in the classics. The condition of unanimity at the first stage is not met. But they are sufficiently like the historical contracts for weaker conclusions to be drawn. If the state, as it addresses its citizens in the appeal for obedience, can point to something akin to an original settlement, it has made a good start. Of course there will be many qualifications, and some of these will emerge later when we consider how far the citizen's participation in democratic politics can be taken as consent. But for the moment we can accept that those who take part in the institution of government have the responsibility of contractors to accept the legitimacy of the institutions they have endorsed.

Before we close our discussion of actual contracts let me mention one wrinkle in the account which may be of some interest. I stated dogmatically above that successor generations cannot be obligated by contracts made by an ancestor generation. Is that always true? Consider this example: it was my political generation that voted heavily for a devolved assembly in Scotland. The assembly can claim legitimacy, at least partly, in virtue of that quasi-contractual social act. I find it hard to believe that these (now historical) credentials have no moral force in determining the obligations of those who have reached the age of majority and become full citizens in the period since that referendum was conducted. We are by now well-used to the idea that persons have duties to succeeding generations. It is a nice question whether those succeeding generations have duties so to say *backwards*, to respect the terms of contracts made by their forebears. Having posed the question, I suspect that there is no simple articulation of the intuition that there may be such backwards duties, and I suspect that further discussion would carry me towards the splendid but murky depths of Burke's vision of society as a partnership of the living, the dead and the yet unborn – a vision that true conservatives would curse me for trying to analyse as rational. So we shall move on.

Actual consent

Express consent

We have already explained the rock-solid philosophical plausibility of actual consent arguments. Let us look at the different varieties. Actual consent in its most obvious form will be express or explicit. The clearest example of this is the naturalized citizen. In the United Kingdom such citizens formerly had to fill out a form solemnly attesting that they will be obedient citizens of Her Majesty Queen Elizabeth II and all heirs begat therefrom (or some other such antiquated form of words). And nowadays they must attend a 'Citizenship Ceremony' at which they must swear or affirm allegiance and make a pledge in these words, taken from the UK Home Office website:

Oath of allegiance

I (name) swear by Almighty God that on becoming a British citizen, I will be faithful and bear true allegiance to Her Majesty Queen Elizabeth the Second, her Heirs and Successors, according to law. [or]

Affirmation of allegiance

I (name) do solemnly, sincerely and truly declare and affirm that on becoming a British citizen, I will be faithful and bear true allegiance to Her Majesty Queen Elizabeth the Second, her Heirs and Successors, according to law. [and]

Pledge

I will give my loyalty to the United Kingdom and respect its rights and freedoms. I will uphold its democratic values. I will observe its laws faithfully and fulfill my duties and obligations as a British citizen.

(http://www.ind.homeoffice.gov.uk/applying/
nationality/citizenshipceremonies/)

What could be more explicit than this as an instance of giving consent?[20] No doubt there are other examples including those undertaking government or military service of express avowals of allegiance, and these may be across the board, or limited in their applicability – as when, in the United Kingdom, one signs the Official Secrets Act. One understands that in other countries citizens affirm allegiance on a regular basis, standing to attention, putting their hands across their hearts and pledging allegiance. Do these (often unthinking) rituals signal the attestation of express consent? I don't see why not, so long as the standard validating conditions are met. (I take it that these would exclude the Boy Scout oath – Dib, Dib, Dib and all that.)

This brief discussion signals that the identification of express consent in a variety of behaviours and the articulation of the scope and contents of the consents expressly adduced will be a delicate matter of political and sociological self-understanding. But these issues go to the Political Problem as much as to the Philosophical Problem. So far as the Philosophical Problem is concerned we should record that the state can fairly claim that it has got one argument securely in the bag and that it can properly impute some range of political obligations to all those citizens who have expressly consented to undertake this range of duties. We should not ignore, however, what every other philosopher has noted with respect to this argument – that this argument does not apply to very many citizens in the modern state who address to themselves the Political Problem. Does this argument capture me in the net of political obligation? As a matter of fact it does not. And I'm confident that it does not capture very many of my contemporary fellow-citizens who have never had the occasion to give express consent to the regime which imposes duties on them. Arguments from express consent are good arguments; they refute the radical sceptic who claims that no arguments are available to the state. They amount to one acceptable solution to the

Philosophical Problem. But as a matter of fact it is unlikely that they solve the Political Problem for many citizens. The resourceful state will seek other varieties of actual consent which may be imputed to its citizens.

Tacit consent

Tacit, or implicit, consent is silent. One tacitly consents to some institution, arrangement or proposal by doing nothing, or by doing something other than expressly consenting which is taken to be an act of consent nonetheless. This latter has been termed 'indirect consent'. Examples will illustrate both silent and indirect consent. First, imagine you are in a committee meeting. Following a discussion the convener says, 'I think the sense of the meeting is clear: we should buy the property. I take it no one disagrees?' And no one speaks. We can fairly conclude that each member of the committee has consented, tacitly, to the decision although no-one other than the convener voiced the decision. This is a useful convention which expedites the business of committees – which is not to say that the boundaries or particular applicability of the convention are always clear.[21] Second, imagine you go into a pub and join some friends. Straightaway one of them says 'It's my round' and asks everyone what they want. You say 'a pint of beer please' and drink it when it comes. The rounds continue and you continue to take the offered drink. When all but you have paid for a round, you drink up and say, 'Thank you very much for your kindness. I've enjoyed your company. I have to be going now' and promptly leave. Let's agree that you've done wrong. How best do we describe your wrong-doing? We should invoke rules of boozers' etiquette governing the buying and taking of rounds of drinks. The rules which govern our behaviour in circumstances of this sort are not written down at the pub entrance nor stated in some Field Guide to British Pubs. They are pretty general, rough-and-ready conventions amongst folk who are well prepared for surprises and the curiosities of local customs. For all I know they may do something different in Dorking or Dornoch. But as stated, these rules imply that those who take a drink have undertaken to buy a pint when their turn comes round. Of course one can explicitly debar oneself from incurring a reciprocal obligation by saying something like, 'That's very kind, but you should know that I'm broke. I can't buy a round in turn.' Such a one can properly accept a drink, under mild protest, as a gift given in good grace. In the normal case it's fair to conclude that in joining the round the willing drinker who is well aware of the rules has tacitly consented to buy drinks in his own turn.[22]

Of course the normal qualifying conditions apply. In this case, notably, the person to whom the obligation can fairly be imputed must have full knowledge of the conventions which apply. The newly arrived man from Mars should be excused his failure to reciprocate on the grounds that he was entirely ignorant of how boozers behave in the Pear Tree Inn (just as he could deny being complicit in the committee decision if it was true that he was ignorant of how these things work). Putting these qualifications to one side, I take it that we have before us clear cases of tacit consent giving rise to obligations in virtue of the social rules or conventions which govern the circumstances of their occurrence.

The key to tacit consent is the existence of conventions which determine just which behaviours (both acts and omissions) entail that persons actually consent and what it is to which they have consented, notwithstanding the absence of express consent. John Locke sees this point exactly when he asks directly 'What are the marks of tacit consent?' He sees the problem: grant *a fortiori* that tacit consent is actual consent, then

> The difficulty is, what ought to be look'd upon as a *tacit Consent*, and how far it binds, *i.e.* how far anyone shall be looked on to have consented, and thereby submitted to any government, where he has made no Expressions of it at all.
>
> (Locke 1960: Ch. VIII, §119)

We know how things work in committees and in pubs. How are they supposed to work in political life? In virtue of what behaviours on the part of citizens may the state conclude that they have undertaken the duties of citizenship? There are two traditional answers to this question and both have ancient origins. These echo the examples given above. The first concerns lack of dissent, the second concerns the receipt of benefits. Let us discuss these in turn.

LACK OF DISSENT

It is suggested that citizens consent to their government in cases where they do not expressly dissent. There is good sense in this thought. It picks up the intuition behind the judgement that the committee members who say nothing consented to the decision as voiced by the convener. So we must ask: is it a rule of, or a convention bearing on political life that if subjects do not dissent from the claim of the state to determine how they shall act they are thereby obliged to accept its authority and fulfil the requisite duties? Surely not. It is an obvious thought that dissent may be onerous or dangerous – as it is in numerous countries nowadays. If the cost of dissent is one's life or one's decent living, the sensible citizen will keep quiet. The heroic citizen will dissent but may well not survive her brave act of defiance. But exceptions of these sorts immediately invoke the constraints on legitimate consent. If lack of dissent is to equate to consent then the lack of dissent must in turn be competent, knowing and uncoerced. And it is not uncoerced if the expression of dissent is (likely to be) costly. We can put cases like these to one side. It may still be true that some cases of lack of dissent, or some typical circumstances in which it is adduced, yield a judgement that citizens tacitly consent therein.

A hard case for the philosopher is that of the citizen of the (generally) decent regime, who goes about her private business in full knowledge of the political powers of the state and the circumstances of its regular exercise who does not dissent when dissent is possible and not costly. We often impute complicity to citizens by saying 'You didn't complain at the time'. Generally we are attributing some responsibility to them when we charge them with silent complicity, and we imply that they must put up with the outcome that their silence produced or licensed. We suggest that such a one must accept the consequences of her omission – which is to say she must fulfil the duties incumbent on her. Obviously in political life in the modern state the normative links between the average citizen and the state and its doings are severely attenuated for a thousand and one reasons. Duties are quickly cast off and easy to disavow. Nonetheless it is important for citizens to be alert to the thought that their political insouciance, their lack of explicit dissent may have ethical consequences.

When John Plamenatz is discussing John Locke's political theory he makes this charge: He says 'If you begin by assuming that only consent creates a duty of obedience, you are only too ready to conclude that whatever creates that duty must be consent' (Plamenatz 1992, Vol. 1: 352). Plamenatz is dead right and in Chapter 4 we have already diagnosed the source of this dialectical manoeuvre in the confusion of voluntarism – the thought that the legitimacy of political authority derives from the expressed will of citizens – with what I dubbed the 'good reasons thesis' – the thought that political authority is legitimate if and only if there are good reasons why citizens should accept it as the source of obligations. If this is correct we should not be surprised to find compliant voluntarists being prepared to identify tacit consent in the most mundane circumstances. Plamenatz evidently accepts that if citizens can go about daily affairs in an atmosphere of security, benefiting from the protection and stability provided by the state, they have an obligation to obey the state. This is an important thought that we shall examine in what follows. He goes on to state that Locke's mistake is to suppose that 'consent is given whenever citizens go about the ordinary business of their lives' – this consent being of course a type of tacit consent.

It is a good question whether this is a mistake.[23] To answer it we have to ask whether in the circumstances of life in a particular state there is such a convention, and this is an empirical matter. Do we understand ordinary citizens to accept that the orderly and unprotesting conduct of their daily affairs implies an actual, but tacit consent to the state that governs them? Before you dismiss this question out of hand, think of a slightly different case. When you go on holiday to France, no-one asks you whether you consent to the duties incumbent on you in virtue of temporary residence, so you certainly do not expressly consent to be bound by the laws of France and to obey the officers of the state. But does your willing visit, in full knowledge of the duties to abide by the laws of that regime that will be imputed to you, imply a tacit consent on your part? I think it does. The case is different with one who is kidnapped and deposited unwillingly on French soil. No doubt when they are released they must accept the same set of duties as the tourist when they work their way home and so some different story will have to be told about the source of their duties (if they have any). There is no ethical rule book for travellers to consult; I simply take it that willing consent can be fairly assumed on the part of the tourist.

Of course one might fairly object that the difference between the home-based citizen and the tourist is not slight. Tourists *ex hypothesi* don't just find themselves subject to a regime in the way that the run of citizens do. Indeed the normal citizen may judge that he is more like the kidnapped traveller than the tourist, so I certainly don't want the example of the tourist to suggest that citizens take on obligations in just the way that tourists do. My point is different. I use the example of the tourist merely to illustrate how the ordinary person, blessed with a modicum of common sense, can take on board a complex story concerning the duties that may fairly be imputed to them. One doesn't need to be an ethical virtuoso to grasp the implications of a modest and uncomplaining daily life. So the question bears repetition: is there a convention governing your life or mine to the effect that the lack of dissent apparent in the life of an ordinary citizen evinces a tacit consent to the authority of the regime? The best answer that I can give in my own case is that I'm not sure – which answer itself tempts me to conclude that there can't be, since it is surely a condition on an operative convention governing the relations between state and citizen that it be reasonably clear and transparent to all parties.

There is one further wrinkle to the issue of whether lack of dissent adduces tacit consent that we should explore. Both Plato and Locke suggested that one reason why one might impute tacit consent to those who enjoy property under a regime is that they have a clear opportunity of dissent by way of emigration. The Laws of Athens specify the operative convention in Plato's *Crito*:

> we openly proclaim this principle: that any Athenian, on attaining to manhood and seeing for himself the political organization of the state and us its Laws, is permitted, if he is not satisfied with us, to take his property and go away wherever he likes . . . On the other hand, if any of you stands his ground when he can see how we administer justice and the rest of our public administration, we hold that by doing so he has in fact undertaken to do whatever we tell him.
>
> (Plato, Crito 51d)

John Locke echoes the point:

> whenever the Owner, who has given nothing but such a *tacit Consent* to the Government, will, by Donation, Sale or otherwise, quit the said Possession, he is at liberty to go and incorporate himself into any other Commonwealth; or to agree with others to begin a new one, *in vacuis locis*, in any part of the World, they can find free and unpossessed.
>
> (Locke 1960: §121)

This is a dangerous argument, as Hume saw, if it implies that a government can tell citizens that their continuous presence within the territories of a state marks their tacit consent. Such a claim deserves Hume's mocking response:

> Can we seriously say that a poor peasant or artisan has a free choice to leave his country, when he knows no foreign language or manners, and lives, from day to day, by the small wages which he acquires? We may as well assert that

a man, by remaining in a vessel, freely consents to the dominion of the master; though he was carried on board while asleep, and must leap into the ocean and perish, the moment he leaves her.

(Hume 1963: 462)

Hume's strictures are just, but there is a rider to the dialectic which he did not acknowledge. There have been plenty of cases where citizens have possessed the resources to emigrate and have identified a state which would welcome them, a state they, too, would welcome as infinitely better than the one they want to quit, and yet they have not been permitted to emigrate, or else the process of emigration has been made hazardous, over-costly or humiliating. One thinks of the predicament of Jews in the former Soviet Union. This episode makes it clear that states which frustrate their citizens' wishes to emigrate cannot attribute to such citizens a tacit consent deriving from the lack of dissent attested by their continuing residence. Nor can it use such an argument in the case of citizens who do not wish to leave. That these conclusions are obvious shows that the argument for tacit consent from the lack of explicit dissent need not be as crude as it is in Locke's statement, nor quite as vulnerable as Hume's counterexample suggests.

RECEIPT OF BENEFITS

Locke's discussion of tacit consent, brief though it is, emphasizes that a tacit consent is given by all those who 'enjoy' property within the domains of a sovereign. We are to take such 'enjoyment' as entailing tacit consent 'whether his Possession be of Land, to him or his Heirs for ever, or a Lodging only for a Week; or whether it be barely travelling freely on the Highway' (§119; see also §§120–2). The implication of Locke's discussion is that those who enjoy property enjoy such 'Priviledges and Protection' as the state affords, which is to say that those who enjoy property are the beneficiaries of the state. The state presents its bill for the enjoyment of the benefits by demanding obedience as the proper duty of the property-owning citizen (as well as the transient or resident alien). In the background therefore is a convention closely akin to the rule of boozers' etiquette described above. It can be stated roughly as follows: if you enjoy security in your possessions and person (as do property owners and travellers), you must reciprocate your willing acceptance of these benefits by obeying the laws of the protective regime. Your voluntary receipt of benefits is a mark of your tacit consent.[24]

I should say at this point that those who defend the authority of the state and its imputation of duties to citizens frequently appeal to the empirical fact that citizens benefit to a greater or lesser degree from the state. This putative fact is appealed to by utilitarians who defend the institution of state authority, by those who espouse the 'Principle of Fairness', and by those who argue that citizens have duties of obedience as an expression of the gratitude that they ought properly to feel. These are each distinct arguments and they will all be discussed in what follows. We have to hand an argument that is distinct from each of these, to the effect that the active receipt of benefits on the part of the citizen attests their tacit consent. A second obvious point to make – and this is relevant to all of the argument types mentioned above – is that the applicability of any such argument, granted that it is cogent and passes the test of being a solution of the Philosophical Problem, will depend upon the facts of the matter. In the case of any particular state, does it provide the touted benefits? Unless we are as pessimistic as Thomas Hobbes concerning the state of nature and as optimistic concerning the limits on the damage that the state can do, we should not enter any benefits (or costs) on the balance-sheet of a state if we have no evidence of how it treats its citizens. So all arguments which refer to the benefits which citizens receive should be treated as conditional, as draft responses to the Philosophical Problem which, if successful, may be drawn upon to answer the Political Problem faced by citizens of any particular state as they ponder their obligations in light of facts that may obtain in the circumstances. If it transpires that they do receive, on balance, significant benefits from their state, these different arguments deduce that they should acknowledge their political obligations. Is this correct in the case where it is claimed that the citizen's receipt of benefits adduces their tacit consent?

To answer this question, let us assume that the citizens have received significant benefits.[25] We don't need to go into detail on the nature of these benefits. Let us suppose that they include the benefits that John Locke had in mind – peace and such security as enables folk to enjoy their property. Obviously, the more benefits citizens enjoy as a result of state activity, the more solidly anchored is the argument, though it may well apply to tourists or transient foreigners 'who barely travel freely on the Highway'. The crucial ingredient, however, is the existence of a convention to the effect that those who thus benefit thereby assume the duties of citizenship. Is there such a convention?

Notice first of all that there is no quite general convention in place to the effect that those who are in receipt of benefits from some person or institution thereby incur some obligation to their benefactor. It's no good showering benefits on me, your teacher; no amount of goodies will give me an obligation to tell you the questions in the forthcoming philosophy examination. And as one of my otherwise non-philosophical daughters told me, the young fellow who was indignant that her favours could not be bought for the price of a *couscous royale* was making a big mistake concerning the ethics of obligation.[26] The proper response to the provision of benefits is a matter of very great moral delicacy, as we shall see in what follows. One cannot cite the receipt of benefits as a blunt instrument to compel the recipient's submission to a regime of duties as specified by the benefactor. Notice further that this question must be put to you, the reader, individually as representative of the citizens of your state, or perhaps as member of a sub-group of citizens that has a firm view on the matter on the basis of some belief that you all share. As a representative citizen it calls for a delicate and knowledgeable understanding of political sociology, which is not to say that such knowledge may not be available to the average citizen – the man on the Clapham omnibus, to cite the judicial test.

I shall conduct such a test for you, supposing you to be a citizen of a state broadly similar to the United Kingdom. Politicians often argue that 'rights imply responsibilities'. This is rough-and-ready rhetoric. If there is any actual reason behind the rhetoric it lies surely in this thought: 'You appeal to the state to protect your rights. You can't expect the state to grant you the benefit of protection of your rights unless you in turn are willing to accept the concomitant responsibilities – the duties of citizenship'. This claim doesn't strike me as unreasonable. It is exactly the kind of case that the state can be expected to put to the philosophically scrupulous but non-rebellious philosophical anarchist (e.g. Robert Paul Wolff, A.J. Simmons *et al.*, whom I suppose to be law abiding citizens). Do they require the state to do anything for them in the circumstances of their daily vulnerabilities? Do they 'phone the police when they are burgled? Suppose that they do call the police (remembering always that as anarchists they may in fact not do so: what do we know of how such folks conduct their daily lives?), is there a convention in place which attests such seeking after benefits as a tacit consent to assume the duties of citizenship? I suspect that there is, though again, as with the lack of dissent criterion, the position is not altogether clear and that lack of clarity is a very defect in the argument. (It is also possible that in identifying a convention that grounds tacit consent one is confusing the argument from tacit consent with one of the other arguments which proceed from the citizen's receipt of benefits – the argument from fairness, or gratitude.) What is important is that the convention governs not merely the fact that one is in receipt of the benefits but that one seeks them out. The citizen who as a new-born infant was given life-saving surgery by the National Health Service has not incurred a life-long duty of obedience. If that same adult seeks out medical treatment as an adult, the convention may then become operative.

We should notice an obvious implication of this argument concerning the range of its applicability. If there is such a convention in place then one who feels that they have accepted benefits from the state, believing that this brings with it an obligation to obey, may fairly judge themselves to have consented to the regime. Contrariwise, some who *accept* this argument may then make every effort to dissociate themselves from the benefits, detaching themselves physically from the state which provides them. They may exile themselves to the wilds of Montana or Idaho, living a life which is self-sufficient apart from periodic trips to the local rifle store. This is Militia Man, the bane of all theories of political obligation which rely on the citizen's consent or receipt of benefits. Whatever grounds may be cited in favour of his consent he will disavow sincerely – which is not to say that all other arguments that can be adduced in favour of his having the duties of the citizen must fail.

We should draw a cautious conclusion concerning tacit consent. Throughout my discussion I have emphasized that tacit consent is a real phenomenon but that its successful imputation relies on the actual existence of operative but unwritten social conventions governing citizens' behaviour. The description and identification of such conventions is a delicate exercise and the results are bound to be controversial. I am confident that the citizen who recognizes such a convention as binding on her and who in consequence accepts that she has tacitly consented to a regime of political obligations through her lack of dissent or her willing acceptance of benefits has made no philosophical mistake. On the other hand, because such conventions are of their nature nebulous and imprecise it is easy for recalcitrant citizens to find the dialectical space to dispute the imputation of duties in their particular case.

Quasi-consent

In *Democracy and Disobedience*, Peter Singer discusses the specific question of whether citizens of a democratic state have particular reasons to accept the duties of the citizen as determined by majority rule. Thus far, we have spoken of the state and ignored the nature of its constitution. We could have been discussing any old state – so long as it is decent or just. The only question in hand was whether the citizens actually consented through the mechanisms of original contract, express or tacit consent. The argument that participation in democratic decisions yields a form of consent is of particular importance, however, since we stated in Chapter 5 that we shall attempt to find arguments that solve the Philosophical Problem only for citizens of just states and we considered one important criterion of the just state that the state be (roughly) democratic. Singer introduces the notion of quasi-consent to explain the distinctive form of not-quite-consent which is implicit in the behaviour of voters. Their behaviour, he believes, mimics consent. They act *as if* they consent and the same normative conclusions may be drawn from their behaviour as are drawn in the case of actual consent (Singer 1974: 45–9). If we describe the basic action of voting – taking the polling card and handing it over to the polling officer, receiving a voting slip and putting a cross a box in a private booth, then placing the voting paper in a ballot-box for counting – nothing amounts to express consent. It would be easy to require valid papers to include a signature affirming that the voter consents to abide by the outcome of the ballot. To my knowledge, such a statement is never demanded as a condition of participation. So if voting attests consent, it is not express consent.

Singer attempts to distinguish tacit consent from quasi-consent, stating correctly that the attribution of tacit consent, as explained by Locke (or some of his prominent interpreters) implies that citizens actually give it – if not expressly, then 'as saying in their heart' that they consent, as acknowledging at the moment that they act in the manner from which consent can be inferred that they do so willingly (Singer 1974: 48–9). The phenomenon of quasi-consent, by contrast, attests the *implications* of voting behaviour, specifically that citizens should accept that their participation in the voting process requires them to abide by the majority result, whether or not they realize that this is what they have committed themselves to. I don't see the difference, not least since I think that the requirement that those who tacitly consent 'say in their heart' that they consent (whatever that means exactly) is over-strong. If one had flown in from Mars and had been entertained by a group of hospitable students, if one was truly ignorant of the ruling conventions of pub visiting, tacit consent could fairly be repudiated. The same is surely true of the ignoramus who does not understand the conventions governing voting behaviour. The only points at issue are (i) is there a rule in place governing everyone's behaviour, (ii) did the Martian or the voter know the rule, and (iii) in case they didn't, ought they to have done so? Should the Martian or the lucky teacher have done their homework before they entered the pub? Generally, ignorance, as displayed by a 'No' answer to (ii), will excuse, though the excuse stretches the point if the answer to (iii) is deemed to be 'Yes'.[27] If we conclude that the drinker or the voter either does, or ought to, understand the ethical implications of their behaviour we will judge that they have the same duties as one who expressly consents, whether or not they said anything in their heart when they accepted the drink or when they voted.

But this is to pre-judge the substantive issue. I endorse Singer's terminology of quasi-consent, not because it has a normative structure different from that of tacit consent – it does not – but rather because it signals a distinctive argument which finds application in the specific context of voters' behaviour. The quasi-consent the voter attests is attributable on the basis of a convention which is unique to the context of democratic decisions. I have no dispute with the philosopher who insists that participation in democratic decision procedures is a third mark of tacit consent, indeed that is what I believe myself. But it is worth insisting that this mark is distinctive. It is not a case of dissent forgone or benefits accepted.

The argument for the conclusion that the voter has consented to abide by the decision taken by the majority elaborates our understanding of the voting process. It articulates what the voters believe (or ought to be able to work out) that they are doing. Think of any occasion of voting: for or against a strike by the workers who are being balloted, for a representative to serve in a parliament or a local council, for or against a policy proposal put to a referendum. In every case it is supposed that the majority decision is binding on all those who take part. This is an assumption that can be challenged. I once spoke, for example, to a colleague who voted in a strike ballot and did not accept that he was obliged to accept the outcome. He thought that, since striking would violate a personal obligation of service to the university authorities, he should do everything in his power to prevent others from striking, which efforts included voting against a strike, whilst not accepting the outcome when (as happened) the majority decision went against him. Such are the frustrations of the picket-line at a university.

All I can say, of what is repeatable, against the voter who repudiates the majority decision, is that they do not understand the point of the exercise in which they are engaged. In a reputable democracy, no-one is compelled to vote pro or con a particular policy. Anyone can abstain, or, where filling-in a voting paper is compulsory, spoil the voting paper – all these things without penalty. Perhaps this is an innocent construction of the reality of voting in all regimes in the modern world. All that the philosopher can do, given the many ways things can go wrong, the many resources of the corrupt manipulators of any decision-procedure, is to insist that whatever reasons there may be for deciding issues by democratic processes should commend themselves to participators. Where these reasons are acknowledged, those who take part in democratic procedures should abide by the outcome.

This may not be obvious. Certainly, as we have seen, there is no rule book which states the convention and those who have the right to vote do not have to pass a test establishing that they understand the ethical implications of voting. There is no way of making a case for the thesis that voters consent to abide by the result of the ballot other than by insisting, lamely, that 'there is a conceptual connection between voting and consenting' (Singer 1974: 50). The conceptual connection can be articulated by explaining the point of the voting process. It is not a method of canvassing opinion, a poll designed to establish which policy or representative is most favoured, which information may be taken into account when a decision is taken. It is *itself* a way of taking a decision. Once the votes are counted, the decision is made. There is no logical space for further decision-making of the sort that might provide an opportunity for demurral between the act of voting and the announcement of a decision.

It is a feature of democratic decisions that those who participate in the making of them bind themselves to an acceptance of the result. Where the result is the establishment of a government, voters have assumed the duties of citizenship as these will be defined by the state. Although I cannot think of any objections to this argument it should not be thought that it directly entitles any specific regime to claim universal allegiance. The real world is a messy place and there are many qualifications that need to be registered.[28] Most obviously, since the argument establishes that those who participate as voters take on the duties of citizenship, this entails that one clear way of repudiating the obligations is not to participate. If you don't want to be bound by a decision to strike, don't take part in the ballot.

This limits the scope of the state's appeal since we can be sure that some – Militia Man again – will refuse to enter the polling booth, or entering it, spoil their paper or, indeed, strip off in protest as Jerry Rubin advised voters to do in the 1968 Presidential Election in the United States.[29] But the story gets messier still. If we are thinking of elections to a representative assembly, the assembly may have structural flaws which limit the legitimacy of its decisions. It may represent an entrenched majority, directing its policies towards the violation of minority rights. It may, subsequent to election, contravene an explicit mandate, either failing to introduce policies announced in the manifesto or introducing policies (deliberately) concealed and unannounced at the time of its election. Considerations such as these reveal that the consent adduced by voting does not amount to the issue of a blank cheque to the winning party. The consent will, in practice, be qualified by further understandings of what it is rational for the citizen to accept. Some qualifications, e.g. the requirement of respect for minority rights, may lead to the withdrawal of all authority with respect to the state's decisions. Others, concerning the detail of the mandate, may lead citizens to challenge the validity of specific laws or policies. Thus some in the United Kingdom were led to protest against the Blair government's decision to go to war in Iraq – 'Not in my name' – and qualify their allegiance. Any alert citizen will be able to produce a long list of qualifications to the thought that those who take part in the election of a government must accept all the duties which that government imputes to them – including all those newly created by the election winners.

Having advanced and supported the argument adducing quasi-consent on the part of voters, we can now review the argument from contract and consent. I conclude that actual consent to the powers of the state entails that those who give it must accept the duties of the citizen. Such consent may take several forms: there may have been an actual social contract or something much like it – a founding constitutional referendum; consent may have been express as when the naturalized citizen or the state official swears allegiance; consent may be tacit, depending entirely on the conventions which hold in any particular society. Tacit consent may be adduced from a lack of dissent, a receipt of benefits or, in the specific case of quasi-consent, from an act of voting in a democratic decision procedure. It is obvious that the argument from consent applies only to those citizens who actually give their consent in one of these fashions. The state which employs it cannot seek to extend the reach of this argument beyond the range of consenters. This is not a weakness of the consent argument. As we argued in Chapter 5, an argument can solve the Philosophical Problem without aspiring to be universal in scope.

It will be a feature, too, of consent arguments that they need not entail a complete set of citizens' duties. Consent as given may reach no further than some subset of duties as is explicit in the case of the civil servant who signs the Official Secrets Act. Likewise if one expressly dissents from some specific policy, say the introduction of a particular tax, one may evade that tax or pay it perforce, whilst willingly paying other taxes that the state may levy.[30] One may thus be an outlaw with respect to that tax legislation, whilst consenting to other duties that the state may impose.

To conclude: consent arguments are good arguments, though it is always to be specified when considering the Political Problem who exactly has consented, in virtue of what convention if the consent is tacit, and what regime of duties this consent commits the consenter to accepting. These are all problematic issues in the real world, but once the argument forms are sketched and the possible range of their applicability is reviewed, settling most of these questions is not a task of the philosopher. It is a predicament faced by the conscientious citizen who quite naturally will wish to review the provenance of the duties imputed to him.

At the start of this chapter I distinguished arguments from actual consent and contract from hypothetical consent and contract arguments, indicating that the 'hypothetical' arguments were radically distinct from the 'actual' versions. I shall make good this claim and examine the credentials of the hypothetical forms of argument in the next chapter.

Chapter 8

Hypothetical contract

Hypothetical consent

The first thing we must do is distinguish between hypothetical consent and hypothetical contract. Hypothetical consent is best understood by looking at the context in which it is most frequently invoked: the practice of medicine. In medicine, hypothetical consent works like this: hospital patients are generally asked to consent to surgical procedures being carried out on them. Otherwise, legally the invasion of their bodies would be an assault. The surgeon will take a view on what course of treatment is in the best interests of the patient and explain a recommended plan of action. At this point the patient can either consent to the treatment or decline. Some patients, notably those who are comatose, cannot give such a consent. How is the surgeon to proceed? It may appear that the answer to the question is obvious. The surgeon should make exactly the judgement as to what is in the best interests of the patient and proceed on the basis that the patient would share this view. At this point we should notice that there is an alternative course of deliberation that the surgeon may follow. Instead of asking simply what is in the patient's best interests (as considered by the surgeon), the surgeon may ask a different, hypothetical, question: would the patient consent were he conscious, rational and fully informed of the nature and likely success of the proposed operation? Surgeons' temperaments dispose them to intervene, to save life or cure illness or advance medical science, so it is important to see that the answer to the hypothetical question may be 'No' when the surgeon's judgement of the patient's best interests may lead her to say 'Yes'.

The way to answer the hypothetical question is to gather the sort of information that friends and family can provide so that the surgeon has as good an idea as is possible of how the patient would decide. This may be easy – the patient may have clear religious beliefs which proscribe surgical procedures of the sort envisaged. Or perhaps the patient has told his family that he does not wish any more expensive, painful interventions which have little chance of success. Or perhaps he has told people that he would grasp at any straw to have a longer life of even meagre quality. In a particularly clear case, imagine that the patient was in the same hospital a month previously, with the same medical condition, and refused consent to the treatment that the surgeon judged to be in his best interests on religious grounds. Suppose he was a Jehovah's Witness and refused a transfusion. In the event, against the odds, he survived. Using this sort of information, the surgeon takes the decision she believes the patient would have reached, substituting his judgement, as she believes it would be, for her own. In the example before us, the surgeon would not give the comatose Jehovah's Witness the blood transfusion.

It is useful to speak of hypothetical consent here because it signals that the decision is being taken from the point of view of the patient as hypothesized, mustering the sort of information that would have been relevant to his decision, were he in a position to make it. In cases of this sort, the different questions as put by the surgeon yield different answers. Many believe that in such circumstances it is the hypothetical consent test that should be used because this is the proper way to respect the patient as an autonomous (though comatose) patient. We don't need to enquire whether this conclusion is correct.

Hypothetical consent, thus construed, looks as though it has little part to play in working out whether citizens have duties to the state. Why should one seek to establish it if there exist mechanisms for finding out whether or not citizens actually consent? What kind of information about citizens' preferences could be a substitute for that elicited by asking them? The only sort of presumption that could motivate the investigation of hypothetical consent is that of widespread irrationality. One must assume that citizens, like the patient, but for different reasons, are incapable of judging rationally whether or not they have the obligations with which they are charged by the state. I can think of only one sort of case where arguments from hypothetical consent might have some purchase in the investigation of citizens' duties, and my thoughts are prompted by the curious remarks of Thomas Hobbes that we quoted in Chapter 4.

Hobbes, in a passage we have already noticed, is discussing the acquisition of 'Dominion' – think of this as rightful authority. He says

> Dominion is acquired two wayes; By Generation, and by Conquest. The right of Dominion by Generation, is that, which the Parent hath over his Children; and is called PATERNALL. And is not so derived from the Generation, as if therefore the Parent had Dominion over his Child because he begat him; but from the Child's Consent, either expresse, or by other sufficient arguments declared.[1]
>
> (Hobbes 1968: 253; Part II, Ch. XX [102])

Nature, the 'begetting', cannot of itself generate relations of rightful authority, Hobbes believes, taking a swipe at those who believe political dominion is a natural relation, much like, if not indeed metaphysically akin, to the natural authority of the parent to the child. For not even parental authority is natural. It must derive from the consent of the child, 'either expresse, or by other sufficient arguments declared'. Pretend that you understand how parental authority may derive from the child's express consent; how are we to understand the reference to 'other sufficient arguments declared'? I believe this should be understood in terms of hypothetical consent, yielding judgements of this sort: '*were* the infant to be fully rational and knowledgeable it *would* accept that parents' decisions should be obeyed immediately'. If so, this suggests that hypothetical consent arguments might find a use in the very limited case of children and adults who for one reason or another are deemed morally incompetent (for want of rationality or full knowledge, say) and yet are still deemed to have political duties – payment of taxes on a private income, for example. I shall not pursue this argument any further since in the standard case of adult citizens the assumption of incapacity or incompetence which motivates the use of considerations of hypothetical consent just does not hold. Who would openly acknowledge that any such assumption holds for himself? Just because we understand so clearly the extreme, unfortunate and untypical circumstances which call for the investigation and imputation of hypothetical consent, we should be very reluctant to use this strategy in seeking to derive citizens' duties.

Before we move on to discuss hypothetical contract arguments, I should mention one other type of hypothetical consent argument which has featured in the literature on political obligation. In recent times it has been found in the work of Jean Hampton and others.[2] According to Hampton, who takes herself to be expanding on remarks made by G.E.M. Anscombe (1978), political authority is an invention, a human contrivance. Hampton develops

> a model explaining how political authority is created. This model is not meant to be a detailed historical account of actual state creation: histories are complicated, messy, and full of irrelevant contingencies. A model of state creation allows us to cut through the historical undergrowth and see the deep structure of state generation underlying all histories of state formation.
>
> (Hampton 1997: 71)

The 'model' is an ideal 'Just-So Story' of how the state emerged from the state of nature (a condition of anarchy that we shall consider in more detail later) and central to it is what Hampton dubs 'convention consent', the consent that can be presumed from the citizens' presumed acceptance of a convention that established a political mechanism which solved the conflict and coordination problems endemic to the state of nature. Once the convention is in place, tacit consent can be presumed on the part of those who recognize how the state solves problems which are severe and pressing, and more particularly on the part of those who actively support the state for these reasons (Hampton 1997: 94–7). This account, Hampton believes has both *explanatory* power and *justificatory* force.

Hampton's theory deserves much more attention than I can devote to it here.[3] Nonetheless we can identify some very great difficulties with this approach.[4] First we should ask what purpose the model account serves. It definitely does not give us a historical *explanation* of the creation of the state in any particular case, unless the reader has to hand an example of a state that was created from the state of nature in consequence of citizens' recognition that it would solve the problems caused by violence and the lack of cooperation that all citizens are presumed to share. So far as history goes it is uncontroversial that the beginnings of almost all states have been in force or fraud. In fact I am prepared to say that the model account carries no historical weight at all. If so, how can it explain 'how political authority is created'? I should say, too, that I find it a complete mystery that the model Hampton articulates is meant to disclose 'the deep structure of state generation underlying all histories of state formation'.

If we follow her account through we can see that the model of state creation through convention consent in fact models a familiar story concerning the benefits achieved through the institution and maintenance of political authority. We can see how the state delivers the goods – peace, personal security and commodious living according to Hobbes, the solution of conflict and coordination problems of the Prisoners' Dilemma and Battle of the Sexes types for the modern analyst – which rational citizens can be safely presumed to desire. We can supplement the Hobbesian thought that life in the state of nature would be 'solitary, poore, nasty, brutish and short' (Hobbes 1968: 186; Part I, Ch. XIII [62]) with game-theoretic insights into the structures of seemingly intractable social problems. Once we have delivered a story of how the state makes possible a life for man that is truly social, wealthy and productive, humane, civilized and long, we can identify the unique virtues of a state with political authority – so long as that story is true. (We have seen that it is challenged by the anarchist.) If the state does deliver the goods as specified, the history of its emergence does not matter a whit. The fact that the state does deliver the goods, does solve problems that would be intractable without it, is the familiar factual premise for a range of arguments that seek to justify the state. We do not need a deep explanation of this fact about the state unless we have an interest in conjectural or speculative history. The explanation of how the state has, or speculatively might have, arisen is ethically impotent. It is just as likely to have had its origins in fraud as in the informed consent of rational persons, as Rousseau saw.[5] The enterprise of finding a *justification* for political authority is entirely different from any historical study, though obviously the two tasks are not disconnected for those who believe that history (or a knowledge of current affairs) attests that the state can offer conspicuous advantages to citizens, advantages of which they would not be able to avail themselves if they had to live without it in a state of nature.

As I read Hampton's theory, the account of convention consent elaborates one way of demonstrating the utility of political institutions. This account then serves the further task of underpinning the attribution of tacit consent to the citizen who understands and embraces the functionality of the modern democratic state. This is an argument that we encountered in the last chapter where we reviewed its strengths and weaknesses.

Hypothetical social contract arguments

Hypothetical social contract arguments work in a very different way from the standard form of hypothetical consent, and Hampton stresses that notwithstanding her debt to Hobbes the social contract as traditionally understood, actual or hypothetical, has no part to play in her theory. The social contract has a very distinguished history in political philosophy, as we noted in the last chapter. Most famously, hypothetical social contracts were employed by Hobbes, Locke (perhaps), Rousseau and Kant to vindicate the authority of the state and to justify a regime of citizens' duties. More recently variants of the hypothetical contract argument have been employed by John Rawls to establish the principles of justice, and by a host of other writers, notably Russell Grice, David A. Richards and, latterly, Thomas Scanlon ('contractarians' or 'contractualists' all, to demonstrate the jargon) to construct a normative ethics quite generally.[6] In what follows I shall stick rigidly to the project of the great, dead, philosophers who attempted to use a hypothetical contract argument to articulate the ethical relationship of state to citizen.

In what is now a well-known quotation, Ronald Dworkin states that 'A hypothetical contract is not simply a pale form of an actual contract; it is no contract at all' (Dworkin 1975: 18). This tells us that there is some work to be done in establishing the credentials of arguments that rely on a hypothetical contract. Such arguments cannot rely on the normative implications of instances of actual consent or contract which standardly entail obligations. Their moral force must derive from elsewhere.

When philosophers speak of hypothetical contracts we should recognize that they are referring to arguments with a distinctive *form* rather than arguments which cite a distinctive occurrence. A hypothetical contract is not an actual contract, it is itself a form of argument. If there is no contract and no contractual obligations why speak of a contract, albeit one that is hypothetical? The answer is that such talk of contracts alerts us to a feature of the argument form, an argumentative device which enables us to see how a course of reasoning which individuals undertake when they work out how they should behave can have universal implications. When we were discussing tacit consent, we insisted that the imputation of tacit consent depended on there being in place operative conventions to the effect that behaving in one way (or doing nothing) implied that one was also doing something else, that one actually but tacitly consented. The conclusion of hypothetical contract arguments must be stated in a different fashion: if the argument is successful it will demonstrate, not that the citizen *does* consent in some way, but rather that she *ought to* consent. Which is to say: she ought to take on the duties of the citizen. Political obligations can be justly imputed to her.

So let us adopt the perspective of the ambitious state. Suppose that we have failed to establish consent where its attribution matters most, in the case, that is, of the recalcitrant citizen. If we haven't established that she does consent, can we show her that she ought to? Can we get her to accept that she ought to agree to the state's imposition of the duties of citizenship although she hasn't in fact done so? Can we claim that other things she believes require her to accept the conclusion she has not yet reached, or perhaps that she disavows?

We have emphasized that accepting the duties of citizenship is costly. The state exacts its severe impositions. It imposes heavy burdens on citizens and it threatens them with heavy penalties for non-compliance. As we saw when discussing the challenge of the anarchist, these powers are unattractive to anyone in their reach. The hypothetical contract argument attempts to show that a rational citizen should accept these powers as legitimate as the cost of achieving goods that she values more. The decisive move is made when the citizen recognizes that she faces not so much a personal dilemma as a social problem, when she realizes that an acceptable solution embraces other persons besides herself, all of whom face exactly the same problem. The simplest way to outline this model of reasoning is to bowdlerize Hobbes, the master of this line of argument.

First, suppose that we are living without the state, in the 'state of nature'. In the hypothetical contract argument this technical term does not refer to some period in the mists of time before the state was invented or 'just grew'. It invites us to conduct a thought-experiment, to imagine how life would be for folk like us if *ex hypothesi* there were no state – no government and no law, no police, no courts of justice and no gaols. Hobbes believes that the way to conduct this thought experiment is to investigate human nature in our own persons, to discover what kind of creatures we are and, crucially, to describe how we would typically behave by identifying our basic motivations, by detailing our psychology. He states (most controversially) that we are both psychological and ethical egoists. At bottom we seek to advance our own interests, placing a premium on the preservation of our lives, and having a standing concern to enjoy 'commodious living', to do as well as we can. Yet we find ourselves systematically thwarted. We find, each of us as individuals, that our own pursuit of such power as is necessary both to satisfy our desires and to protect ourselves from others who seek to use our powers for their own ends is continually frustrated by the power-seeking activities of others, who are just like us in the single-minded pursuit of their own interests. Hobbes finds, 'for a generall inclination of all mankind, a perpetuall and restlesse desire of Power after power, that ceaseth onely in Death' (Hobbes 1968: 161; Part I, Ch. II [47]).

In the social condition in which we currently live this relentless power-seeking takes a host of peaceful and civilized forms. In chapters 10 and 11 of *Leviathan*, Hobbes describes this competition for power in terms of the upstairs-downstairs machinations of the great country house.[7] Thus to take one example, 'Riches joined with liberality is Power; because it procureth friends, and servants: Without liberality, not so; because in this case they defend not; but expose men to Envy, as a Prey' (Hobbes 1968: 150; Part 1, Ch. X [41]).

No doubt you could give a similar account of the sociology of the various rat races in which you are engaged – the politicking of the business world or the student union or the university department.

When we ask ourselves what form would this power-seeking take if hypothetically there were no coercive political authority of the kind that you or I enjoy we can deduce that it would be a condition of endemic war.

> It is manifest, that during the time men live without a common Power to keep them all in awe, they are in that condition called Warre; and such a warre, as is of every man against every man . . . not in actuall fighting; but in the known disposition thereto.
>
> (Hobbes 1968: 185–6; Part I, Ch. XIII [62])

In the state of nature, *nothing*, not even morality, constrains this pursuit of power. Since the unimpeded pursuit of our own interests inevitably undermines its own achievement, the rules of the game need to be revised. Since as things stand, no-one is getting what they want, the circumstances of human interaction need to be changed.

Supposing there are just two persons, you and I, involved in this desperate state of nature, we can identify four possibilities: the first, the *status quo* wherein we each of us struggle for power, is hopeless for both of us since we are roughly equal. The second possibility is that I have all the power, but you will not accept that (and nor would anyone else) – and I know this. The third possibility is that you (or someone else) have all the power, but that won't suit me – as you know equally well. The final possibility is that neither of us has power over the other. We can achieve this outcome by both of us renouncing our private pursuit of power and handing over our powers to some third party who will establish the conditions of peace. We can rehearse this argument for any number of people because, being rational, we all think along the same tracks: we value the same things (life and commodious living), we can each work out how each of us is frustrating the achievement of these goods by the other, and we can each of us work out how to escape this desperate condition. We conclude that it is rational for agents who wish to preserve their lives under conditions of commodious living to give up their powers and accept a sovereign power to rule over them, a common power to keep them all in awe. It's as though we wish to make a bet with one another but can't since neither of us trusts the other to pay up. We finally manage to do so by agreeing to give our stakes to a third party who will pay out the winner. That way, neither of us can renege. In the political context, the result of our several deliberations is that each of us judges that if we do not have a sovereign we should institute one; if we do have a sovereign we should support and keep it by recognizing its authority. On this we agree.

You will have plenty of reservations about this story. But look at the outcome. We have portrayed an exercise of practical reason undertaken by each party to the conflict as giving rise to a mutually acceptable solution. It is not that everyone has agreed with each other in the way of shaking hands or signing a treaty. The agreement that has been modelled is agreement in the minimal sense of congruence in the reasoning undertaken and the conclusion reached. We each reach the same conclusion, since we all reason in the same fashion from the same premises. Matters stand *as if* we had made a contract. It might be objected that this is a poor sort of contract. After all, if we are all asked to write down the answer to the following sum: $2 + 2 = ?$, and we all write down 4, what is gained by representing the agreed answer as the outcome of a contract? It is *as though* we had agreed (I could say, truly, 'haven't we all agreed that $2 + 2 = 4$?'), but what are the implications of this? We should certainly *not* conclude that $2 + 2$ equals 4 on the basis of a hypothetical contract.

This objection forgets a central feature of the Hobbesian story. Unlike the mathematical case, as each person in the state of nature reviewed the possible outcomes, they were forced to consider the responses of others and restructure their priorities in line with their judgements of what outcome others could reasonably be expected to accept. Each person conducted the moral arithmetic separately, but each person found themselves having to take into account the anticipated responses of others. The first preference of each, that he or she has all the power, could not survive the obvious thought that this would not be acceptable to others. So each 'contractor' trimmed their aspirations, seeking only some solution that would be mutually agreeable, knowing that that would be the only kind of solution that could work. A hypothetical contract works as a device for modelling the practical reason of individual agents seeking an answer to a common problem where it is a condition of the acceptability of a solution that everyone reaches the same conclusion. We can say everyone agrees to it because agreement is the only way forward. We can represent the conclusion to our deliberations as follows: *Rational persons who seek to live decent lives in peace and security ought to accept a sovereign political authority*. I find this model of reasoning explicit in Hobbes. It specifies a deep and important reason that each person has to accept the authority of the state.

Hobbes's account is richer than I have sketched it, but it raises a huge variety of questions, most of which I am unable to tackle here. In the first place, you might question the 'moral' theory in the background – the postulate of ethical egoism. This thought – that it is never wrong to compromise one's own best interests – is indeed hugely controversial. Indeed I think it is false. Nonetheless, it stands as a useful assumption in this context because it is plausible to think that if one could solve the problem of establishing the terms of peaceful co-existence amongst a population of egoists one has solved it in the most difficult case. 'The problem of establishing a state, no matter how hard it may sound, is soluble even for a nation of devils (if only they have understanding)' Kant tells us in his essay 'Toward Perpetual Peace' (Kant 1996c: 335 [8: 366]).[8]

A second objection is more pressing, and it is prompted by reflection on Kant's 'devils'. These may be misanthropic creatures but when the stern voice of duty speaks out to them, being rational they heed the call. It is very doubtful that Hobbesian man would follow them in this. As I read the main thrust of Hobbesian ethics, Hobbes's man has no moral duties at all. The laws which the sovereign commands are positive (in the sense of 'actual') laws, not moral laws, and they prescribe positive, not moral duties. The (nineteen) laws of nature which Hobbes deduces and elaborates in chapters 14 and 15 of *Leviathan* are 'counsels of prudence', maxims to be adopted by those concerned to govern their lives in accordance with principles of enlightened self-interest: 'they are but Conclusions, or Theoremes concerning what conduceth to the conservation and defence of themselves' (Hobbes 1968: 217; Part I, Ch. XV [80]).[9] It follows that the conclusion we reached above: *Rational persons who seek to live decent lives in peace and security ought to accept a sovereign political authority* does not express a moral demand and does not frame a moral duty. If we grant that Hobbes's argument is sound, we should recognize that it offers the citizen a perfectly good reason to institute and maintain a sovereign authority – but that reason is not at bottom a moral reason. It is a strongly prudential consideration, and as I claimed in Chapter 4, such an argument cannot establish the legitimacy or moral authority of the state. It might be true for each of us severally that we are better off for having a state, but this conclusion is insufficient (on its own) to ground a regime of citizens' duties.

Normative hypothetical contract arguments

This conclusion does not signal the end of the hypothetical social contract argument. It has deeper resources than the scanty materials furnished by Hobbes. And these deeper resources were employed effectively by Locke and Rousseau. In what follows I shall sketch the more powerful argument that they offer without defending the attribution of it to these authors.[10] For Hobbes the goods that are threatened in the state of nature and protected by the state are the preservation of life and 'commodious living' which we may think of as property. It is common ground to *all* the contract thinkers that individuals are concerned to protect their persons and property. Locke differs from Hobbes in that a clear moral law operates in the state of nature: 'no one ought to harm another in his Life, Health, Liberty, or Possessions'. In addition, man in the state of nature has a duty of care to come to the assistance of his fellows: 'when his own Preservation comes not in competition, ought he, as much as he can, *to preserve the rest of Mankind*' (Locke 1960, Ch. II, §6). We can translate this moral law into a regime of natural rights – each person has an equal natural right to life, to personal physical integrity, to liberty and to property, and a further right to the assistance of others. But notwithstanding this constituent morality, the state of nature will eventually degenerate into a state of war since the inhabitants have no way to adjudicate the disputes that will inevitably arise concerning the proper punishment of those who violate the law of nature.

Rousseau's argument is not so easy to reconstruct, since the hypothetical contract argument is employed in *The Social Contract* and the values to be protected and promoted are not described there explicitly.[11] Fortunately, these can be traced in other sources, notably in the *Second Discourse on the Origins of Inequality* and in the *Emile*. Here Rousseau claims that persons naturally pursue their own well-being (*amour-de-soi*), have a concern for suffering of others (*pitié*), see themselves and recognize others as equals, and prize their independence and liberty. So we can say that men place a moral value on life and property, on equality and liberty. The hypothetical state of nature is not described in the *Social Contract*. Rousseau says casually

> I suppose men to have reached the point at which the obstacles in the way of their preservation in the state of nature show their power of resistance to be greater than the resources at the disposal of each individual for his maintenance in that state. That primitive condition can then subsist no longer; and the human race would perish unless it changed its manner of existence.
>
> (Rousseau 1973 *The Social Contract*, Bk I, Ch. 6: 190–1)

This analytic formulation of the intolerable circumstances of the state of nature frames the purpose of the hypothetical social contract:

> The problem is to find a form of association which will defend and protect with the whole common force the person and goods of each associate, and in which each, while uniting himself with all, may still obey himself alone, and remain as free as before.
>
> (ibid.)

So we can put the point of the Locke–Rousseau argument this way: men who seek to preserve their lives and property, who think of themselves as morally equal and independent, having no natural relations of dominion and servitude to one another, and who value their liberty, will inevitably find these goods and values compromised in a state of nature. Putting this argument in a clear hypothetical contract mode, we assert that, as citizens of some state or other we hypothesize that, were we to find ourselves without a state that preserves our persons and property under conditions of maximal liberty and equality, we would find our circumstances intolerable. Even those who share a set of values and hypothetically place themselves in a state of nature will deduce that in such circumstances their lives and well-being would come under threat, their equality would be compromised and their liberty would be diminished. However strong their commitment to these values, they would be unable to enforce them and would have no secure or stable way of doing so. However much goodwill and commitment to the moral law they each judged themselves to manifest, their human fallibility would lead to a lack of trust and this in turn would force them to take a protective and defensive stance. They would have to *think* their way out of such a condition. But since they all value the same things, and since they see, as in the Hobbesian scenario, that the root cause of their problem is each other (including importantly their expectations and perceptions of each other as potential threats), they think along parallel tracks when they use their reason to find a satisfactory alternative to the state of nature. (Hopefully) they reach the same conclusion. Since everyone would understand what is happening, everyone would see that the only solution is to empower a state to protect persons and property in a fashion consistent with their liberty and moral equality. They would agree on this. It is as though they had made a contract.

I shall call this a *normative* social contract argument since the goods which the contractors seek include the satisfaction of moral, as against purely prudential, values. The contractors value not only their own persons, property and liberty but those of other persons, too. I suggested above that the Hobbesian argument cannot transmute the base metal of self-interest into the gold of a conclusion which ascribes a moral duty, but I think the normative social contract argument can do this since it includes clear moral values among the goods that the contractors aim to secure.

I say 'hopefully' since in this more complex version of the hypothetical contract argument there are more and different values in play than self-interest, and these may be prioritized in different ways should they come into conflict. Some may prioritize liberty over well-being; some may accept this priority in one sort of circumstance but not another. Some may value liberty higher than equality, and others *vice versa*. These sorts of issue are the staple of current discussions of social justice and may lead individuals to different solutions to the same problem at different times and in different circumstances.[12] This is a severe problem, but it is mitigated by the thought that everyone who deliberates in hypothetical social contract mode, considering how best to avoid the state of nature, does so in an (at least) two-stage fashion: first of all working out that the only general solution lies in accepting the authority of a legitimate state, and then second (and perhaps third, fourth, etc.), working out the details of how exactly that state should be constituted in order to deliver the goods. If this is true, then we can avoid the problems of having to secure a variety of independent goods, having found at least one basic element common to all possible solutions, that is, the ground-level acceptance on the part of all citizens that it is better to be live under the authority of a state and accept the concomitant duties of the citizen than to live in the state of nature.

We should notice that both Locke and Rousseau argued for the state as the solution to the problem of the state of nature but then argued for very different constitutional settlements – Locke for a constitutional monarchy within an attenuated representative democracy (nowadays, still, the 'Queen-in-Parliament' is sovereign in the UK) and Rousseau for a radical, direct democracy as legislature with an (over-powerful) executive to serve it. I am sure that they would both reject my proposal that there is a two-stage process of reasoning at work here if that implies the Hobbesian thought that *any* state is better than the state of nature, but that some constitutional arrangements are better than others. For both of them, some constitutional arrangements are quite impossible for a rational citizen to accept; deliberation about the necessity of the state and the optimum, or better, minimally acceptable constitutional settlement, must proceed together. For Locke, a tyranny which violates citizens' rights must be overthrown – and then one can start to pick up the pieces, since a Civil Society (not *pace* Hobbes, a state of nature) will still be in place (Locke 1960, Ch. XIX, §212). But for Rousseau not even a representative democracy will be tolerable to rational citizens – who would never assert for themselves a portion of the sovereign will, then immediately alienate it to a representative (e.g. a Member of Parliament or Congressman) (Rousseau 1973, Bk II, Ch. 1: 200).

I think that both Locke and Rousseau, in their different ways, are right about this. We can agree with them because we have already insisted that we are not in the business of finding good reasons that one might have to support any kind of state however iniquitous. I argued in Chapter 5 that we must assume that it is only the 'just' state that can advance claims to be legitimate. If this is so, then we can finesse the difficulties I have raised, though we should notice that since the 'just' state as I characterized it was a representative democracy, Rousseau would not accept this conclusion.

This argument is cogent but it is weaker than the Hobbesian hypothetical social contract argument since its wider assumptions represent greater hostages to fortune. The Hobbesian identification of rational conduct with behaviour designed to most effectively secure one's life and the conditions of living well is hard to dispute. As soon as one adds to this list values of equality and liberty, one has the additional problems of first spelling out the nature of these values, second, of defending them, and third, perhaps of assigning priorities to them to adjudicate alternative candidate solutions. One who defends the normative hypothetical social contract must take these problems on board. The task is forbidding, but it must be attractive to anyone who values liberty and authority as well as personal security. Nonetheless if we ask: what is the scope of the claim to authority that the state makes on the basis of this argument we should notice that there are some individuals who will resist it.

As put, in both the Hobbesian and normative forms, the hypothetical social contract argument requires acceptance of a small set of personal goods and social values. As we have seen Hobbes's goods – the preservation of life and the conditions of living well – can be represented as a very weak assumption. One might think that the list is still uncontroversial when it is lengthened by the addition of the values of liberty and equality as espoused by Locke and Rousseau. But this is not so. We are *not* all liberal democrats nowadays. Some might object that crucially important values are not on the list and name salvation as understood by some specific religious creed as an obvious candidate. If the dogmas of such a religion exclude non-believers from possible citizenship we cannot assume that all contractors will be thinking along parallel lines and seeking the basis for an agreement with each other. There are many in the modern world who would insist further that the values of life and liberty are as nothing when put on the scales with salvation. Such religious enthusiasts do not seek common ground if that prescinds from the articles of their faith. At bottom such believers will not accept political sovereignty as an institution independent from theocracy. This is a deeply unattractive position, but one cannot pretend that it does not exist. If this is so, the normative hypothetical contract argument will not reach out to them.

Hypothetical contract arguments in one or other form might work, however, with the Militia Man who abjures all the conventions that underpin tacit consent. We can test this thought by seeing how such an argument applies to Militia Man. Note that although he has withdrawn to the wilds of Montana or wherever, he hasn't succeeded in inoculating himself from the contagion of other members of his society. He still makes claims against them, notably that they keep off his land, and reinforces these by threatening to use his automatic rifle. He makes a claim even in this restricted domain, so it is important to work out how it might be adjudicated when it comes into conflict with the claims of others. If he is wise, he will not rely on physical force or weaponry. An alliance of rival claimants will get him sooner or later, as Hobbes foresaw. He can't insist that he isn't a threat. His neighbours will no doubt give a wide berth to his territorial boundaries but they may still worry that he may take pot-shots at straying cattle or children. Whatever his antecedent principles about big government and the like, he should realize that he has to make an accommodation, which amounts to accepting a procedure for the arbitration of conflicting claims. He has to do this because otherwise everything he holds dear is threatened. The state puts itself forward to recalcitrants such as Militia Man as adjudicator of disputes and enforcer of valid claims. Hobbes would accept any third party as long as it can settle disputes effectively. Just in case Militia Man distrusts the state, it can offer him a place in the making of rules and the settling of claims as a participant in democratic decision procedures. He would do well to accept the offer, but if he doesn't its terms may fairly be imposed upon him anyway.[13]

It is a feature of hypothetical contract arguments that they figure the state as the deliverer of goods. It should be unsurprising to find other arguments which use this putative fact as the basis for the ascription of authority to the state and duties to its citizens. In the next chapter, we shall examine several more of these positions.

Chapter 9

The provision of benefits
Arguments from fairness and gratitude

In this chapter I shall review two broad arguments that proceed from the putative fact of the state's providing benefits to the citizens. I shan't argue for a general proposition to the effect that states benefit their citizens since if there are any facts hereabouts they can only be, or derive from, facts about particular states at particular times. It is true that one could construct a model of the modern state and list or categorize typical benefits or services that the model state provides. But the contents of the list and certainly the extent and range of provision (how much of the good and to how many people it is made available) will vary from actual state to actual state. We should expect the modern state to provide personal protection and external security – the traditional function of the nightwatchman who patrols the streets and guards the city walls. Beyond this, the state will generally make available (or indeed compel citizens to take) a great range of benefits and public goods.[1] But the provision of these goods will incur costs, which will also vary from state to state, and besides the costs of benefit provision the state may also impose severe burdens on some if not all of its citizens. For these reasons, in any particular case where a citizen is reviewing the benefits provided by the state, the final judgement will always be one concerning net benefits (or costs). This is important because we understand perfectly well that the costs and burdens in particular cases can greatly outweigh the benefits. In such a case any argument from the receipt of benefits by the citizen will be a non-starter. For these reasons, we should regard all arguments based on the citizens' receipt of benefits as conditional, having the form: 'If the citizens benefit significantly from the activities of the state, then . . .' In what follows we shall assume that this condition is met; if it is not met, the conclusion which is supposed to follow from it will be unsound. We shall also have occasion to notice that this initial conditional statement may need to be more specific. Whether some or all citizens benefit, and if only some, which ones, may make a difference to the question of whether or not citizens have duties imputed to them.

The principle of fairness

In the broadest terms, this argument states that considerations of fairness require those in receipt of benefits from the state to reciprocate by accepting the appropriate burdens, by accepting the duties of citizenship.[2] In modern times it was first sketched by H.L.A. Hart:

> When a number of persons conduct any joint enterprise according to rules and thus restrict their liberty, those who have submitted to these restrictions when required have the right to a similar submission from those who have benefited from their submission.[3]
>
> (Hart 1955: 285)

The argument was used in Rawls's (1958) paper 'Justice as Fairness' and his (1963) paper 'The Sense of Justice'. It was further developed by Rawls in 'Legal Obligation and the Duty of Fair Play' (1964). In *A Theory of Justice* Rawls stated the principle as follows:

> when a number of persons engage in a mutually advantageous cooperative venture according to rules, and thus restrict their liberty in ways necessary to yield advantages for all, those who have submitted to these restrictions have a right to a similar acquiescence on the part of those who have benefited from their submission. We are not to gain from the cooperative labors of others without doing our fair share.
>
> (Rawls 1972: 112)

The principle of fairness was mauled by Nozick in *Anarchy, State and Utopia*. It was reported, expanded, defended and ultimately dismissed by Simmons in *Moral Principles and Political Obligations* (and later in Simmons 2001). A qualified version of the principle has been defended by Greenawalt in *Conflicts of Law and Morality*. The argument has been revivified, developed and endorsed by Klosko in *The Principle of Fairness and Political Obligation* and in his latest book, *Political Obligations*. Hart is clear that this account of the grounding of political obligation should be sharply distinguished from those that derive obligation from consent or promises. If the argument works, it has the same power as the arguments from hypothetical consent and utility to attribute obligations to those who expressly disavow consent. The argument has an obvious surface plausibility since there are clear cases where it does apply. To see this, consider the following example.

Bridge is a card game that is played in partnership – two players playing against two opponents. One can't play the game without a partner. Partners are sometimes ill, sometimes absent. One may not have a regular partner. How then can a single person regularly play the game? My bridge club solves the problem by using a stand-by system several times a week. Individuals sign up to be stand-by at a tournament. This means that anyone can turn up for the tournament without a partner and be sure of a game. If there is another 'single' looking for a partner when they arrive, they play with them. If there isn't, they wait to see if another single arrives. If one does, they have a partner. If no-one else turns up, they play with the self-designated stand-by. This system is burdensome for the stand-by because it means that they may have to go home without a game if an even number of singles arrive, that is, 50 per cent of the time. Many, but not all, members of the club use the stand-by system on those occasions when they haven't arranged a partner or when a regular partner has to withdraw at the last minute. It is a useful facility that maximizes the number of club members who can find a game. The success of the system requires that members volunteer to be the stand-by, signing up for a specific date and thereby guaranteeing a game to others.

Do club members have an obligation to volunteer periodically to be the stand-by? I think they do have such a duty if they themselves actually benefit from the stand-by system, having turned up on occasion without a partner and having found a game as they anticipated. I also think they have a duty to volunteer to be a stand-by if, counterfactually, they would use the system were it ever necessary for them to do so. It is doubtful that they have a duty to volunteer if they never have nor ever would use the system. But where I say there is a duty on the part of those who do or would use the system it is worth considering why. The answer, surely, is that periodic volunteering is a requirement of fairness where the demand of fairness in this context is spelled out by Hart's principle – put roughly: we shouldn't seek to gain from a cooperative system which is intended to benefit all unless we are prepared to pay our fair share towards the maintenance of this system. In this example, I have spelled out the benefits of the stand-by system. 'Paying one's fair share' amounts to volunteering periodically alongside others. Thus I take it as a datum that members of the club who benefit from the system by turning up occasionally in full knowledge that they will find a partner yet never themselves volunteer to be stand-by do wrong because they are acting unfairly.[4]

Robert Nozick addresses the principle of fairness with a very different example to the forefront of his argument:

> Suppose some of the people in your neighbourhood (there are 364 other adults) have found a public address system and decide to institute a system of public entertainment. They post a list of names, one for each day, yours among them. On his assigned day (one can easily switch days) a person is to run the public address system, play records over it, give news bulletins, tell amusing stories he has heard, and so on. After 138 days on which each person has done his part, your day arrives. Are you obligated to take your turn? You *have* benefited from it, occasionally opening the window to listen, enjoying some music or chuckling at someone's funny story. The other people *have* put themselves out. But must you answer the call when it is your turn to do so? As it stands, surely not. Though you benefit from the arrangement, you may know all along that 364 days of entertainment supplied by others will not be worth giving up *one* day. You would rather not have any of it and not give up a day than have it all and spend one of your days at it.
> (Nozick 1974: 93)

This example is as persuasive in its own way as the one that I introduced, though it is more contrived and less realistic. It is hard to reject Nozick's conclusion in respect of this particular example, not least since we are naturally wary of others' foisting gifts on us and then expecting us to reciprocate in some fashion. Does your use of the pen enclosed in the letter from the charity oblige you to send them a donation? Surely not. Is the woman obliged to take to her bed the man who has just paid for the *couscous royale* in the restaurant to which he had invited her? Once again, surely not.[5]

How would Robert Nozick's story need to be amplified in order for us to agree that an obligation had been created? The most obvious ways would be to describe the reluctant payer agreeing to set up such a scheme, or voting for (or against) its institution in a neighbourhood poll which they judged to be a decisive way of settling the issue, or else failing to dissent when an invitation to do so had been extended – silence understood to be a mark of complicity. But then the argument would attest some sort of consent. Perhaps one could fill out the story so that the dissenter gets great pleasure from listening, looks forward to transmissions and then seeks to avoid doing her stint. We can elaborate the story to show that she is a poor neighbour, ungenerous and miserly, but unlike the non-payer in the pub, I don't think we can accuse her of being unfair to the point of failing an obligation unless we can articulate some convention that she understands and violates. And then, as we saw in Chapter 7, if there is a convention in place, this may fairly be taken as tacit consent.

Now that we've sorted out the ethics of the bridge club, the musical neighbourhood, gifts from charities and dating in restaurants, we can move on to bigger things. None of the examples that we have discussed should license a simple argument from analogy of the form: 'Just as members of the bridge club/musical neighbourhood . . . so then should citizens recognize/not recognize a duty to. . . '. We should address more directly the question of whether the principle of fairness applies to the relationship of citizen to state (or the relationship of citizen to fellow citizens, as both Hart and Rawls insist (Hart 1955: 285; Rawls 1999: 123).

At this point we should look more carefully at the benefits that serve as premises for the argument. In the first place, these should be substantial. If the goods or services that are provided by the state are insignificant, absolutely or when weighed in the balance with the costs of assuming the range of citizens' duties, the argument from fairness will not get off the ground.[6] Second, we should note that the types of benefit that the state is providing differ widely. In particular there is a great difference between:

(a) benefits (public goods) that are 'open',[7] that citizens cannot help receiving and cannot be excluded from, such as national defence, law and order and clean air, and

(b) benefits that are 'readily available' at no cost to the user and from which the citizen cannot be excluded, such as public parks, and in the United Kingdom, public education and health services. In contrast to open public goods, the citizen needs to seek these out. One needn't visit public parks and one can choose to pay for private education and health services.

(c) In addition, there may be open goods and readily available goods that are accessible to, and usable by, only some fraction of the population. (I guess plenty of us have not been able to make any use of lighthouses.) Sometimes the state might limit access: notoriously 'Negroes may not sit on this park bench'. Other goods may be directed to some evidently needy section of the community, e.g. Braille IT equipment for the blind.

There are lots of distinctions to be made amongst the goods and services provided to some or all by the state. For our purposes, the important distinction is between (a) the open goods and (b) the readily available goods. There is a concomitant distinction to be drawn in respect of the manner in which the goods are received. If citizens can be described as merely 'in receipt' of the open benefit, because like the rain from heaven it has been showered upon them, gifted willy-nilly, then the case is different from the benefits they have 'accepted' in the positive sense of having solicited or sought out. If I apply for a pensioner's bus pass, and then use that bus pass to travel freely throughout Scotland, I have made an effort to gain a (conditional)[8] benefit from the Scottish government. I have done nothing to benefit from the well-swept streets in my locality. In different ways I can be merely in receipt and positively accept the same benefit. I merely receive the benefit of personal security which I enjoy due to effective policing. I positively accept that same benefit when I phone the police for assistance, believing that someone is attempting to steal my car.

I believe that those who readily seek out benefits that are made freely available by the state are captured by the principle of fairness. They have a concomitant duty to maintain the system from which they choose to benefit. They are in exactly the same moral position as the bridge player who attends the bridge tournament as a single in full knowledge that they will get a game. In the bridge case, fairness required that the club member volunteers to take a turn. What is required of the citizen who applies for and uses a bus pass, 'phones up the police when he is frightened, turns up at the local hospital with a broken wrist, etc.? The obvious answer is that they should accept within reason the duties ascribed to them by a just government. (I say 'within reason' to remind readers that the cheerful consumer of readily available government services is not required to hand over a blank cheque of unconditional compliance to even a just government.) But by and large this means being law-abiding and cooperative, generally a good citizen.

There are several objections to this conclusion which I should address. First, it will be objected that my description of the relation of state to citizen is mistaken. I have been speaking as though first the state provides goods and services for its citizens – on a plate, as it were. Next, citizens decide in light of these benefits whether fairness requires that they comply with any demands that the state makes of them. Then, if citizens decide that the argument from fairness is sound, the citizens comply with these demands. This, it will be claimed, is not how things work. Rather, the state makes available goods and services which citizens pay for through their taxes. This is not, at bottom, a moral relationship to be explained in terms of fairness and consequent duties; it is a straightforward commercial transaction between a service provider and a client.[9] Those who take up benefits are required to pay for them either in cash terms through taxes, or in kind, as when they forbear from doing actions of kinds that they want the state to protect them from on the part of others.

There can be no doubt that many folk view their relationship with the government at least in part in just this way. 'I pay my taxes, so the government should . . . ' sometimes takes the commercial reading it bears on its face. In the same way some tax payers say 'Why should I pay for schools through my taxes when my children go to private schools?' And this commercial perspective is often correct; citizens do pay directly for some state services. They buy maps from the Ordnance Survey and books from Her Majesty's Stationery Office. Energy, water and many transport and communications services in the United Kingdom were in national ownership 25 years ago and the Post Office still is. What has emerged here is a tension between communitarian and commercial views of the state.[10]

This issue will re-emerge in Chapter 11 when we discuss associational accounts of the duties of the citizen. For the moment, we should notice that the difference between the two (moral and commercial) perspectives is overstated in just those cases where the principle of fairness is seen to apply most perspicuously. These are cases where the citizen seeks out a good or service for which no charge is directly made, but for which payment or some other contribution to the maintenance of the system is necessary in order for benefit provision to be readily available to those who need it or otherwise choose to make use of it. In these circumstances (as against, say, the purchase of postage stamps) there are many reasons why charges are not made at the point of use. It may be that such a payment system is inefficient. More likely considerations of justice intervene, as they do where those who need the service most cannot afford to pay for it, or where it is deemed just that those with greater wealth and income contribute more to the maintenance of the system than those who have less. It is in just these circumstances, where 'free riding' in the manner of tax evasion is iniquitous, that the principle of fairness can be employed to explain why this so.

A different objection is less challenging. According to Simmons, the application of the principle of fairness will only work as an improvement (in the sense of its being a strong supplementary argument) over arguments for consent if it can capture some significant number of citizens who have not consented, actually or tacitly. This is true. He goes on to argue that this

> would not be the case, however, if accepting benefits in the right sense required having an understanding of the moral consequences of such acceptance, for certainly most citizens who receive the benefits of government do not have such an understanding.
>
> (Simmons 1979: 117)

Simmons is correct to claim that the principle of fairness could not be used to ascribe duties to those who take benefits without understanding that in consequence the duties of citizenship may fairly be ascribed to them. This would be a problem if the argument supporting the principle of fairness were unsound or if the gist of the principle of fairness were not perfectly clear to the citizens who stand to be captured by it. I think the argument is sound, but more importantly in this context, I think it is the statement of a principle which can command widespread acceptance in the fashion required by the 'Publicity Condition' which I introduced in Chapter 5. It is well-understood by members of my bridge club and they didn't need any lessons in ethics to grasp it. In fact, I daresay the applicability of the principle of fairness to the success of the stand-by system has never been explained in words of one syllable to anyone: first, because it has never had to be and second, if some officious pedant attempted to do so, members would find her efforts patronizing.

In like manner, I take it that most citizens are capable of understanding how the principle requires that they contribute their fair share towards the provision of benefits which they solicit. Simmons may not be denying this, for he makes a slightly different point, confidently asserting that 'certainly most citizens who receive the benefits of government do not have such an understanding [of the moral consequences of their receipt of benefits]' (Simmons 1979: 117). Now this of course is not a philosophical conclusion. It is a statement of fact. Is it true? I don't know and I suspect Simmons doesn't either. Yet again we come across a bit of guesswork which addresses not the Philosophical Problem concerning the philosophical credentials of the principle of fairness, but the Political Problem of judging whether or not that principle applies in some specific circumstances.[11] The conclusion that Simmons draws from his discussion of 'acceptance' is that 'citizens generally in no actual states will be bound under the principle of fair play' (Simmons 1979: 139).[12] But defenders of the principle should not worry about this unless they aspire to use the principle to assign duties to citizens generally in some actual state. But then they would not be working as philosophers but as commentators on public affairs and there is no reason to think that philosophers have any expertise to offer in this area.

We should notice, however, that in drawing a distinction between merely receiving benefits and accepting them the applicability of the principle of fairness is limited in principle. The principle of fairness would be much stronger if it could be extended to circumstances in which persons merely receive benefits, but I do not believe that this is possible. We have seen in the case of Nozick's counter-example how the scheme for a community public address system might be elaborated so as to generate an obligation to contribute. Basically, one has to demonstrate that in some fashion those who benefit from it have consented to act as the service provider when their turn comes round or one has to simply assert that there is a *de facto* convention of fairness in place which citizens understand. If just as a matter of fact we are talking about a community that operates such a convention, well and good. What is needed at this point is an argument to the effect that citizens ought to be operating such a convention. One can't upon pain of circularity use a contingently operative convention to demonstrate that one must exist.

Exactly the same is true with respect to the state. No matter how much one expands on the detail of the open benefits provided by the state, unless one can demonstrate that there is some widely understood convention in place that explains how those who receive benefits willy-nilly take their receipt of unsolicited benefits to be a ground of political obligation, one cannot impute obligations to them. I think this is true, no matter how many benefits are showered upon the recipients and no matter how important these benefits are to them. Even if it is a matter of the provision of basic needs, one can't deduce that fairness demands that the recipient should fulfil the duties that the beneficient state ascribes to him. Think of the Good Samaritan case. Imagine that the man who fell among thieves is in fact wealthy. The Good Samaritan has saved his life, dressed his wounds and taken him into the nearest town. Does fairness demand that he should pay something to the Samaritan as just recompense for his time, trouble and out-of-pocket expenses? I'm sure not. There may well be other reasons why the Samaritan should be rewarded – gratitude is the obvious one and we shall discuss gratitude in the next section. Indeed prudence will probably dictate that those in receipt of substantial goods that meet vital needs should support the state that provides them. But the issue is not one of *fairness*.

In the same way, if one elaborates on the idea that the state is a cooperative venture or scheme (to use Rawls's terms) to the point that those party to it – the intelligent, active cooperators – must in fact understand that their mere receipt of benefits is a ground of obligation, one is once more begging the question at issue. If they do understand this, that is because, as a matter of fact, in a particular society a convention to that effect is in operation. And again, one can't use the fact that there is a conventional principle of fairness in operation in a particular society to explain why that principle should guide the behaviour of citizens in all other societies who stand in receipt of benefits. If the citizens of these other societies just do not understand that their receipt of benefit has a liability to the duties of citizenship as a moral consequence, then there are no such moral consequences.

We should conclude that the argument from fairness works well in the case of those who actively solicit the benefits that the state makes readily available. Some may fail to understand this implication of their conduct, but they are obtuse, to speak kindly. Again, just like the argument from consent, the principle of fairness will capture some but not all citizens. It will not capture those, such as Militia Man, who deliberately avoid taking up the optional benefits that the state makes available to them despite the fact that they benefit in other ways from the provision of goods and services from which they cannot be excluded and from which they cannot avoid benefiting.

Where the principle of fairness applies, we should consider the extent of the moral consequences. Does fairness demand that those who actively seek out benefits should accept all the duties that may be ascribed to them? Suppose that in extremis Militia Man has no alternative but to seek the attention of the State Medical Service to treat a dangerously infected wound. Does this mean that he loses his political virginity, becoming liable thereafter to all the duties fairly

imputed to average citizen who happily accepts a full range of benefits? My inclination is to say things that may prove to be incompatible, namely that Militia
Man has taken on board *some* liabilities in accordance with the principle of fairness. He cannot say that he repudiates the principle; he does not, since it is in
virtue of the principle that as a rule he avoids taking up the benefits that the
state makes available. Nonetheless it is reasonable to think that his liabilities
must be in some reasonable proportion to the benefits he has sought and received
if these are significantly less than those accepted by the average citizen. At the
same time, it would be quite unreasonable to grant Militia Man a licence to pick
and choose just which duties he will, in fairness, fulfil. How far philosophy can
take us in the resolution of these problems, I do not know.

Gratitude

A second argument that the state may advance on the basis that the citizen has
been in receipt of substantial benefits from the state is the argument from gratitude. This argument has an ancient and distinguished source; it was outlined by
Socrates in the *Crito*. Socrates imagines that the Laws of Athens ask him:

> "Well, have you any [objections] against the laws which deal with children's
> upbringing and education, such as you had yourself? Are you not grateful to
> those of us Laws which were instituted for this end, for requiring your father
> and mother to give you a cultural and physical education?" "Yes", I
> [Socrates] should say.
>
> (Plato 1959: 50b)

If successful, this argument extends even further the range of citizens who should
accept the duties imputed to them by the state. Since it is premised on the
receipt of any benefits, whether they are solicited or not, it nicely supplements
the argument from fairness. This argument claims that citizens ought to be grateful for what they have received from the state, and, further, that the gratitude
should be signalled by the citizens' acceptance of their proper duties. Again, the
first step in the argument is a claim that the citizen has received benefits (and
once again we assume that this is true). The next step in the argument is the
claim that citizens ought to feel grateful to the state. The final step is the claim
that acceptance of the duties of citizenship is the appropriate expression of gratitude. We can see the distinctness of steps two and three in the details of an
immigration case, reported in the British newspapers in the late 1990s,[13] which
captures this structure nicely.

An army officer's life was saved by one of his Gurkha soldiers. Properly, he felt
grateful and expressed his gratitude by promising to educate the soldier's son in
Britain. As these things go, the son was refused the necessary immigration credentials, so the former officer (a wealthy man) said he would leave the country,
too, taking his millions with him. In the first place, the officer was right to feel
grateful. In the second place he chose to express his gratitude by taking on an

obligation to the father, and to the boy, to see to his education. Having taken on board this obligation, the officer judged correctly that he was morally required to fulfil it. One can think of other ways in which the officer could have expressed his gratitude, ways which did not place him under an obligation – indeed, this is a nice example of how acts of gratitude can be as generous as the services that give rise to them.

It is important that steps two and three in the argument are distinguished. They can easily become conflated when we speak of 'debts of gratitude' as though the government pursues payment of these debts when it holds us to our obligations. Rousseau stated that 'gratitude is a duty to be paid, but not a right to be exacted': not exacted, that is by parents against children or by the state against its citizens.[14] Since many of the duties of the citizen are enforceable, Rousseau thought they could not be derived from gratitude. As we shall see, this is a mistake. For the moment, though, we should register the philosophical oddity of speaking of *debts* of gratitude, of announcing feelings of gratitude (as against duties of reciprocity) in the language of 'I owe you one'. The payment of debts can be insisted on as an obligation of the debtor, whereas however appropriate or felicitous gratitude might be, it can't be the proper object of a demand or claim, the issue of a special right.[15]

It is perfectly clear, on the other hand, that we can insist that persons *ought* to be grateful, taking gratitude to be a distinctive feeling or attitude appropriate in one who has received a benefit. We teach our children that gifts cannot be claimed as rights and that they ought to feel appropriately grateful. We train them to feel grateful by making them act out the rituals of gratitude, minimally saying, 'Thank you', and undertaking the chore of writing conventional 'Thank you' letters following birthdays and Christmas. We trust that in these ways we teach them what to feel as well as how to behave. We teach good habits as a way of inculcating good dispositions of character.

These commonplaces are worth bringing to mind because they effectively refute one line of argument against the claim that political obligations may derive from gratitude. The bad argument goes as follows:

> If political obligation is an obligation of gratitude, and if an obligation of gratitude is an obligation to feel certain things, there can be no political obligations (on these grounds, at least) since we cannot make sense of obligations or duties to feel certain things in a certain way. Feelings cannot be the objects of obligations. In any case, political obligations are obligations to act, not to feel, to act obediently, for example, rather than to feel obedient.
> (Simmons 1979: 166–7)

This argument runs together the different steps in the argument that I have been at pains to distinguish, but at the heart of it is a claim that should be disputed to the effect that we cannot be required to have specific feelings since feelings aren't the sort of things we can be expected to command and control by way of trying to have or inhibit.[16] This is a blunder of a crudely Kantian sort. Feelings can be taught and learned, modified, sharpened or quietened by effort on the part of the sufferer and her educators – and this includes feelings of gratitude. Indeed, if feelings were not, in some measure, in the control of those who exhibit them, it would be odd to criticize folk for the lack of them. In the case of ingratitude this is particularly obvious. I accept that it is odd to speak of obligations to feel gratitude but that is not the claim that I am trying to establish. Rather I seek to show that one can claim that people *ought* to feel gratitude without committing a philosophical blunder.

The next claim that needs to be defended is that it is philosophically accept-able to say of citizens that they ought to feel grateful for the goods and services they receive from government. I don't want to claim that any such judgement is true – who knows which government is being discussed? – just that the proposi-tion makes sense. This claim needs defence because there are objections in the field. The first objection begins with the plausible thought that feelings of grat-itude are only appropriate as a response to benefits which have been conferred with a suitable motive. If you give me a fast motor-bike in the hope that I will soon come a cropper, I will feel no gratitude as soon as I learn of your devious plan. To generalize, the identification of goodwill in the provision of the benefit is required before gratitude is appropriate.

In the case of gratitude for the services of the state, we must therefore be able to impute motives to the state. But 'the attribution of motives to a government may be impossible or incoherent' (Simmons 1979: 189).[17] The only possible reply is that we do it all the time. And we are equally cavalier in our imputation of motives to other institutions. This firm cares (or doesn't care) for its staff, this uni-versity takes seriously (or ignores) its task of teaching students, this hospital is help-ful to (or hates) patients' visitors. One could reply that this talk is metaphorical, but this would not be a statement of the obvious. Rather, I suspect, it would indi-cate a strong and controversial philosophical position, most likely some variety of methodological individualism. We can shelve these discussions and move on, fairly assuming that when, for example, it is claimed that 'This government really cares for old age pensioners' the claim may be true or false but is not incoherent.

Let us accept that motives can be fairly attributed to the state. A further dif-ficulty is encountered. In attributing, minimally, motives of goodwill to the state, we are thinking of the state as Lady Bountiful (or more likely Big Brother), view-ing its disposing of goods and services in the manner of gifts. On the contrary, the state is our servant; it has nothing but duties to fulfil. And we should not be grateful when it complies with its duties to its citizens. We should not be grate-ful to the policeman who rescues us from the football fans who are just about to beat us up; he is doing his job.

This, too, is an error, but it is understandable. We should resent the posture of the statesman who speaks as though he is spending his own money. Nonetheless, the ancient analogy with the family can be usefully employed here. Parents have duties to their children willy-nilly, as children nowadays are prone to remind them. 'I didn't ask to be born!', you might have heard. This does not disqualify the thought that children should be grateful for what they have received of right. The duties of the parent can be fulfilled with love and grace, but even a grudging concession to a legitimate demand can merit gratitude. After all, as we know too well, some parents can't manage even this.

Isn't the same true of governments? Don't we recognize the difference between an ethos of genuine service and a time-serving reluctance to respect claimants? And shouldn't we be grateful even to heartless bureaucrats who are efficient and conscientious in the delivery of goods they are appointed to distribute? I can imagine – indeed have heard – arguments pro and con, but I don't believe that the logical space for such disputes is the product of fallacious reasoning. I don't see, in principle, why one who does their duty to us should not merit our gratitude.

The final objection to the idea that one may be grateful to the state for the goods and services it provides draws attention to the constitution of the state. It asks, in the first place: to whom or to what should one be grateful? Some, abhorring the possibility that an exotic metaphysic may be imputed to them, insist that the citizen who has grounds for gratitude should be grateful to her fellow citizens.[18] This strikes me as an evasion. One should not be grateful to all of one's fellow citizens severally. Some, we should remember, have resolutely avoided paying their share towards the provision of services of which they have been massive beneficiaries. Others have been net recipients only perforce, being too poor to make any payment towards social provision. Shame on the first, damn shame for the second – but in either case, feelings of gratitude would be misplaced. So if we should be grateful to our fellow citizens, we have to think of them collectively, which on my reading amounts to our being grateful to the state.

Critics are right to believe that there is something creepy about sentiments of gratitude being directed towards the modern state, but part of this may be due to a reluctance to see the state as 'other'. Aren't we all democrats nowadays? And should we not recognize that one element in democratic thinking is the claim that we all have equal political standing? Regarding the state as other and in some measure alien to us, seems to pre-suppose a hierarchical relationship between state and citizen which does not sit well with the democratic ideal. The instinct which grounds the suspicion that there is something undemocratic about institutions to which one may direct gratitude expresses a truth which is hard to weigh.

The only form of state in which gratitude seems to be inappropriate would be a direct democracy which takes all decisions by plebiscite, a simple Rousseauian model wherein all are equally citizens and subjects. In this model, citizens should be viewed as providing goods and services for themselves. Like members of a winning football team, they should feel pride rather than gratitude for their success in self-provision. But even in these circumstances, gratitude might not be entirely out of place. Citizens may think of their democracy as a unity which serves all its members. Players in winning teams may feel grateful to the team and their fellow members for granting them the opportunity of success, as well as pride for the part they have played in achieving it. In any event the modern representative forms of democracy do not work like this. The structures of decision-making and the bureaucracies created to put policies into effect are sufficiently alien to citizens that gratitude may be appropriate when they perform their assigned functions conscientiously and well.

I conclude that one who feels grateful for the provision of state services has not committed a philosophical error, though in particular circumstances gratitude may be misplaced, may indeed be witness to the citizen's capture by a successful ideology. If this is right, we can now move on to the next question: what does gratitude require of the citizen who properly feels it? Here, there are two routes we can take. The first is indirect, arguing that one who fails to comply with the duties of citizenship harms the state. The focus is not so much on the requirement of gratitude but on the evil of ingratitude. As Hobbes saw, ingratitude is often imprudent; the fourth law of nature thus requires that 'a man which receiveth benefit from another of meer Grace, Endeavour that he which giveth it, have no reasonable cause to repent him of his good will' (Hobbes 1968: 209; Part I, Ch. 15 [75]). But as many have taught us, as well as being imprudent, it is also a great vice to harm a benefactor.

Is this what we are doing when we fail in our political obligations? We certainly may be. The state is harmed directly if we evade payment of taxes, commit treason or encourage others to break the law. But not all law-breaking is like this. It is surely a matter of fact whether the state is harmed when citizens break the Licensing Laws or drive beyond the speed limits, and often such acts will be harmless. I don't see any argument that could take us to the conclusion that all law-breaking amounts to ingratitude since it always harms the state or one's fellow citizens.

The direct way of arguing will serve us just as well. The only thing that gratitude to the state could require is that citizens do their duty by it. It is entirely disingenuous to suggest that we might willingly take the benefits the state provides, send a 'Thank you' letter, then dodge the demands of the state, refusing to take compliance as an obligation. But on the other side, as I stated before, we should not be too po-faced about these duties, identifying them as an all-or-nothing requirement that citizens obey all the laws all the time. The good society and the sensible state can afford to be relaxed about the incidence and severity of law-breaking. Individuals should not be worried that their standing as good citizens is forever impugned by an episode of after-hours drinking or opportunistic speeding on an empty motorway.

Before we leave this question, there are a couple of qualifications that ought to be made. The first of these concerns the conclusion that citizens who receive benefits from the state *ought* to feel grateful for them. This conclusion then served as the premise of the next argument to the effect that those who feel gratitude in the way that they ought should express this gratitude by assuming the duties of citizenship. Unfortunately there are reasons for believing that citizens can exclude themselves from this 'ought' although they receive the benefits that would normally ground it. If the benefits are open, non-optional and quite unavoidable in the way that for example the personal security which is effected by a successful regime of law and order would be, we can envisage that some strange folk would counterfactually reject these inescapable benefits. That is, they would understand how the argument runs and, because they have such strong objections to the conclusion which attributes citizens' duties to them, they will insist that, were it possible for them to forgo the inescapable benefits they would definitely do so. This is the (philosophical) return of Militia Man. He genuinely believes that he is quite capable of providing for his (it is always 'his') own security, and as a matter of principle he would (counterfactually, but if possible, in fact) disavow any benefits that would entail his allegiance. In other words, he accepts the philosophical credentials of the argument from gratitude in just the way the same way that he accepts the argument from consent, but he insists that it does not apply to him. Militia Man is quite capable of telling the government that this is what his principles dictate (by letter or loud hailer). I do not see that the government can insist that Militia Man should feel gratitude in these circumstances any more than the aunt who has been politely told that her gifts from a collection of ivory carvings are unwelcome can expect a 'Thank you' letter from her elephant-friendly nephew if she persists in sending them. We should conclude that the argument from gratitude does not capture everyone who is willy-nilly in receipt of benefits, though it will succeed with a good few.

The second reservation about the success of the argument invokes the Justice Constraint as described in Chapter 5. Gratitude is the appropriate response to *good* government, not merely government that provides us with the goods and services we value. Suppose a state has two classes of citizens, those who receive benefits and those who are excluded from benefits. Should those in the lucky class feel grateful and endorse the political obligations which are thereby incumbent on them? My inclination is to conclude that they should not. To use the analogy of the family: Should the Ugly Sisters feel grateful to their parents for the benefits they have been granted (and thereby accept an obligation to follow their parents' wishes or obey their commands) if they know that their good fortune has been achieved at Cinderella's expense? Nothing has been spent on poor Cinders, and the only reason the Ugly Sisters have time to paint their faces and primp their hair is because Cinders is busy doing the chores. Probably the Ugly Sisters feel grateful, but ought they to?

For all that the duties of parents have their foundations in love and other sloppy sentiments, they can be partly specified as duties incumbent on them in virtue of an institutional role, a position of moral responsibility in which they stand to all of their children equally. Something has gone wrong in a family where there is a grossly inequitable division of labours and favours. Whereas parents can't be commanded to love all their children equally or in the same fashion, all the children should recognize that something has gone drastically wrong if it is always one of them who has to sweep the hearth. The Ugly Sisters should be ashamed of themselves, and this shame should banish their gratitude. They should feel unworthy of the favouritism they enjoy.

I shall take it that this example finds a consensus of approval, having found that in pantomimes, we all 'Boo' in the same places. I claim something similar should be working with respect to our attitudes to the state. If some (in a democracy, it will generally be a majority) receive benefits which others do not enjoy, or receive benefits in conspicuously and comparatively generous measure, they should regard the benefits as a poisoned chalice, morally tainted by the inequity of its distribution. They should regard themselves as morally compromised, shamed in a fashion the Ugly Sisters ought to recognize. This is a particular case of the operation of the Justice Constraint that we introduced in Chapter 5. Gratitude is not appropriate for benefits with an unjust or immoral provenance.

Conclusion

We have examined a couple of arguments that attempt to ground the duties of the citizen, widely construed, on the fact of the citizen's receipt of substantial benefits from the state. These are useful arguments, so long as they are not advanced in the expectation that they must be accepted by everyone, so long as they are not taken to be universal in scope nor, I suspect, complete in respect of the range of duties ascribed to citizens on the basis of them. In the real world, where there are some very strange creatures, there will always be citizens who can properly repudiate the duties imputed to them by the state on the basis of these arguments. These will be the citizens who will reject the argument from fairness on the grounds that they do not seek any benefits from the state however many benefits are foisted upon them. The list of recusants will also include those who reject the applicability to them of the argument from gratitude on the grounds that, were it possible for them to reject or avoid the benefit on the grounds that acceptance entailed the unacceptable consequence that they would incur a regime of citizens' duties, they would definitely do so. If this avowal is sincere, I do not see that they should feel grateful for what they describe as a moral burden notwithstanding the truth of the claim that it derives from a material benefit.

The arguments we have reviewed thus far, with the exception of the argument from hypothetical consent, have all been addressed to a constituency of citizens who willingly receive benefits, although as in the case the argument from gratitude, they may not solicit them. It is integral to these arguments that they do not aspire to universality since how far they extend is a matter of fact. This is not a philosophical weakness any more than it is a philosophical weakness of arguments which derive obligations from the fact that persons have promised to do something that not everyone has in fact made such a promise. But it is a weakness from the perspective of the ambitious state which seeks to capture all of its citizens. In the next chapter we shall investigate two arguments which share this ambition.

Chapter 10

Utility, justice and Samaritan duties

In this chapter I wish to discuss two very broad styles of argument which have been used to defend the authority of the state and the attribution of duties to citizens. In each case we shall encounter a style of argument which proceeds from a classical account of normative ethics: in the first place we shall examine utilitarianism; next we shall examine accounts that have their origins in the natural law principles that the good state is the just state and that citizens have a duty to support just institutions. I shall discuss both John Rawls's argument that citizens have a natural duty to maintain and support a just state, and Christopher Heath Wellman's argument that both the legitimacy of the state and the citizen's obligation to obey the law are grounded in a Samaritan duty of care to fellow citizens.

Utilitarianism

Utilitarianism is a consequentialist theory of normative ethics stating, at its broadest, that right actions maximize utility. Its grounding intuition is the thought that human happiness and suffering are the important things to focus on when we seek to determine whether actions are right or wrong. It is a theme on which a great number of variations are played. There are many utilitarianisms. Versions differ along several dimensions. Some insist that utilitarian calculation must be directed at particular actions. Others say one should calculate the utility of adopting moral rules, and the rules in question may be of different types, as we shall see. On this account, the right thing to do would be whatever action is required by the best moral code – that moral code the adoption of which promises the greatest amount of utility. Some utilitarians would have us calculate maximum aggregate utilities – a sum total – for different outcomes. Others argue that we should compute maximum average utility – dividing that sum total by the number of beneficiaries and sufferers. These issues frame the *formal theory* of utilitarianism.

There are equally strong disputes concerning utilitarian *value theory* – how best to characterize what I referred to in the minimal formula above as 'utility'.[1] Very broadly, utility refers to the good which is to be maximized. The good has been explained in various, importantly different, ways. The 'classical' utilitarian theorists (Bentham, Austin, James and John Stuart Mill) analysed the good as happiness and this, in turn, as pleasure net pain, although there are important differences amongst them. Others analyse the good as 'desire- or preference-satisfaction' – this is an understanding of the good that has proved useful for welfare economists in particular. Yet others list a variety of independent goods: happiness, personal autonomy, knowledge, close personal relationships and the experience of aesthetic beauty being typical candidates. G.E. Moore, for example, claimed with Bloomsbury aplomb that acquaintance with beautiful people and beautiful things were notable features of a good life.

All of the issues that I have signalled – and more – are contentious and need settling. And once we have arrived at what we believe to be the best version of utilitarianism, we shall find that we have few philosophical friends. Utilitarianism is widely rejected. Clearly it would take us too far afield to even broach the question of whether or not utilitarianism is an acceptable theory of normative ethics. If utilitarianism is badly mistaken as an approach to determining the morality of how one should behave quite generally, then it can have no bearing on the problems we are tackling in this book. It would not be a fit theoretical instrument for determining whether or not the state should be granted authority or whether or not individuals should accept the duties of citizenship under some specification. So here I want to engage a different task from that of evaluating the utilitarian position. I want to investigate how utilitarian theory might get a grip on these central questions of political authority. And for this purpose we can just assume that the philosophical credentials of utilitarianism are sound. We shall put the utilitarian case for state authority at its clearest and strongest and leave the cogency of this position to rest on the plausibility of utilitarian theory quite generally. And if, as I believe, one can be a pluralist in normative ethics, it may well be that utilitarian assessment has a particular aptitude for resolving problems in the political domain, concentrating as it does on the total good that can be produced for the community of those affected by actions and policies. So, for the purposes of the argument, I shall assume that we are all utilitarians.

How does the utilitarian approach the problem of political obligation? A first shot would be to suppose that the citizen asks herself, whenever the question arises, whether or not she ought to obey the law or break it.[2] On any occasion when the citizen feels that a duty calls, she should judge whether or not she should respond positively to it. If she judges that in the circumstances more benefits will accrue from breaking the law than from complying with it – considering benefits and costs overall, not simply benefits and costs to herself – the right thing to do is to break the law. If we take this to encapsulate the utilitarian approach to the problem, 'then' as Jonathan Wolff points out, 'a moment's thought reveals that it is a law-breakers' charter' (Wolff 1996: 55). In any circumstances where law-breaking would benefit me and do no significant harm to anyone else, say stealing a book from a large bookshop (Wolff's example) the right thing to do would be to steal the book since overall the world is a better place. The citizen's moral duty is to steal the book because that would lead to a net increase in happiness, impartially considered.[3]

This conclusion will be unpalatable to many, but if this is the correct way to tackle the problem, the utilitarian will have to swallow it. Fortunately for the utilitarian there are good reasons for thinking that this is not the best way to proceed. In the first place, as we noticed above, it is disputed whether the utilitarian should be focusing her attention on a calculation of the happiness that may accrue to the particular alternative actions in prospect. Consequences can be hard to foresee with any prospect of accuracy, and if we make great efforts to foresee them whenever a moral decision is in prospect we shall find ourselves spending an inordinate amount of time processing the calculations. And careful calculation imposes its own costs. The standard response to this line of objection is to recommend that the utilitarian fix his attention not on individual actions but rather on a system of rules, as noted above. This was the tack chosen by John Stuart Mill when he addressed the objection that 'there is not time, previous to action, for calculating and weighing the effects of any line of conduct on the general happiness'. He continued,

> there has been ample time, namely the whole past duration of the human species. During all that time, mankind have been learning by experience the tendencies of actions; on which experience all the prudence, as well as all the morality of life, are dependent . . . the beliefs which have thus come down are the rules of morality for the multitude, and for the philosopher until he has succeeded in finding better.
>
> (Mill, Utilitarianism, Ch. II, 1968: 21–2)

In the discussion that follows, Mill dubs these rules of morality 'subordinate' or 'secondary principles' and he is quite correct in ceding an important role to rules or principles in the determination of how one ought to behave. It looks as though we can now shift the utilitarian focus from an investigation of the consequences of each possible individual act of disobedience or compliance with the law to an investigation of the utilitarian credentials of some appropriate moral principle. Here are two candidate rules:

1   Citizens should respect the claims to authority made by the state.
2   Citizens should accept the duties of the citizen as specified by the state.

If we read these principles not as injunctions to all citizens of all states, but as ostensive principles to be examined by citizens as governing their moral relations to their own state, the problem of calculation now looks a good deal more tractable. They can review the balance-sheet of costs and benefits and decide whether or not the greatest happiness will or will not be promoted by their acceptance of the state's claims to authority or the concomitant regime of citizens' duties. If they judge that the facts of the matter (the expected utility) support the state, they will adopt the candidate principles as moral rules. If by contrast a greater happiness could be expected in a state of nature, the principles should be rejected. If the best outcome could be achieved by dismantling the present state and, following rebellion and revolution, by constructing another, then again the principles should be rejected.

This looks to be a neat solution. Since we are assuming for the purposes of argument that the state does provide on balance significant benefits through its provision of goods and services to citizens, we can see how the utilitarian argument can in principle support a state which claims authority over its citizens and the regime of duties which it legitimately imposes. Everything depends upon whether the facts of the matter support this conclusion – which is to say that we no longer have a moral debate on our hands, but which is not to say that we have an easy task; the factual judgements may be difficult and controversial.

Unfortunately the neatness of this solution conceals a nest of deep and genuine philosophical difficulties which the utilitarian cannot evade. Following Mill, we have been speaking of moral rules or principles as though these were unproblematic phenomena. We cannot help ourselves to this assumption since there are at least three different conceptions of rules in play. The first sort of rule is the 'ideal' rule – a technical device unique to utilitarianism. We introduce ideal rules when we claim that actions are right if they are in accordance with those rules which would promote most good, were they to be complied with generally.[4] Ideal rule utilitarianism has been effectively criticized.[5] A first difficulty is this: Suppose our car is stuck just below the top of the last hill before we reach our destination. The rule for all five passengers to follow is clearly, 'Push', given that a quick push will see them over the summit and into a comfortable bed. Four passengers either don't work this out or don't follow the rule. If ideal rule utilitarianism were the best decision procedure to follow, the fifth passenger should push even when her solitary efforts will prove ineffective. This is clearly irrational. And it doesn't look like a utilitarian strategy either, since no benefits would accrue and the diligent rule follower will suffer for her hopeless efforts.

A second difficulty follows. Alter the scenario so that only the pushing of four passengers is needed to get the car over the summit. Why should the fifth passenger push? Isn't utility maximized if the fifth passenger loiters alongside rather than lending her shoulder to the task? Again ideal rule utilitarianism suggests that not pushing would be wrong, although it is hard to see how her unnecessary expenditure of effort could maximize utility. (I accept that other things might be wrong with her not pushing. Perhaps it is unfair of her not to shoulder her share of the burden. But now it looks as though fairness conflicts with utility.) The central point of both these examples is that real utilitarians would not stick to ideal rules if the circumstances dictate that utility is best advanced by breaking them. In J.J.C. Smart's terms, either one is a utilitarian or a rule worshipper – one can't be both.[6]

In the context of the problem of political obligation these objections are surely decisive, too. We can easily amend the examples to display this. Imagine that Adam is a citizen of a just and decent state which is suddenly plunged into chaos and civil war by an army coup. It might be true that if citizens generally were to obey the commands of the properly constituted authority: 'Lay down your arms and fly the national flag outside your house' the civil war would immediately cease and the just and decent government would resume. Nothing has changed with respect to the calculation of whether it *would* be best if citizens generally *were* to obey the constituted state. Now suppose that Adam's laying down his arms and flying the flag would expose him and his family to very great danger, without any compensating gain since few others will obey the commands of the failing state. '*Sauve-qui-peut!*' is the rule of the day. In this case it would not be reasonable for Adam to do as he is commanded nor would it maximize utility. Adam would be one of Smart's 'rule-worshippers'. I conclude that 'ideal rule utilitarianism' is an unsound basis on which to base the authority of the state.

The second conception of rules identifies them as useful rules of thumb.[7] A better example here than Mill's example of the sailor who consults the *Nautical Almanac* (which we should treat as infallible!) is a rule for hill-walkers such as 'If you are in a mist and cannot see the point to which you are heading, take a compass bearing and follow it'. Accepting such a rule will lead you to take a map and compass on your walk and generally help you to escape difficulties in route finding. But it is important to recognize that the rule should not be followed slavishly. It should be quickly broken if walking along the bearing takes you to the top of a cliff.

Are moral rules like this? The act-utilitarian believes that they must be. 'Keep promises', we say, but we recognize lots of cases where exceptions may properly be made. Sometimes we cite a specific qualification to the rule which suggests that the rule is more complex than the original simple formulation. We can add a clause: '. . . unless the promise has been extorted'. We can gather together exceptions, as when we add: '. . . and unless disproportionate harm will be caused to some third party'. Or we can make exceptions on a case-by-case basis whenever exigencies seem to require the breaking of the promise. When these things happen, the utilitarian says we are justified if we can maximize well-being by breaking the rule.

It has been argued, successfully I think, that this rule-of-thumb variety of rule utilitarianism reduces to act utilitarianism since the bottom line in each of these calculations is that the right action is the one that maximizes utility in the particular circumstances. And it has been objected that if we see the moral rule or principle in this way we fail to recognize the distinctive normative force that such rules or principles carry. But this is a mistake if the implication is that the resolute act-utilitarian should not take advantage of such rules of thumb in order to avoid the difficulties and costs of calculation. We can expect the rules which we employ in the face of uncertainty to develop the force of inhibitions. We may be taught them in the secure expectation that they will develop this motivational power. But whatever the motivational push or pull exhibited by the rules we endorse, we should not expect them to be either immune to revision or privileged against exception wherever utility dictates. The utilitarian claims, with some justification, that the effects of spontaneous good judgement are so positive that we should be reluctant to break rules without compunction; the purposes served by having rules in the first place will not be easily subverted if the rules are strongly internalized. Thus although this variety of rule utilitarianism is consistent with (because it is reducible to) act utilitarianism, there remain strong reasons for supporting the induction of moral rules like 'Keep promises' or 'Obey the law' in the consciousness of agents – just as there are strong reasons for getting walkers to make a *habit* of using a map and compass.[8]

This variety of utilitarianism is well suited to issues concerning political obligation since it can articulate the law-abiding disposition of the citizen of a just state without requiring the compliant response to be absolutely rigid. Here, as with promises, one finds a permanent tension between the firm commitment to a rule and the practical necessity of reviewing that commitment when circumstances prompt. As a rule of thumb, the utilitarian might perfectly well accept the claims of the state to authority, treating its commands as pre-emptive, content-independent, and generally binding as we saw in Chapter 3. And as we also saw in Chapter 3, this creates a tension given that we all know that force of circumstance can pull us up short in our habit of obedience. However strongly committed we are to a state or a particular government the impact of some policy can cause alarm bells to ring. I take it that this has been the experience of many citizens who have found themselves reviewing not simply a policy they believe to be misguided, but the extent of their allegiance in consequence of the gravity of the error. When hundreds of thousands of British citizens demonstrated against the 2003 war in Iraq many carried placards stating: 'Not in my Name'. This registered more than a policy disagreement; it was a clear and public act of dissociation with their state. And many citizens who didn't say it, felt it. And many citizens who neither said nor felt these things at the time, came to agree with their disaffiliated fellow citizens later when they discovered that their political leaders had been either liars or shameful incompetents – all of these otherwise dutiful citizens being in some measure outlaws, conducting a little rebellion in so far as they regarded some of their acts of compliance as motivated not by a sense of allegiance, but grudgingly, in the face of *force majeure*.

This sort of tension is a fact of political life which every theory of political obligation must accommodate. Almost all alert and thoughtful citizens who regard themselves as committed in their allegiance will regard that allegiance as vulnerable if not fragile. The great strength of rule-of-thumb utilitarianism is that it both explains the commitment to rules and offers a way of resolving the problem when that commitment comes under severe pressure. If there is a weakness to it, it is not philosophical but phenomenological. It is a good question whether moral rules of the sort that underpin political obligation are treated as rules of thumb by those who observe them. Perhaps the comparison with the rule that enjoins hill-walkers to use a compass is misleading, not least because there is no strain in breaking the rule when one arrives at the top of a cliff and no occasion for serious review of the rule once one has negotiated the obstacle. One should respect the thought that the commitment of the dutiful citizen to his state is altogether stronger and more serious than that – not so easily cast off or qualified and not so simple to reassume. With this thought in mind, we should look at a third conception of rules that the utilitarian might employ.

This third conception of rules is of particular importance in political philosophy. This is the category of rules which are constitutive of institutions – institutional rules.[9] Many of these rules will have the force of law and will be backed by legal sanctions, although there are non-legal institutional rules and non-legal sanctions. For an example, we can expect most societies to have an institution of private property. Such an institution is best understood in terms of an inter-related set of rules establishing rights, duties, powers and privileges. The core rules will be expressed in law, such as prohibitions against theft. But there will be associated non-legal or non-enforceable rules, too. 'Do not write in books that you borrow from friends' is one which I expect most readers to accept. Other institutions which comprise a mix of legal and non-legal rules include marriage and family life, arrangements for treating the sick and educating the young, and of course the political life of the community as embodied in the state. This is the institution that we are seeking to understand.

The 'ontology' of the state as a law-governed institution is complex. As I suggested in Chapter 2 we should understand the state to be constituted by a structured set of rules which, at the sharp end, command the behaviour of members and prescribe punishment for non-compliance. H.L.A. Hart distinguishes two very broad types of rule: first, primary laws of obligation which address citizens directly. Criminal law consists chiefly of rules of this sort. The second type of rule he dubs secondary rules, comprising rules of recognition, change and adjudication. Constitutional law will be amongst the most important secondary rules (Hart 1961: 77–96). Hart further explains that this is a system of rules with respect to which one may take an internal or external point of view. Internally, members (insiders) identify with the institutions whose rules they recognize as valid. The external perspective is taken by observers (outsiders) who describe institutions on the basis of members' conduct. Of course, the same person may be both insider and outsider; these terms describe roles or perspectives and so all depends on the stance from which he is describing or evaluating the rules in question (Hart 1961: 55–6).

Constitutive institutional rules differ from rules of thumb in two significant ways. In the first place, they will be justified as necessary for the effective functioning of the institution, serving as means to given ends. Suppose we take the state to be justified on the grounds that living in the state maximizes utility. Suppose further that we explain this in terms of the state's effectively providing a range of benefits to citizens which would not be available in the state of nature. Suppose finally that the state which most effectively provides these benefits is a just state with the constitutional shape roughly described in Chapter 5. Now we can see that the various rules will not need to be justified piecemeal. Rather they will articulate the constitutional and regulatory requirements for the state to carry out its specified function.

Let us assume that the state which maximizes utility is the state which protects persons and their property under conditions of maximal liberty and equality. We are now using several secondary or subordinate principles (to employ J.S. Mill's terms) to direct the pursuit of utility through the political activity of the state. Of course the appropriateness of these principles will need to be demonstrated, but some fine philosophers including Hume and J.S. Mill have shown us how this might be achieved. We can now move on to justify the structure of primary and secondary rules and if we are utilitarians we find that we have two options. First, we can adjudicate candidate rules directly in terms of their utility. It's plausible to claim, for example, that individual rules serving to protect individuals from harm at the hands of others ('Don't kill or injure') will straightforwardly promote citizens' happiness. Second, we can endorse institutional sub-systems on the grounds that such intermediate institutions promote utility. This was how Hume defended private property as an integral element of justice.[10] These sub-systems will themselves be constituted by rules which either directly or indirectly in virtue of their location within the system promote utility directly or indirectly satisfy a secondary utility-promoting principle. Finally, we shall adjudicate individual actions not directly in terms of whether they promote utility but in terms of whether or not they comply with the rules.

In this respect the utilitarian treats the state in the same way as any other institution that comes up for assessment. Suppose we are concerned with the way domestic arrangements should be governed. We may ask: should children be brought up in a nuclear family, an extended family or as a group, say in a kibbutz? Having assessed the respective utilities of these different domestic arrangements, we can then go on to fix, for example, the rules for assigning responsibility for child care or the allocation of appropriate income tax allowances or some other means that we might employ to support what we have concluded is the optimal domestic unit. Institutional rules differ from rules of thumb in that the primary focus of justification is often the institution or the institutional sub-system rather than the particular rule.

The second major difference is equally important. This concerns the justification of particular actions. We have already stated that the rightness of actions is to be determined not by a direct application of the principle of utility but indirectly through the value of the institution and the secondary principles (if any) which govern its structure and dictate its primary rules. This gives the problem created by acts of non-compliance which promote utility a different shape than it took with respect to rules of thumb. Assume that we have in place a system for the legal regulation of private property which includes rules governing inheritance and bequest. My family are hard up. Am I morally justified in forging alterations to Donald's will so that his estate will give my family the security they deserve rather than support the drug addiction of Donald's intended beneficiary, given the evident fact that greater happiness will be produced by the forgery?

If the rules governing bequests were rules of thumb, immediately the question would be open: What does utility dictate in these circumstances? With the facts as described it is clear that the right thing to do is to forge the will. Matters are very different when we are thinking of institutional rules and it is important to work out just why this so. Here is one immediate difference. In the case of rules of thumb, the rules have standing in the deliberations of the moral agent as ready-reckoners which obviate the need for hard, often fallible, calculation – but when the alarm bells ring and the circumstances scream out for judgement outside the normal response of compliance, direct calculation of the appropriate utilities is the only rational response. In the case of institutional rules, these have an authority quite independent of their service as guides to conduct for the unsure or hard-pressed. In the case of institutions that carry genuine authority the rules will bind pre-emptively and independently of their content, as we saw in Chapter 3. They are not open to scrutiny except as elements of institutions which find their justification in terms of their operation as a whole. One may certainly question an authoritative institution, demanding whether or not it promotes utility. But if it does then the authority of the institution becomes entrenched, and it acquires a social reality which cannot be dissolved by the exercise of deliberation. In the above example we should obey the law, complying with the institutional rule governing bequests. We should not fraudulently amend Donald's will, since the law proscribing this conduct is justified by the utility of the institutions of property and legality of which it is an element.

For sure, one may seek to alter the institutional rules. Maybe different and better rules will serve the institution more effectively. The just state, broadly democratic and responsive to its citizens, has the means to effect changes. And this kind of tinkering goes on all the time, conspicuously in legislative activity. But suppose an institution promotes utility in the way its defenders claim and suppose the rules of the institution effectively secure this. If the utilitarian accepts these claims, it is not open to him to violate the rules in order to promote utility directly. If two people decide the most worthwhile way to spend their time is by playing chess, so long as the game is proceeding it is not open to one of them to cheat on the grounds that both of them will better enjoy subsequent play. It might indeed be true that it will make for a better game if the rules are changed, and this may prompt them to change the rules, giving a handicap to one of the players. But as the rules stand at the beginning of the game, cheating cannot be vindicated by rule changes it may be sensible to introduce later. The cost of subscribing to institutions which promote utility is that one sacrifices the opportunity of breaking rules on occasions which suggest that rule-breaking promises utilitarian gains.

So, if I am caught out in my forgery of Donald's will, I should not expect the officials of the legal system to listen carefully to my utilitarian defence. They will follow the rules which utility has dictated should be followed in all cases. The just utilitarian state will not have a Great Utilitarian Ombudsman serving as a last resort of the judicial process with a duty to review all instances of individuals claiming they broke the rules in the service of some over-riding utilitarian purpose. Nor should this kind of pleading persuade us that one should be installed. Readers can work out for themselves the disutility of introducing such an institutional role.

This is not to say that in emergencies, in cases of disaster or catastrophe, the rules of institutions should not be broken. You may justifiably break the speed limit when driving a badly injured person to hospital. But then you should not expect to get punished either, since an institution which is justifiable and maximally effective will make provision for such cases by, for example, specifying allowable defences against the charge of wrong-doing. If such defences are not in place, then the rules of the institution should be altered to permit them. It is always possible in the interim that the system may find some space for the exercise of discretion. Contrast this with the rule of thumb about following compass bearings. We don't alter or amend the rule when we find ourselves at the top of the cliff. We disregard it until we have circumvented the obstacle – and we pick it up later. We are not in the business of formulating optimal rules of thumb with guidance for each contingency; such rules would quickly become unwieldy and just as difficult to apply as pristine act utilitarianism. But we *are* in the business of designing and sustaining optimal institutions and there is something desperately wrong with institutions which cannot be remedied in the face of conspicuous disutility. Commanding officers, we are told, may decorate soldiers for bravery – then punish them, if their heroism involved disobeying orders. 'Change the rules', the utilitarian should insist.

There is one further problem that the utilitarian faces in this area which should be mentioned. From what I have said it might be thought that the utilitarian has no problem calculating the utilities of institutions. But one should ask whether the utilitarian can conduct a convincing audit of institutions of the type we have been discussing. How would one start to weigh the pros and cons of the state as against the state of nature, or a system of private property versus a communist system, with the means of production, distribution and exchange in common ownership? Utilitarian calculations are everywhere distrusted; for many 'cost-benefit analysis' is a rogues' charter, and welfare economists are particularly suspect when environmental issues are being addressed.[11] It is interesting, however, to note that Hume and J.S. Mill did not see a problem hereabouts. Hume and, to a lesser degree, Mill are best read as 'conservative utilitarians' (Knowles 2000). Mill, as we have already noticed, believed that much of commonsense morality ('rules of morality for the multitude') can be trusted as the product of a course of learning undertaken by mankind throughout history as to what sort of rules and social structures are most likely to produce happiness – which is not to say that they may not be improved. Hume, before him, had argued throughout all his works that history had been a testing ground of the institutions of justice, insisting that we could trust the institutional framework of our (developed, modern) society as the successful outcome of centuries of experimentation, the repository of historically acquired wisdom concerning which domestic, social and more specifically political institutions work best in the context of time and place to promote happiness and well-being. But again, as with Mill, he too can find a necessary place for reformist proposals and practical criticism, as well as resistance and rebellion *in extremis*.[12]

Of the three varieties of rule utilitarianism that I have examined, I believe the third version which invokes institutional rules ('practice rules' in Rawls's terminology, 'rules of justice' in Hume's) is best suited for tackling the problem of political obligation since it addresses directly the comparative question of whether we are best served, whether our well-being is best promoted, by living under a state that has the authority to determine our duties as citizens. This approach can also be used to determine the specific rules, primary or secondary, that constitute any particular political system. The rules can be fixed either directly by applying the principle of utility to the various sub-systems of government as component institutions or to specific legal directives, or indirectly by working out how they can best promote what Mill called secondary principles (including in this the liberty principle) which serve as indicators of how utility can be maximized.

The utilitarian defence of a regime of state authority and citizens' duties is clear and ambitious. It seeks to embrace all citizens and all duties but it does not apply to all states. The theory will apply only where it fits the facts, hence it must be used on a state-by-state basis and would not justify the political obligations of citizens in a state which is second-best in circumstances where improvements could be efficiently effected. Of course the theory is no better as a theory of political obligation than is attested by its philosophical credentials as a normative ethic. And these are notoriously controversial. Nonetheless, I hope to have demonstrated that it is not a flaw of utilitarian ethics that it cannot serve in this area of political theory. It surely can.

Justice

In Chapter 5, I argued that it was a necessary condition of citizens accepting a full or unqualified range of duties towards the state that the state be just. I gave a sketchy and no doubt controversial account of the different elements of political society that are liable to an evaluation in point of justice. I now want to consider whether the fact of a just state might operate as a sufficient condition on the legitimacy of the state and the ascription of duties to its citizens. I shall discuss two very different theories: first, the account of a natural duty of justice as given by John Rawls; second, Christopher Wellman's 'Samaritanism' account.

John Rawls: the natural duty of justice

Suppose that one finds oneself[13] a citizen of a just state; does the fact that the state is just entail that the citizen has a sound moral reason to accept the duties which are ascribed to him by the state? There is an old tradition of natural law which suggests that he should. And this way of thinking has been endorsed in recent times by John Rawls who argues that 'a fundamental natural duty is the duty of justice. This duty requires us to support and to comply with just institutions that exist and apply to us' (Rawls 1972: 115).[14]

According to St Thomas Aquinas,

> Humanly enacted laws can be just or unjust. To be just they must serve the general good, must not exceed the lawmaker's authority, and must fairly apportion the burdens of the general good amongst all members of the community. *Such laws oblige us in conscience, since they derive from the eternal law.* Laws however can be unjust: by serving not the general good but some lawmaker's own greed or vanity, or by exceeding his authority, or by unfairly apportioning the burdens the general good imposes. Such laws are not so much laws as forms of violence, and do not oblige our consciences except perhaps to avoid scandal and disorder, on which account men must sometimes forego their rights.
> (*Summa Theologiae* I–II, 96: 4 (Aquinas 1991: 291), my italics)

According to this tradition of natural law, citizens must (i.e. morality requires that they) obey the just laws of a just regime which aims to promote the general good of the community. We must obey just laws because they are derived in accordance with right reason; right reason enables us to understand God's law and follow His commands. Of course there may be other routes to determining the principles of justice. For Rawls 'the principles of natural duty are derived from a contractarian point of view . . . those that would be acknowledged in the original position . . . understood as the outcome of a hypothetical agreement' (Rawls 1972: 115). For the purposes of our argument it doesn't matter what provenance is established for the principles of justice. We can simply assume that the state is just, abstracting from the grounds on which we reach this conclusion, and ask whether this is sufficient to ground a regime of citizens' duties.

So we should consider at this point whether we need a further argument to demonstrate that the just state possesses the authority to prescribe duties to its citizens. Will it not suffice for any dialectic between state and citizen that if the state can assert *truly* that it bears the credentials of justice then the citizens are liable to the duties of citizenship? I think not, since evidently this condition does not meet the publicity condition as outlined in Chapter 5. There are a variety of scenarios that we should consider.

First, suppose Plato is right about the quality of justice in the state – it consists in each member of society doing the kind of work and accepting the concomitant duties appropriate to his natural station as this is revealed in a careful process of education. Suppose further that Plato is correct to believe that the ordinary folk, the *hoi polloi*, would never be able to understand the rationale for asserting that a particular state is just. Then they need to be told the Noble Lie.[15] Suppose finally that they believe the Noble Lie – that the philosophers alone have the metal to rule. Here we have a just state with the citizens believing that it is a just state, though most of them would be unable to give a sound explanation of why this is so since they are the unwitting victims of a carefully inculcated ideology. I conclude that, although this state is just (*ex hypothesi*), since the publicity condition is not met political obligations cannot be imputed to the citizens.[16]

Suppose next that the state is just, that most or all of the citizens believe it to be just, and that this belief is based on their acceptance of a plausible theory of what justice requires. Say they accept Rawls's two principles of justice believing that 'justice as fairness' requires this specification of justice. In these circumstances I cannot see why anyone who accepts that the state is just in accordance with principles they endorse should reject the imputation to them of duties which the state prescribes to citizens. In these ideal circumstances I cannot find any ethical space within which such citizens could either register an objection to the state's authority or deny that this furnishes them with a strong reason to maintain and support the state which they accept as just. This is not, of course, a guarantee that they will in fact act justly, absent a strong argument against the possibility of such weakness of will.

The case is different if the state is just, and there is a public account of justice which is widely accepted, and yet some citizens fail to accept it as just. Perhaps they espouse some idiosyncratic theory of what justice requires: they are Platonists maybe, or their conception of justice is entirely dictated by some religious doctrine which they know will be unacceptable to those others in their community who do not share their faith.[17] Should these recalcitrant citizens accept the duties of citizenship? The way that I put the issue supposes that there is a theory of justice which yields an objective fact of the matter as to whether any particular state is just or unjust. This is a massive assumption but I do not need to settle these issues here since we can set out the alternatives. If there is a fact of the matter, and reasonable grounds can be given for asserting it which satisfy the publicity condition, it does not matter that the benighted ignoramuses disagree. It is reasonable to require that the demands of morality as expressed in the rules of the just state bind them regardless of the sincerity which funds their recalcitrance. Of course things are very different if there are no facts of the matter to be had concerning justice, and readers should understand that there are many meta-ethical positions which take this view. But still, I think there is one conclusion that can be fairly drawn: whatever the meta-ethical standing of a citizen's judgement that a particular state is just, even if *de minimus* it is encapsulated in the subjectivist bleat, 'But that's just my own opinion', the citizen who accepts that the state is just is committing himself to accept the regime of citizens' duties.[18]

Simmons has raised a different problem for those who accept that the natural duty of justice commits citizens to accept their political obligations: the argument from justice does not meet 'the particularity requirement'.[19] The particularity requirement operates on arguments for political obligation as a condition that such arguments must explain 'those moral requirements which bind an individual to one *particular* political community, set of political institutions etc.' (Simmons 1979: 30). As he explains matters, this seemingly trivial requirement has important implications:

> Suppose we accepted . . . that we have an obligation or a duty to support just governments, and that is what our political obligation consists in. And suppose that I am a citizen living under a just government. While it follows that I have an obligation to support my government, it does not follow that there is anything *special* about this obligation. I am equally constrained by the same moral bond to support *every other* just government. Thus, the obligation in question would not bind me to any particular political authority in the way that we want. If political obligation and citizenship are to be related as I have suggested they should be, we need a principle of political obligation which binds the citizen to one *particular* state above all others, namely the state in which he is a citizen.
>
> (ibid.: 31–2)

I confess that I am blind to the reasoning employed here since I do not see that the argument from justice is constructed in this way. The argument does *not* employ as a major premise the general principle that 'citizens have an obligation or a duty to support just governments' wherever they may be, mine own or any other, as stated explicitly in the above passage. (That said, this is an interesting suggestion that might underpin a person's duty to obey the law in states which he visits, or to press his own government to support a just neighbouring state which is being attacked by rebels who promise tyranny.)[20] The full principle of justice giving both necessary and sufficient conditions should be stated in general but explicitly self-referential terms, as follows: citizens have a duty to support *their own state* if and only if *that particular* state is just.[21]

There is nothing illicit in such a formulation. Indeed it is *because*, as Simmons states, 'we need a principle of political obligation which binds the citizen to one *particular* state above all others, namely the state in which he is a citizen' that we frame the principle of justice in this fashion. Consider this analogous problem: we wish to determine the grounds upon which children should respect their parents. (Imagine you have a horrible disrespectful child to deal with.) We propose the answer: children should respect their parents if and only if their parents treat them with tender loving care. We would never be tempted to think that an answer of this kind is flawed in principle because it entails that children should show respect to all parents (other children's parents included) just in case those other parents treat their own children with tender loving care. That wasn't the issue in which we were interested, though again, as with the citizen's duties towards states other than his own, it is a different issue that merits examination. Exactly the same logic of self-reference applies in the case of the state.

It is because Simmons frames the argument from justice in such a misleading fashion that he makes such heavy weather of Rawls's discussion of the natural duty of justice – the requirement that we are to 'support and to comply with just institutions that exist and apply to us' (Rawls 1972: 115). Simmons asks 'What, after all, does it mean to say of a just institution that it "applies to us"?' (Simmons 1979: 147).[22] The answer to this question is that there is no perfectly general answer. All depends upon the 'us'. If it is 'us citizens' then we have the duties imputed to us as citizens, or to emphasize the technical relativity, us '*qua*' citizens. If we are a member of the 'us' as a resident alien, or *gastarbeiter*, or overseas student, or a tourist then we have the duties imputed to us *qua* tourist or whatever. I expect that the duties will vary from case to case, but we can see that in each case a role is specified, a role constituted in important part by the duties incumbent on the bearers of the role. To say that an institution 'applies to us' is to say nothing more than that the institution determines a range of duties, rights and responsibilities as constitutive of a variety of roles and that this particular role fits us.[23]

I concede that some may insist that something further needs to be said with respect to citizenship that draws out the link between the legal and moral standing of the citizen and the state which binds him. Evidently there is a lot more that could be said about the nature of citizenship and this will amplify our understanding of why the citizen is required to accept the duties of his station. What I dispute is that such amplification, or a further argument, is needed to demonstrate that the citizen has a political obligation towards his state if that state is just.[24] We shall return to this topic in our next and final chapter.

In the meanwhile we should notice that there is a severe limitation on the applicability of the argument from justice. In Rawls's formulation the natural duty of justice applies to a state that is just, or a state that is 'as just as it is reasonable to expect in the circumstances' (Rawls 1972: 115), or 'a nearly just society, one that is well-ordered for the most part but in which some serious violations of justice nevertheless do occur' (Rawls 1972: 363). These latter qualifications are important and they point to a real problem for Rawls. I believe the argument from justice works only for just states, not for states that are nearly just. Imagine a citizen who fails to comply with an unjust law of a nearly just state. If the state insists upon compliance, or seeks to punish the recalcitrant, why can't he resist, saying 'Nearly sorry' in the manner of the parent replying to the child who complains, 'You nearly hurt me'. There may be plenty of other reasons why the citizen should comply with a state which is nearly just but strictly unjust. These may be prudential reasons or indeed moral reasons. Disobedience may lead to prison and prison may lead to one's children being neglected. Perhaps I made a promise to my mother never to disobey the law. But if the justice of the state is to do any work as a sufficiency claim, justice itself serving as the ground of citizens' duties, we would need a separate, additional argument if we wished to claim that the nearly just state has the same authority. We would need an argument from near-justice, but the prospect is almost comical. To the state which claims authority on the basis that it is nearly just we can all too easily imagine the citizen replying that he nearly has the duties of the citizen – but not quite.

I conclude that the sufficiency claim fails for the nearly just state. But we should recall from Chapter 5 that this is not true of the necessity claim. That can perfectly well be reformulated as a necessary condition on the state's authority that it be just, or nearly just. There are no strict or simple rules governing how much injustice disqualifies a claim to authority and validates the citizen's rejection of imputed duties. We saw that justice in the state has many dimensions. The state may be just in some respects but not others; some types of injustice are more significant than others; some infractions of justice of a specific type will be more serious than others.[25] These differences will justify different types and degrees of recalcitrance as we saw earlier.

Moreover, given the absence of strict and simple rules hereabouts, it is likely that there will be a great deal of dispute concerning alleged infractions of justice by the state which it is hard to imagine might be resolved. Consider the arguments put by a resolute follower of John Stuart Mill in respect of the illegitimacy of paternalism who challenges the justice of the state's (or, more likely, the local government body enacting the by-law) prohibition of smoking in the fresh air of a public park.[26] Am I being pessimistic in supposing that arguments to- and fro- will go on forever? If the argument from the natural duty of justice is the only argument in the field, for better or worse, it will invite a great deal of controversy about the fact and the range of citizens' duties. But, as a philosopher, I suppose it is no worse for that, though obviously the state will hope for something stronger. Maybe the argument for 'Samaritan Duties' on the part of both state and citizen can improve matters.

Samaritanism

In a series of recent publications Christopher Heath Wellman has developed a novel defence of the theses that:

1   just states may be legitimate (thus countering anarchism in all its forms – political and philosophical, weak and strong) and
2   all citizens of just states have a political obligation to obey the law.

We shall call his account 'Samaritanism', in keeping with his own favoured terminology.[27]

Notice the distinction of (1) and (2) above. Wellman is one of those philosophers who distinguish the question of whether the state is legitimate from the question of whether the citizen has a duty to obey the laws of a legitimate state. I don't distinguish between these problems. The concepts of legitimate state authority and political obligation are evidently different, but I argued in Chapter 2 that they are systematically related. In particular, it is not possible that a state be a legitimate authority yet its citizens have no duty to comply with its prescriptions. Nor do I believe that citizens can have political obligations to a state which is not a legitimate authority. As I set out Wellman's position I shall respect his use of this distinction but I intend that my discussion of it will bring it into question once again.

Wellman's answers to both of these questions invoke what he calls a Samaritan duty – a duty of care for others. A common element of Wellman's arguments both for the legitimacy of state coercion and for the proper attribution of political obligations to the citizens of the just state is the familiar Hobbesian claim that the condition of anarchy, life in a state of nature, would be intolerable. The state provides citizens with the very great benefit of political stability through the rule of law and does so in a way that is not unreasonably costly. The costs may be great, but the benefits of stability far outweigh them. These net benefits could be secured only by a state with coercive powers.

The Samaritan account of the legitimacy of the state

These facts provide the basic 'descriptive component of a benefit theory of political legitimacy' (Wellman 2001: 743): '(1) states provide important benefits and (2) these benefits are unobtainable without a state . . . Coercive states . . . offer the only viable solution to the perils of a state of nature' (ibid.: 743). The *normative* element of the theory is provided by an account of Samaritan duties: 'The common understanding of samaritanism is that one has a duty to help a stranger when the latter is sufficiently imperilled and one can rescue her at no unreasonable cost to oneself' (ibid.: 744). The state is not justified in coercing me on the grounds that this coercion is to *my* benefit. Such an argument would be impermissibly paternalistic, Wellman believes. Rather the state is justified in coercing *me* in order that *other* citizens should not stand in peril of the state of nature. We are to see the state as exercising a Samaritan duty of care which makes it permissible to coerce each citizen in order to benefit every other citizen. The particular form that benefit takes is that citizens are rescued from, or are guaranteed security in face of their imperilment by, the state of nature.

Thus far, this strikes me as a strange argument, but that may be because of its undoubted novelty. I shall record some aspects of the argument that can be endorsed and also register some worries. First, I am not concerned about the descriptive premises. Wellman insists that the deal is a good one as far as citizens are concerned – 'by producing benefits that far outweigh its costs, it is as if the state forced each of its constituents to give up a hundred dollar bill but in return gave back ten twenties' (Wellman and Simmons 2005: 17).[28] Whatever the sums involved, I regard the argument to this point as being conditional, resting on facts of which the philosopher is no master. In the face of the inevitable anarchist challenge, the best the philosopher can do is to muster an argument of the form: 'If the benefits procured by the state can be achieved at no unreasonable cost, then . . .'. So let us assume that the facts are as stated (in one or other version) and proceed to examine whether the argument that follows is cogent.

My worries are different. Let me register an oddity in the argumentation. A standard example of a Samaritan duty is that of the bystander who can rescue the drowning infant by wading into a couple of feet of water. Notice that in this case we confidently speak of a Samaritan *duty*. The bystander does wrong if she doesn't rescue the child. Philosophers may disagree over whether this is a *perfect* duty (failure to comply with which may be sanctioned by punishment) or an *imperfect* duty (failure to comply being pathetically and shamefully immoral, hopefully a source of persisting feelings of guilt, but not liable to penal sanctions, legal or otherwise). In many legal jurisdictions the citizen has a legal duty of care, with failure entailing a liability to punishment if she fails to rescue the child because, e.g. she claims that this would have soiled her Armani trouser-suit. Wellman (1996, 2001, 2005) speaks in terms of Samaritan duties in his presentation of the general duty of care, but then he describes the normative position of the state in terms of its possession of a liberty-right: 'the state is *at liberty* to coerce individuals in a way that would ordinarily violate their rights only because this coercion is necessary to rescue all those within the state's borders from peril' (Wellman 2001: 745, my italics). This is an inexplicable shift.

Before we investigate what is going on here, I should give the details of an analogy that bears enormous weight in Wellman's argument (and turns out to be a great source of confusion). Beth has a heart attack. The only way that Alice can get Beth to hospital is to commandeer Carolyn's car without her permission.[29] Wellman argues that

> In extraordinary conditions like those involving Beth's peril, however, Alice is at liberty to take Carolyn's car, and Alice's liberty-right correlates to Cathy's lack of claim-right [to exclusive use of the car] in these circumstances . . .. As the case with Alice, Beth and Carolyn demonstrates however, samaritanism need not always be spelled out exclusively in terms of duties; in this instance it explains Alice's liberty right and Carolyn's lack of claim-right.[30]
>
> (2001: 744–5)

He concludes,

> In sum, just as Beth's peril and the necessity of using Carolyn's car to rescue Beth combine to justify Alice's action, the perils of the state of nature and the necessity of constructing a state to rescue anyone from these circumstances combine to justify the state's coercive presence.
>
> (ibid.: 745)

There are two different concepts of liberty-right in the literature, which is unfortunate since it is a term of art and so at the very least should be unambiguous. On the first account, a liberty-right is exemplified famously by Hobbes's right of nature:[31] to say that 'x has a liberty-right to $\emptyset$' is equivalent to saying 'x has no duty not to $\emptyset$'. It does *not* say that x has a duty to $\emptyset$. Nor does it entail that any other party has a corresponding, consequential, or correlative duty not to prevent x from $\emptyset$-ing. So to say that the state has a liberty-right to rescue its citizens is usually to deny (by implicature) the stronger claim that the state must (= has a duty or obligation to) rescue its citizens just in case they are in need of rescue from the state of nature. To ascribe a Hobbesian liberty-right to the state is a very odd description of the normative position of the Samaritan state *vis-à-vis* its citizens, in just the same way that it would be very odd if the insouciant bystander were to defend her sartorial priorities by analysing her Samaritan duty as a liberty-right consisting merely in her not having a duty not to rescue the drowning child (which right she might have complied with by sauntering past, making sure that the child's flailing and splashing didn't soak her suit). If it is the dire state of nature that threatens, wherein life is solitary, poor, nasty, brutish and short, and if only the state can rescue us from the horrors, doesn't the state have a duty to do so if it can? Similarly, if the claim were rather that it is a Samaritan duty of citizens to concede a Hobbesian liberty-right to the state, this is too weak; surely the Samaritan citizen would require a state with a Samaritan duty to prevent a state of nature. What is the point of setting up and paying for a system of life-guards on the beach in order to make it *permissible* for them to swim out and save the poor souls who might drown? We would ascribe to those whom we appoint as life-guards a *duty* to rescue folks in danger (and we would sack them if they fail). The same is surely true of the relation between citizens and the state.[32]

Second, some have dubbed as 'liberty-rights' negative claim-rights of this form:

'x has a negative claim-right to $\emptyset$ if and only if some y has a duty not to prevent x from $\emptyset$-ing'. Negative claim-rights are also termed rights of non-interference and rights of action. They differ from liberty-rights under the first specification in the respect that they are claimed against some party (often the world at large, as rights *in rem*) that has a consequent duty not to interfere with the exercise of this right. (This is the sort of right of ownership attributed to Carolyn in respect of her car.) On this reading of the Samaritan duty of the state as a liberty-right, it has a claim-right against all citizens (and anyone else) that they not interfere with its coercive efforts to secure them against the state of nature. By inference, they have a duty not to prevent the state exercising this right. If, as described, the Samaritan duty were equivalent to the state's claim-right against citizens, this duty would not quite be equivalent to the citizen's duty to obey the law – if it were, the distinction between the state's legitimacy and the citizens' duties would collapse very quickly. On this account, reading the Samaritan duty as a negative claim-right is to say other bystanders have a duty not to prevent a would-be rescuer from jumping in to save the drowning child. (This explains why Wellman says that Carolyn has no claim-right against Alice which might prevent Alice using her car – on the contrary she has a duty to let Alice use her car to rescue Beth.)

Once more, this implies that the would-be rescuer does not have a duty to rescue, which again is very odd, since the account began with the assertion of Samaritan duties. If on the other hand, the Samaritan duty is the moral duty of citizens to endorse the claim-right of the state to enforce legal duties upon citizens in order to prevent the state of nature, the distinction between the state's legitimacy and the citizens' duty collapses straightaway.

The Samaritan account of citizens' duties

Unfortunately, when Wellman turns to discuss what on his account is the separate problem of citizens' duties, he loses control of this analogy. There he argues that

> just as samaritan considerations explain Alice's liberty-right to take Carolyn's car, they can equally account for Carolyn's duty to lend her car to this effort. . . . Turning to political obligation, we may conclude that samaritanism not only explains the permissibility of state coercion, it also explains a citizen's duty to obey the laws of the state.
>
> (2001: 748)

In 2005 he writes, 'samaritanism can help explain why Beth has a duty to take Amy to the hospital and/or why Cathy has a duty to loan her car to the cause'.[33] He continues,

> The vehicle required to save Amy is Cathy's car, and the vehicle required to save my compatriots is our state; but Beth's *duty* is to drive this car, and my *duty* is to obey the legal commands of our state.
>
> (2005: 31)

At this point we should be asking whether it is Beth or Cathy (or her car) that is analogous to the state or to the citizen, or both.

What are the implications of this? Wellman makes one of the two possible claims outlined above, both of them weak and flabby, when he ascribes a liberty-right to the state to rescue those imperilled by the state of nature. His view should be more heroic: if the state is needed to rescue folk, then it has a duty to do so rather than a liberty-right under one or other of these constructions. Whatever liberty-right the state possesses which makes it permissible to impose a regime of duties on citizens derives from the Samaritan duty of care. But what does my confident assertion of this duty imply for third parties? If all citizens have a Samaritan duty to maintain and support a state conceived as a rescue agency, and if the state can only do its work of rescue by imposing legal duties on citizens, then *those same citizens* who stand to be rescued also have a moral duty to accept the regime of duties which the state imposes on them. What else can their duty to support the state entail? It is not possible to impute a Samaritan duty to the state without imputing a corresponding duty to citizens to support that state.

Some might be metaphysically queasy about ascribing duties to the state as though the state were a moral agent. In which case they should view any such imputation of duties to the state as the ascription of duties to citizens to construct, maintain and support the only institution that can carry out the act of rescue. We should conclude that since exactly the same argument, supposing it to be sound, generates both the legitimacy of the state and the citizen's obligation to obey the law, this amounts to a distinction without a significant dialectical difference.

We can now see clearly where Wellman's example has led him astray. There are not three parties to the state–citizen relation, in the way that there are three persons in his little story. There are only two. Each citizen is both rescuer and rescued. Each party is a man from Samaria, victim and saviour both. In Wellman's political world, each citizen, as both threatening and the target of threats, has a Samaritan duty of care to each other citizen – which duty they fulfil by recognizing a political obligation to maintain and support a just state, which state then has a fiduciary duty to execute that duty of care. Now that we can see these matters clearly, we are in a position to raise the still open question of whether this account of the normative relations between state and citizen is true.

Is the Samaritan account acceptable?

A question of rescue?

A second oddity with Wellman's argument has been pointed out by Simmons. It really is strange to attribute to the state and (derivatively) to citizens the duty to rescue other citizens from the perils of the state of nature as though the state of nature were some pit of mortal doom into which all of us are in imminent danger of falling, as though we are all of us on the edge shouting 'Help', understanding that it is only the state, or (for the metaphysically squeamish) only the state now conceived as a sheriff's posse or a rescue team composed of responsive citizens, which can rescue us from death's door.[34] Simmons expands his point by contrasting on the one hand, general duties of charity, beneficence, or indeed justice, as responses to pervasive conditions of dire need with duties of rescue in desperate circumstances on the other. (Roughly, it is a duty of rescue which explains why the good citizen rushes to resuscitate the fellow who has collapsed on the pavement; it may be a duty of charity, beneficence or justice which explains why a society organizes its public services to ensure that there is an ambulance on hand to assist both of them just in case the need arises.) He concludes by asking us to 'Notice that the very idea of institutions administering such a duty [of rescue, in emergencies] by collection [of taxes?] and distribution [of the taxes thus raised into rescue services?] makes no sense in this case'. He tells us that Wellman's Samaritan duties are a 'curious hybrid' of rescue and charity – which they are, since 'the emergency is not really properly described as an emergency at all' (Simmons, in Wellman and Simmons 2005: 184–5). In all this, Simmons is surely right; there is a clear whiff of philosophical artifice about Wellman's construction which contrasts smartly with both his and standard examples of the duty of rescue and care. Do you, right now, feel in need of rescue to the point of recognizing that emergency services are required to help you and your fellows escape the state of nature? Wouldn't this be just as absurd as mountaineers calling out a mountain rescue team to stand by since they alongside other intrepid fellows are heading off to climb a mountain?

This last example should make us pause since, *pace* Simmons's rejection of an institution such as the state undertaking – indeed having its *raison d'être* as undertaking – duties of rescue, there are plenty such. And indeed, my own example of the ambulance service, sneakily introduced above, is a good example. But so are the fire brigade, lifeboat services, and many more such-like institutions. Indeed the examples of the ambulance service and the fire brigade show that the state can undertake a rescue function, and in many cases it may be the most efficient provider (although it is stretching a point to see them as rescuing us from the state of nature). In which case the weakness of Wellman's argument does not lie in the supposition of funded institutions, as against heroic individuals, undertaking acts of rescue; if there is a serious weakness, it must lie elsewhere.

A question of fairness?

Perhaps we can find it by attending to a distinctive feature of Wellman's argument from Samaritan duties to establish that citizens have a political obligation to the state. In its first, simple formulation the citizen has a duty to obey the law as a Samaritan duty which is '(1) not unreasonably costly and (2) in fact necessary to rescue others from peril'. Unfortunately Wellman notices that it is not true of any individual citizen that *her* fulfilment of a Samaritan duty is necessary in order to rescue other citizens from peril. The jaws of the horrible abyss of the state of nature do not beckon if one citizen fails to comply with her duty to obey the law. At this point Wellman might abandon his project of justifying political obligation; instead he adds a substantial refinement to the theory. He introduces considerations of fairness; all citizens have the Samaritan duty to obey the law since their individual political obligations amount to their 'fair share of the communal samaritan chore of rescuing others' (Wellman in Wellman and Simmons 2005: 32–3).[35]

What is our fair share of the Samaritan chore? We can investigate what this amounts to by each asking of ourselves what is necessary on our part in order that our fellow citizens live the sort of decent life that seems impossible in a state of nature. One might think there is a straightforward answer to this question: I should respect the moral rights of fellow citizens and assist them directly should they be in imminent danger. We can see that this is a fair share because it is clearly true that were everyone else to shoulder the same burden, then peace for all would be secured. Everyone would live in harmony, respecting each other's rights and giving a helping hand should that prove necessary. Notice that, thus far, we haven't mentioned the state.

Of course it will be objected that what has been described is a scenario of moral perfection. We have already conceded that it does not describe a stable practical regime because we know, or suspect, that without the active exercise of the coercive powers of the state there would be plenty of folk who would violate the rights of others. That may be so, but then a different issue is being addressed at the moment, namely, what is one's fair share of the Samaritan chore? If the answer that I gave was reasonable, and if as the world stands one's fair share is insufficient to rescue others because others will not do their fair share, does one's own fair share increase in order that one shoulder the extra burden imposed by the prospective unfairness of others? Wellman's argument pre-supposes that decent well-meaning citizens must assume, as a matter of fairness, the additional burden created by other citizens' immorality: that burden, specifically, is the state with all its coercive apparatus.

The dialectic to this point bears a strong similarity to that exposed by problems concerning international justice. Given a pattern of radical inequalities in the international distribution of goods such as income and wealth, educational provision, sound health and life expectancy, one might ask what fairness demands of those who are comparatively rich in the resources which can fund these goods. Some say that each person in surplus should transfer resources to the amount that, were every other rich person to give a similar amount, the problems of poverty would be solved. (Of course there are many different ways in which such a calculation might be done.) But suppose it is done, suppose the problems of dire poverty could be overcome if every citizen of the OECD countries were to give 20 per cent of their income to Third World charities. Does this tell us what fairness demands of us? Given that we *know* that a great majority of folk will not in fact fulfil this obligation, does fairness require those who are motivated by considerations of fairness to revisit the calculation in order to compensate for the anticipated failure of others?

Surely not, so long as fairness is construed as 'one's fair share of the communal Samaritan chore'. Of course there are other ways of understanding the demands of fairness, just as there are other arguments which might require the citizen who contributes a fair share to contribute even more to the elimination of poverty or the threat of an imminent state of nature. I shall not enquire what supplementary arguments there might be in the case of either international justice or the citizen's duty to protect her fellows from the state of nature. But we should notice that Wellman's account *requires* that citizens assume a greater burden than the notionally sufficient respect for the rights of others and a duty of care should they require emergency assistance (whether this be the consequence of others violating their rights or just the product of bad luck – sickness and the like). His argument *requires* not only that citizens desist from violating the rights of others and care for them when they fall in need of rescue but, in addition, that each citizen actively protect each other by instituting or endorsing a state which will ensure that they never stand in need. As such the state looks less like a mutual-rescue team and more like the mutual-protection associations described by Robert Nozick in *Anarchy, State, and Utopia* (Nozick 1974: 12–25).

At this point, Simmons's criticism that the argument is factitious – idiosyncratic and artificial – takes on greater force, since we are now in a position to consider whether there is any difference in substance between two models of mutuality. The first ('Sweetie-Pie') model is one of universal mutual concern: just as a matter of fact, A declares that she will rescue B and C should they need it; B declares that he will rescue A and C; C declares that she will rescue A and B. In each case the rescue vehicle to be employed is the state. They each make these declarations as avowals of a moral duty of rescue (in more familiar terms, a duty of care). This is a coincidence of moral judgement; one might say an agreement, in the sense of congruence, of moral beliefs or sentiments. The second ('Hobbesian') model is one of universal but conditional enlightened self-interest, an arrangement of the form 'I will, if you will, so will I' as the old song put it. A declares that she will rescue B and C should they need it, on condition that they rescue her should she in turn fall in need, and, most importantly, given that security S is provided by all three of them to guarantee their compliance with the agreement or contract. B declares that . . . (and the story is repeated by each party). (Of course, security S is the state with its big battalions; this is a covenant of steel, backed by the sword.)

Now suppose that all of them, in both models, *are* as a matter of fact in need of rescue, as in the supposition that all of us are vulnerable to the perils of the state of nature. In both cases the rescuing agency is the state, established under the first model as an agency through which rescuers fulfil their duty of care, under the second model as the guarantee of security given by all. Which model gives the superior account of the practical reasoning of persons faced by a common danger? Would they be motivated first, or more strongly, by a prudential concern to save themselves or by a moral concern to rescue others? The prudential account has the virtue of familiarity; it is of course a skeletal version of the (hypothetical) contract argument at the heart of *Leviathan*, as I read Hobbes. The Samaritan account requires more by way of evidential backing; in contrast with the Hobbesian story it looks contrived. Still, I am not persuaded that it should be rejected, not least because whilst these two models have been paraded as alternatives, they are not. Decent souls will find that they are motivated both by self-interest and by their concern for others, and these motives happily converge on the same practical solution: a state with coercive powers is the servant of both self-interest and Samaritanism. Those who are moved by both prudence and care for others will find that these motivating factors pull in the same direction. Both concerns counsel support for the state which is just as well as coercive.

Before we leave the topic of Samaritanism, I want to draw attention to two further, related, worries. The first is raised by Wellman himself: he considers whether a state as justified by the Samaritan duties of citizens to rescue fellow citizens from the hazards of a state of nature might be unable to justify its exercise of wider powers, 'anything like a full-blown, liberal welfare state' (Wellman 2001: 757). As matters stand the state which has responsibilities to rescue citizens from the state of nature has (legitimately) only those powers sufficient to the task. These will be the traditional 'night-watchman' functions of internal security and external defence, plus whatever powers of coordination are required to prevent prisoners' dilemmas and other sources of chaos in the pursuit of common goals. And these functions, as stated, do not extend to the standard agenda of the liberal welfare state; in particular they do not include a prospectus to achieve distributive justice: to deliver equality or constrained inequality or to allocate resources according to need or any other criterion of urgency short of rescue from imminent danger.

At this point Wellman concedes that this point is well taken, but it does not amount to an objection. His thought is that 'once a state is in place, the moral relations among compatriots change . . . once a minimal state is in place, values other than those associated with samaritanism may come to the fore and justify additional political activity' (Wellman 2001: 758–9). Once we have demonstrated that the state is legitimate and that citizens have political obligations – both of these on the grounds that they are necessary to fulfil the Samaritan duty of states and citizens to prevent the state of nature – other state functions may acquire legitimacy and the duties of citizens may be rightfully extended for reasons other than Samaritanism. Thus Wellman argues that there are sound independent arguments to the effect that the minimal state should be a democratic decision-making body, and this is turn may require a measure of redistribution in order to achieve an informed, well-educated electorate wherein citizens exercise equal political powers, and so forth. We have argued that it is a necessary condition of the state being legitimate that it be just or nearly just. Justice has many modalities. Samaritanism tells us that a state is legitimate and that citizens have duties in order to rescue folk from the perils of the state of nature. But the state thus instituted must be just if it is to command obedience, and justice may require more of the state than that it fulfil the traditional functions of the night-watchman and road traffic coordinator. In my book, it is a splendid result that arguments from Samaritanism, fairness and justice bolster each other so neatly.

A final criticism of Wellman's Samaritanism has been put with force and in great detail by Massimo Renzo. Renzo argues that the argument from Samaritan duties has a wider scope than Wellman's theory is able to accommodate. In particular, he claims that any argument which succeeds in establishing the legitimacy of the state as the agency of Samaritan duties amongst a community of fellow citizens will also require that state to extend its Samaritan efforts beyond its own citizenry. Indeed the Samaritan agency (the state of Italy is his example) should direct its efforts to wherever it can do most good. Renzo, on the other hand, supposes that the Italian government does have a special duty 'to pay special attention to Italian needy with regard to such [redistributive] policies'. Wellman's argument has no explanation of this widely held view, hence it fails by *reductio* (Renzo 2008).[36] If it can rescue more citizens (and from a more desperate condition of need) of some other state than Italy, then it should do so. The same is true for citizens taken individually. If they have a Samaritan duty towards their own fellow citizens, they also have a Samaritan duty to anyone who is in a condition of very great hazard – indeed this is the very point of the New Testament parable: 'Who is my neighbour?' asks the legal scholar, and the answer of course is that it is the one who shows mercy to *whoever* is in great need, whatever their origins (Luke: Chapter 10). If an Italian citizen could rescue the starving citizens of some other state by evading the taxes imposed on him by the Italian state, Samaritanism would seem to offer him a reason *not* to obey the law.

This is a very strong argument and Wellman is aware that it is in the offing. Two responses are available to him, both separately and in combination. The first is to defend the special duties that states have to their own citizens and the special obligations that citizens have towards their own state and their own fellow citizens. This response has a good deal of plausibility. It is obviously acceptable with respect to those Samaritan duties which motivated the account in the first place – the duty to protect folks from the state of nature. Who would doubt that the Italian state is much better at maintaining peace and stability in Italy than in Iraq or Somalia? Wellman believes that there are good reasons why states should acknowledge further (and redistributive) special duties to their own citizens, but I shall not attempt to adjudicate the issue.[37] The second response, which Wellman concedes may be appropriate, is to acknowledge that the same Samaritan instincts which call for support of the state as necessary for political stability also require it to be a much more active agent of international justice.

If neither of these responses is persuasive, Wellman's theory of Samaritan duties must fail. But I see no reason to be pessimistic on this score. Let us summarize my discussion of the Samaritan theory. We should welcome this approach as an additional element in the repertoire of arguments which support the legitimacy of just states and the concomitant obligations of the citizen; it works well as a supplement to, and in combination with other arguments and should not be quickly dismissed. If we take the facts of the matter as given and understand the state to be the only agency capable of preventing a society collapsing into a state of nature, it makes sense to attribute to citizens a Samaritan duty to help each other if the cost of doing so is reasonable. It is a conceit to speak of 'rescue' in these circumstances and the conceit becomes more strained as we understand that the rescuers stand in need of rescue themselves. There is no emergency. That said, it does us no harm to remember that even in settled Western democracies the carapace of civility may be brittle, appearing to be little more than skin deep. In my lifetime there have been riots in Los Angeles and Washington, in Brixton, Bristol, Manchester and Liverpool, and most recently in Paris. These may have their origins in political protest, but as soon as the police retreat, shop windows are smashed, white goods are looted and the premises burned. Responsible citizens who have a care for their neighbours will generally support the state which acts as a barrier between them and a lifetime of fear and mayhem. In this light, they will assume the duties of the responsible citizen. For sure this argument is not sufficiently water-tight to capture every citizen or to under-pin every duty that may be ascribed to them. But it does capture an orientation towards the state and one's fellow citizens that is displayed by the committed and diligent citizen. And maybe these commitments should be more readily extended to citizens of other states who are hard-pressed and in need of help. That thought, generous when actively acknowledged, should not be thought to weaken the argument.

What these concluding considerations have prompted is a closer examination of the special relationship in which many have claimed citizens stand to their own state. Some have deemed that this relationship, once correctly understood, will itself explain the essential duties of citizenship. We shall examine these claims in our final chapter.

Chapter 11

Communities and citizenship

Up to this point I have framed the governing dialectic of arguments for and against the authority of the state and the concomitant duties of citizens in terms of the slogan expressive of modern liberalism: 'the state proposes; the citizen disposes'. For a number of philosophers, notably those who, first, believe that the standard set of arguments in favour of the state's authority and citizens' concomitant obligations all fail and yet, second, resist the move to scepticism or the brands of anarchism discussed in Chapter 6, the alternative has been to reject this dialectic. Such a strategy identifies the fault of such approaches in the search for a justification that can be made good to the citizen who demands one. Let us purloin without attribution a term of contemporary jargon and dub this position 'communitarian', though I well understand that those who advocate it may reject the label as confusing.

So the account I have given of the liberal dialectic does not go unchallenged. The slogan recited above characterizes the citizen in the first place as a philosopher who seeks to satisfy the reflective requirement that the arguments be got straight and second, as an enquirer into the facts, charged with testing whether or not in the actual world of their lived experience these philosophical arguments apply to themselves, and to some subset or to all of their fellow citizens. Whether as philosopher scrutinizing arguments or as empirical investigator looking into the facts, the citizen takes an intellectually detached position, assuming the role of rational enquirer. This is what 'disposal' amounts to.

The communitarian argues, to the contrary, that this represents a fundamental mistake concerning the task of the philosopher in this domain. Since I believe that there is something important to learn from this contrary position, we shall examine the arguments with some care. The contrary position represents the philosophical task as an interpretative or hermeneutical enterprise. It is the task of the political philosopher to articulate our best understanding of the normative relations which hold between the state and the citizens. We should be engaged in an exploration of the meaning that our allegiance to the state bears to us as citizens since citizenship is a standing condition of our daily lives. It is an error to suppose that philosophers should detach themselves in thought from the fact of any imputed allegiance and assume a critical stance, applying some external moral standards or ideals as yardsticks to determine what conditions must hold for the state to be granted authority and for political obligations to be imputed to citizens.

Hegel the communitarian

Of the great, dead, philosophers, Hegel is the grandest exemplar of this view of political philosophy.[1] He tells us that

> *the truth* concerning *right, ethics and the state* [including whether or not citizens have moral duties to each other and the state] is at any rate *as old* as its *exposition and promulgation* in *public laws and in public morality and religion*.
> (Hegel 1991: 11, emphasis in original)

He is claiming that we all *know* that the state has authority over us and that we, its citizens, have duties as prescribed in its laws (and nowadays, perhaps) public morality and (probably not) established religion. Philosophy which purports to *examine* what we already know is a farce. Worse, if it takes a sceptical position towards the authority of the state, it becomes a dangerous game. Worst of all are those professional philosophers who take a salary from public institutions like universities then repay the state which funds them by abusing their positions and pandering to the natural excitability of the young students in their care.

The position Hegel takes in the Preface to the *Philosophy of Right* is extreme because it is political, polemical and motivated by personal hostility.[2] That said, the philosophical orientation of his argument has been rediscovered in modern times. Hegel asks: if we already know that we have duties as citizens, what task is there that remains for philosophers to accomplish? He answers: the task of the philosopher is to *comprehend* this system of duties, to disclose the rationality embodied within the social network of ties that bind, to interpret and understand the practices in which we are, willy-nilly, enmeshed. It follows that there is no philosophical problem of political obligation, as I have framed it: no posing of the Philosophical Problem, no investigation of the Political Problem of how far the acceptable philosophical arguments apply to us.

I suspect that most readers will find this position very puzzling, not to say threatening. Let us try to make it sound persuasive. Let us advance the most plausible case before we subject it to careful assessment.

We can begin with an analogy. Consider family life – or family life that is going well, or best, family life that is going as well as its most fervent apologists tell us it can go: not *The Sopranos*, more *Little House on the Prairie*; not *King Lear*, *Hamlet*, or *Othello*, more the happy, unwritten, sequel to *The Taming of the Shrew*. Mother and father love each other, care for their children and look after ageing parents. Where family matters are concerned they think about things, not as individuals pursuing their own discreet agendas, but as a couple, an organic unity speaking in the first-person plural as 'We', no longer as 'I'. They recognize their evident duties: of fidelity to each other, of loving care to their children and honour to their parents, and they fulfil these duties gladly. They don't pose any evident ethical problem. Ask them why they do things in this way and they are puzzled: 'Because we are a family', they say. 'What other reason could there be?' A similar question could be put to the children. 'Why do you believe that you have a duty to honour and obey your parents?' And we expect these respectful children to be equally stumped.

Then they twig that *philosophical* questions are being asked: 'What are the reasons why you accept these duties? Just why do you think it would be wrong to reject them or fail to fulfil them?' The questioner should realize that she is unlikely to elicit answers that reveal foundations in the sense of deeper principles from which the duties concerned can be derived. What is being probed is the sense of identity of the family members. Their seeing themselves as parents or children amounts to their recognizing the duties incumbent on them in these roles. Some say duties of this kind *constitute* the identity of their bearers – in which case we should not be surprised at the inarticulacy of those who are questioned, or their puzzled repetition of obvious facts like 'But I am their parent', 'But I am their child'.

This conception of duties as constitutive of social roles which persons generally find themselves occupying, which they haven't in many cases chosen to inhabit, receives its most systematic and articulate philosophical expression in Hegel's account of 'Ethical Life' (*Sittlichkeit*) in *The Philosophy of Right*. In a rational state, individuals will find themselves related to other family members in a specific kind of domestic structure, working alongside others in an economy which organizes their relationships with fellow producers and consumers, subject to the rule of law and the disciplines of regulatory bodies, and living in a political world with a constitution that promotes their freedom and is a focus for their patriotic sentiments. These nested relationships comprise an ethical home, complete with a full moral address. The model citizen will just find that, being describable as John Smith, son of Arthur and Margaret, husband of Annie and father of Katy and Helen, colleague of Jones, citizen of Glasgow, Scotland and the United Kingdom, he has duties galore!

Duties of these sorts, some John selected, some he was born with, and some that have just grown, emerge out of every citizen's life story. We have before us the example of the duties of family life – a soft-hearted version of Hegel's own account. I think it makes good sense to accept that one who regards himself as a family member, on the model thus described, may not be able to question the duties ascribed to him, although he can of course decide not to comply, to do what he believes to be wrong.

Arguments of this form gain their plausibility from the reader's approval of the social arrangements which are being described. It is important that Hegel believes he is describing the uniquely rational form of social life, that which best permits humans to express distinctive elements of their nature. The rules of ethical life do not operate as constraints, they liberate persons who would otherwise be unable to develop, in the case of family life, their capacities for loving, long-term commitment to other persons. Marriage on this account is not a ball and chain but rather a natural opportunity for persons to grow out of the bonds of atomized self-concern.[3] Likewise citizens of the modern rational state do not live in chains, as Rousseau believed. Citizenship manifests their freedom.

Hegel believes that he has explained the rationality of the institutions which constitute the modern state. He has traced their history and can explain how they meet the aspirations which mankind has learned to articulate as they have thrown over the institutions which crippled them. The different dimensions of social life (domestic, economic, legal and political) fit together in a fashion he described as dialectical but which we can best understand as coherent and harmonious, making it possible for us to be persons of all these kinds at once, to fulfil the duties of our various stations without generating social conflict or personal fragmentation. He also claimed that citizens could recognize the rationality of their condition (although I doubt that Hegel took this requirement – the publicity constraint as discussed in Chapter 5 – seriously). Endorsement must be given but the reflections from which it issues do not permit the possibility of challenge. But, there again, why should anyone want to challenge institutions which, in their broad framework at least, cannot be improved? At the end of history, 'what is rational is actual; and what is actual is rational'.[4]

It looks as though there cannot be a problem of political obligation any more than there can be a problem of parental duties or the bonds of friendship. Once we understand the nature of the modern state (and by analogy with the account of family life that has been given above), interpreting its distinctive institutions as serving necessary functions given the desires and values humanity has developed through its history, once we acknowledge the state's contribution to our freedom, we find that in describing it, we recognize its legitimacy. Rational legitimation is, as it were, built into the structure of the moral world we inhabit.

From this we can see that it is misleading to interpret Hegel as denying that the philosopher has anything to say about the justification of the state and its citizens' duties. The hermeneutic task of articulating our comprehension of the duties we are taken to recognize, of interpreting the practices which constitute our ethical nature, explains the rationality of these institutions and the duties incumbent on those who are members of them. But then, once we see clearly how and why the state and its relations with the body of citizens is rational, as rational citizens as well as philosophers we are forced to concede that the rational state is justified. It follows, although Hegel did not explore this issue in the modern world, that a state which is irrational cannot justify the demands that it places on citizens any more than a dysfunctional form of domestic life can justify the burdens it places on some family members. We should conclude that the impression given by Hegel's initial characterization of the task of political philosophy, that the problem of political obligation is a pseudo-problem, as they used to say, is thoroughly misleading. In disclosing, as he believes, the rationality of the modern state he makes an effort to demonstrate the grounds on which its authority can be justified to the citizens to whom it imputes obligations.[5]

The pattern of Hegel's discussion is instructive. At first it looks as though the pursuit of a hermeneutics of political life – what John Horton, following Bernard Williams, has described as a 'phenomenology of ethical life' (Horton

1992: 174) – undercuts the straightforward liberal demand for rational legitimation. But it turns out that this is a false impression since the task of comprehension (as well as the details of the only kind of state that is fully comprehensible) consists in showing that the state is rational or, to use a term that means much the same in this context, that the state is just. We shall see that this pattern is repeated in the work of modern philosophers who have taken up Hegel's baton (sometimes with no realization that in philosophy there is very little that is new under the sun).

The conceptual argument

There is another way of making these points, more philosophically parochial, less methodologically explicit, which owes something to Wittgenstein. Some claim that our understanding and endorsement of central elements of our political life is likewise built into the language we use to talk about them. Such language is suffused with normativity, with a recognition of the requirements made on us by the institutions we use such language to describe. It is claimed that if we know what it means to talk about the state, authority, government and the law, if we can play this particular set of language games, we can see that asking, 'Why can't I break the law?' is like asking 'Why can't I move a rook along a diagonal?' whilst playing chess. Thus T. McPherson insists that

> 'Why should I obey the government?' is an absurd question. We have not understood what it *means* to be a member of political society if we suppose that political obligation is something that we might not have had and that therefore needs to be *justified*.
>
> (McPherson 1967: 64, emphasis in original)

In similar fashion, Hannah Pitkin argues that

> The same line of reasoning [as that adopted to dispose of the question 'Why should I keep a promise?'] can be applied to the question 'why does even a legitimate government, a valid law, a genuine authority ever obligate me to obey?' As with promises, and as our new doctrine about political obligation suggests, we may say that this is what 'legitimate government', 'valid law', 'genuine authority' *mean*. It is part of the concept, the meaning of 'authority' that those subject to it are required to obey, that it has a right to command. It is part of the concept, the meaning of 'law', that those to whom it is applicable are obligated to obey it. As with promises, so with authority, government, and law: there is a *prima facie* obligation involved in each, and normally you must perform it.
>
> (Pitkin 1965: 78, emphasis in original)

To be rude, we can recognize the Wittgensteinian tenor of the argument when we hear the heavy breath and table-thumping *sound* of the italics. These arguments derive their plausibility from conceptual connections[6] which are evident enough: once we modify the nouns with the adjectives 'legitimate', 'valid' and 'genuine', 'prima facie' even, there is very little room to manoeuvre. Obligation follows from legitimacy, if, as we have argued, we understand a legitimate government as generally having the authority to impose obligations. But notice, in the Pitkin quotation in particular, how these adjectives slip out of the argument. As soon as we see that we can properly speak of tyrannical governments as well as legitimate ones, of unjust laws as well as valid ones, of spurious authorities as well as genuine ones (the last with only the slightest whiff of solecism), we can see how these arguments trade on the assumption that is explicit in Hegel, namely, that the institutions to which these terms are applied have already passed the test of rational legitimation. If we do not make this assumption, then we shall find that we do not judge that 'it is part of the concept, the meaning of "law" that those to whom it is applicable are obligated to obey it'.

Dworkin on associative obligations

The conceptual argument was too swift, appealing to accounts of the meaning of terms which are defective because they are either controversial, plain wrong or egregiously question-begging. In recent times, other philosophers have taken up the challenge by exploring the phenomenology of membership. A conspicuous example is Ronald Dworkin. He identifies a type of

> obligations that are often called obligations of role but that I shall call, generically, associative or communal obligations. I mean the special responsibilities social practice attaches to membership in some biological or social group, like the responsibilities of family or friends or neighbors.[7]
>
> (Dworkin 1986: 195–6)

Dworkin goes on to argue that political obligation is of this type: 'Political association, like family and friendship and other forms of association more local and intimate, is in itself pregnant of obligation' (ibid.: 206). And he goes on to defend his claim against two objections: first, that such obligations rest on emotional bonds that cannot hold in large political communities like the modern nation state where citizen members have personal acquaintance with a tiny fraction of other members, and second, that the attribution of such special communal responsibilities 'smacks of nationalism, or even racism' (ibid: 196).

What are the features of 'true' or 'genuine' communities on this account? First, they must be 'bare' communities meeting whatever natural, historical or sociological conditions that social practice identifies as constituting a community. Amongst the bare communities, the true communities that yield obligations share these features:

(a) The obligations 'must be *special*, holding distinctly within the group, rather than as general duties its members owe equally to persons outside it'

(Dworkin 1986: 199).[8] I take it that this condition is uncontroversial. (In the context of political association this condition, if met, ensures that Simmons's particularity requirement is also met.)

(b) These responsibilities are *personal*, holding directly between persons. Thus the obligations of family life hold between individual members and not between members and the family taken as a whole. An implication of this condition for the duties of citizens is that they hold directly between citizens, and not between citizens and the state. This is controversial – indeed I argued against a dogmatic insistence on this point in Chapter 2. Some of the duties of the citizen (duties of care, some duties required by principles of distributive justice) evidently are duties to fellow citizens. It will do no harm to think of them all in this fashion. Since the controversy is orthogonal to the discussion here, I shall ignore the point.

(c) These responsibilities are to be seen as

> flowing from a more general responsibility each has of *concern* for the well-being of others in the group . . . within the form or mode of life constituted by the communal practice, the concern must be general and must provide the foundation for the more discrete responsibilities [still to be specified].
>
> (Dworkin 1986: 200)

(d) This manifest concern must be 'an *equal* concern for all members' (ibid.).

We should recognize that conditions (c) and (d) are puzzling. They look very much like psychological conditions, and if they are, Dworkin has no response to the first of the two objections put above. There is no feeling or other conative psychological attitude that all, or even most, citizens of a large modern state (or, I dare say, of a state of any description) direct towards all other citizens.[9] But Dworkin insists instead that such concern is not a psychological condition; it is 'an interpretive property of the group's practices of asserting and acknowledging responsibilities – these must be practices that people with the right level of concern would adopt' (Dworkin 1986: 201).[10] Thus it is possible, if most unlikely, that a group may operate a range of practices without any group members *feeling* concern for others. There are two things wrong with this: in the first place, as Dworkin admits, the practices will be unstable if the community members do not show 'the right level of concern' for each other, and yet we know that not all of them will do so even if the right level of concern is taken to be a most attenuated and watery measure of goodwill. (Thus, for example, those who say, 'Charity begins at home' when faced with the prospect of international aid tend not to be very charitable to their fellow citizens either. Charity often begins and ends at home, literally.) Second, in making this defence, Dworkin has forgotten that his third condition requires that one recognize a 'more general responsibility each has of *concern* for the well-being of others in the group'. Granted that the required concern may be an interpretive condition on practices amongst a community whose members show no real concern for others, I fail to see how the *responsibility* for concern for the well-being of other members can be likewise reinterpreted. The only way such a responsibility can be discharged is by actively feeling concern. One doesn't discharge it by feigning concern or by merely acting as one who does feel concern would act.

Put to one side for a moment the fourth (equality) condition on genuine community. Dworkin recognizes that genuine communities which meet the conditions outlined above 'may be unjust or promote injustice'. They may be unjust in the way of families who believe that equal concern for their children require them to exercise more severe disciplinary control over daughters than sons, notably in the area of sexual conduct. They may be unjust in the way of religious communities the members of which respect each other but discriminate against believers in other religions. Taking the community which commands our interest to be the nation state, we can reconstruct injustices of both of these kinds in the ways citizens may behave towards fellow citizens and aliens. A nation state, as we know too well, may prevent or limit the education of girls and persecute religious minorities.

Dworkin's response to this possibility is characteristically sensitive and nuanced, but the upshot is one we should accept. Basically, granted the existence of grey areas and hard cases, he accepts that one's convictions concerning the justice of the social practices will determine how far these practices are ethically potent, how far members of communities which engage in such practices can be assigned the constitutive moral obligations. His broad conclusion is that unjust communities, most conspicuously those communities which violate the rights of their members, cannot determine the associative duties of members (although this might be a matter requiring explanation and regret on the part of the recalcitrant member of the community she 'has a duty to honor').[11]

The implications in respect of political associations are not clear. It looks as though Dworkin would accept the judgement that it is a necessary condition on the imputation of political obligations that the state be just or nearly just. Does he also believe, along with Rawls (a matter we discussed in the last chapter) that a natural duty of justice serves as a sufficient condition for the attribution of political obligations to citizens? It is not easy to say. He discusses justice in the way of a side-constraint on associations which amount to true communities and hence yield obligations, so it seems that it operates as a necessary condition. On the other hand, we notice that the fourth condition (d) on true or genuine, obligation-constituting, communities is that there be 'an *equal* concern for all members'. This equality condition on the concern for others that members display is glossed as an assumption that 'the roles and rules [constitutive of the group in question] are equally in the interests of all, that no-one's life is more important than anyone else's' (Dworkin: 1986: 200–1). In fact, Dworkin goes on to explain that the only form of political community that satisfies all four conditions is a community governed by a model of principle. This is explained as a common subscription to a scheme of principles, political ideals concerning justice, fairness and due process, which consistently assign equal rights and duties to all citizens.[12] As Dworkin describes matters, this amounts to a general acceptance of political integrity 'as constitutive of political community' (ibid.: 211).

'Concern' for all members by each is to be read as respect for the integrity of the principles which all members accept. On any reasonable interpretation, granted that the values of equality and justice are not articulated in any detail, this reads as a requirement that the 'true' community be a just community.[13]

If this is true, it becomes impossible to distinguish Dworkin's argument for political obligations as associative obligations from the argument that we have a natural duty of justice to support the just state by recognizing our duties as citizens. The account is valuable in so far as it draws attention to the mind-set characteristic of members of true communities large and small, but it is a mistake to believe that this position represents any significant advance on the claim that the justice of a state constitutes sufficient grounds for asserting its legitimacy and attributing political obligations to its citizens. In fact, the position outlined by Dworkin is very similar to that taken by Hegel. In both cases, it looks at first as though the sheer fact of membership of the community generates the obligations constitutive of the association, but upon closer investigation we find that it is the rationale that is given for the particular form of association (in terms of justice or, for Hegel, freedom) that bears the justificatory burden.

Horton on citizenship, membership and identity

In his book *Political Obligation*, John Horton has revived this tradition. He summarizes his position as follows, arguing that:

> [1] Political obligation is conceptually connected to membership of a particular polity; [2] that membership of a polity is not usually a matter of choice or voluntary commitment; [3] that neither membership nor the corresponding obligations normally require further moral justification; [4] that the connection between membership and obligation is mediated through a sense of (partial) identification with the political community; [5] that political obligation requires taking account of the interests and welfare of one's polity; [6] that political obligation is particularly closely connected to acknowledging the authority of the law and the government of one's polity which is the kernel of the terms of the political association; [7] and that recognition of this authority is consistent with particular acts of disobedience.
>
> (Horton 1992: 169–70, my numbering inserted)

There is much in this that is plausible. I shall assume, in particular, that claims [5] through to [7] are uncontroversial and true. As Horton intends, his account captures well an understanding of what allegiance means to the dutiful citizen of the just or decent state. It is perfectly possible that the dutiful citizen never raises to herself the philosophical problem of political obligation as I have characterized it. Such a one is blessed if her membership of the polity never generates any moral problem. Her identification as a citizen of some just state will be secure because it is unreflective and uncritical – blamelessly so. It is not a moral requirement on active citizenship that it be philosophically well-founded in the reflections of all

members of the polity, though I do claim that it is a feature of the modern temperament that citizens do assert the right to subject the claims of authority to
moral audit as soon as these claims generate suspicion or raise controversy.

On the other hand we should make an effort to distinguish what is acceptable
and what unacceptable in the position as stated. At the heart of Horton's position
is his denial of voluntarism as a necessary condition on the validity of political
obligations. He insists that it is deeply misleading to understand the obligations
of citizenship as necessarily the issue of some act of choice or other voluntary
undertaking, and along with many others in this tradition (including Hegel and
Dworkin as we have seen) he explores the analogy of family life to make this
point. So far, so good, in my book – but as I have emphasized from the beginning
there is a very great difference between the denial of voluntarism as a necessary
condition on legitimacy and the rejection of a call for rational legitimation when
that demand is made. Let us see whether Horton appreciates this difference.

It is important to notice that when he attests in [1] a conceptual connection
between membership of a polity and the holding of political obligations this is not
an endorsement of the 'conceptual argument' advanced by McPherson and Pitkin
and rejected above. The conceptual link is much more attenuated, being revealed
through a study of what membership of a political community typically involves. In
the first place (claim [4] above) it is a moral relationship manifested in the ways that
citizens identify with and take responsibility for the activities of their state – even
to the point of feeling ashamed of policies carried out in its name (Horton 1992:
152–3). As a consequence of such identification, citizens can recognize obligations
both to obey and disobey the political sovereign, to endorse and to protest against
what is done, to feel proud or ashamed of their country's deeds. As Horton's case
develops it becomes apparent that the conceptual connection between membership
and political obligation consists in the fact that membership is to be understood in
terms of the citizens' recognition of a regime of duties in the very broadest sense.

So to be a member of a political community is to be disposed to act as citizens
ought on the basis of thoughts and feelings that are 'internal' to their political
standing – to behave as thoughtful citizens feel they should. It follows that one
cannot be a true member of the polity who does not experience the appropriate
thoughts and feelings. (This position contrasts with Dworkin's as discussed
above, but then I argued that Dworkin could not consistently deny that the
required concern amounted to a psychological condition.) But surely one may in
principle hold a passport, be subject to tax and liable to legal punishment, and
be eligible to vote in elections, have legal and political standing in all these ways
and more, yet not have the thoughts and feelings appropriate to the real member.
A citizen may be quite indifferent to his political obligations, yet still be doing
just what has to be done, living as an internal alien or a compliant outlaw might.
To my knowledge, no association has the psychological power to ensure that
'bare' members feel and sincerely act out an appropriate repertoire of thoughts
and sentiments. Even in good families, one finds the black sheep who feels nothing for his parents or siblings, doing nothing obviously wrong, just moving out of
the moral orbit as soon as independence is possible.

Horton seems to recognize this, raising the spectre of the amoralist familiar from the moral philosophy texts and considering whether there might be a political equivalent to one who knows what is the right thing to do (what morality dictates) yet not being at all motivated to do it. Realizing that the possibility of such a case would be disastrous for his conceptual thesis, he asks, 'can the standard conditions of membership be met, yet there be no corresponding obligations?' (Horton 1992: 158). In the manner of Aristotle considering the related problem of whether the rational agent can ever do wrong knowingly – the problem of weakness of will or *akrasia* – he attempts to dispatch the recalcitrant cases as pathological or very rare, as though a tiny baby can be just a little mistake.

First, he tells us that those who explicitly deny their political obligations may still be recognizing the legitimacy of their polities in the 'many and various ways' in which they act (Horton 1992: 160). Of course this is right. Prospective anarchists should recognize that the voluntarist arguments from tacit consent or the knowing receipt of benefits may well be in the offing. Imagine the case of a self-styled anarchist who advertises his political, philosophical, position openly. It never occurs to him that having, as they say, sucked hard on the tit of the state as the funder of the educational provision that succoured him as learner, teacher, researcher and big earner as university professor, from age five to fifty, he has a sin to expiate and a debt to repay. Watch your wallet, I say, if you meet a rich and clever anarchist. But notice in such a case that it is the substantial arguments from tacit consent or fairness that one would bring to bear to convince such a one of his obligations, rather than the fact of mere membership of the polity.

There are other difficult cases which cause Horton to throw up his hands. What of the straightforward dissident with a radically different political perspective? Or, in the most extreme case, the 'unworldly hermit whose understanding of himself lacks any sense of identity with the political community and who exists as far as possible apart from it' (Horton 1992: 160). In these cases, given that these members disavow any imputed political obligations, Horton suggests that

> the political community should recognize that it has no authority against such a person and no reciprocal obligations obtain. In such cases the political community will have the right to protect itself against any serious infraction of its rules and standards, but it may have no legitimate claims on his allegiance and he should, by and large, be left alone.
>
> (Horton 1992: 160)

But what if teenagers attack our unworldly hermit in the street? What if over-zealous policemen charge down the dissidents with horses and then beat them up with truncheons when they demonstrate in public? Are the hermit and the dissidents sufficiently members of the community despite their explicit disavowals of any political obligation to be entitled to legal remedy? I believe so. Suppose in either case that they become so fed up with persecution, official and unofficial, that they decide to emigrate and seek from the state the documentation which is necessary for them to cross its borders. Does this transform them into the sort of members of the community who cannot deny their conceptually linked oblig-ations? Surely not. Horton tells us that 'it is likely that when most denials of political obligation are examined it will be discovered that they are more or less disingenuous' (Horton 1992: 160), but we should ask what is the devious plan behind such clever discoveries. We can be sure that however hard we search the malcontents we shall not discover a membership card.

Put aside the philosophical controversies: do we not need a clean conception of membership, one that is disentangled from disputes concerning political oblig-ations? I believe one ought to be able to decide who is or is not a member of the polity quite independently of issues concerning which members have what oblig-ations. In fact, like most clubs, I suspect that a political community, a nation state, has a good variety of *categories* of membership. Thus it may be useful to think of my membership of the political community of France when I visit as a tourist in much the same way as my *Temporary* Membership of the Buckingham Bingo Club in Blackpool which I visit as a guest. While you're on the premises, just follow the rules and play the game! Likewise my *Associate* Membership of the Buchanan Bridge Club, appropriate to those learning the game and not to be trusted in seri-ous tournaments, may be interestingly similar to my membership of the polity of the United Kingdom as a resident alien who is learning to behave in the manner of the locals – and nowadays my competence as an applicant for citizenship will be examined before full membership is granted, courtesy in the United Kingdom of David Blunkett MP and Professor Sir Bernard Crick, who set the tests.

I see no alternative to judging that a polity may have bona fide members who may, in good faith, reject any political obligations, in which case mere member-ship of the polity does not entail political obligations. This does not mean that members of the polity who reject their obligations in good faith are correct to do so. As Horton suspects, there may well be good reasons to impute obligations to them, but the mere fact of their membership will not serve.

It is time to tackle directly Horton's third claim 'that neither membership nor the corresponding obligations normally require further moral justification'. How does he establish this? Again he makes heavy use of the example of the family, claiming that there are many circumstances in which 'the very demand for justi-fication may itself be thought odd and out of place' (Horton 1992: 147). Thus, if

> I am asked to go to a party one evening and I reply that I cannot because it is my parents' silver wedding anniversary and I must spend the evening with them, though I had not promised to stay with them and I would prefer to go to the party, then frequently no more needs to be said. If I were asked why this was a reason for not going to the party we would mostly find the ques-tion odd and inappropriate. What more does the questioner think needs to be supplied?
>
> (ibid.: 147–8)

Notice first that the speaker seems to have got his priorities right. The right thing to do – attend the silver wedding – is pretty obvious in the circumstances which means that the person pressing the question is likely to be a child, a fool or a philosopher. This is why the questions are 'odd', 'out of place' and 'inappropriate' (to use Horton's terms). Matters would be very different if the speaker were less sure of the priorities. Imagine it is a surly teenager who is asking why everyone thinks he should go to his parents' silver wedding celebration rather than the party his mate is holding where he will meet the girl he lusts after. Now there is some explaining that needs to be done. The teenager will not be impressed if all he is told is that his question is odd, out of place, and inappropriate because going to silver weddings is constitutive of family life. No doubt the teenager is a boor, but the woman of whom he enquires can do better than simply fob off the question. She can mention the distress he will cause his parents if he goes to the party, she can recite the Fifth Commandment: 'Honour thy father and mother', she can articulate the virtue of gratitude or explain the applicability of Hobbes's fourth law of nature: 'That a man which receiveth Benefit from another of meer Grace, Endeavour that he which giveth it, have no reasonable cause to repent him of his good will' (Hobbes 1968: 209; Part I, Ch. 15 [75]). And no doubt there is much more that she can do to promote the teenager's moral education.

Exactly the same is true of the duties of citizenship. There are two (or twenty-two) kinds of case: first, there are the cases of the ignorant, the fools or the tyros, who for one reason or another don't know the answers to obvious questions, but ask them nonetheless. They need putting straight. In these sort of cases, just repeating 'But you are a member of the polity' will not always succeed. Some will be flattered and accept this, but both the dumb and the clever may feel that a better answer is due. And they will be right. In such a case those who would answer the question of why the various recalcitrants should, e.g. do what the law demands, will need to find a better answer than simply, 'That is what your citizenship (membership) requires. Do you not understand the concept of citizenship (membership of an association)'? Just as in the case of the teenager who has a lot to learn about his duties to his family, the ignorant citizen should be given whatever reasonable philosophical arguments apply to his case.

The second kind of case is that of the decent, obedient citizen who has reflective inclinations and a genuinely philosophical curiosity and who recalls Kant's dictum that 'This is the age of criticism'. If the Why-question is put – 'Why do I have a duty to . . .?' – an answer is due. In the modern world, neither priests nor princes nor professors of politics or philosophy can dismiss the question as meaningless or 'odd'. It doesn't matter whether the questioner is a likely rebel or just one of nature's bloody-minded philosophers; once the question is put, the cat is out of the bag. Pandora's box of philosophical goodies is opened up. As Kant noticed more than two hundred years ago, the question is now *open*. It will not answer itself.

If Horton were to ask himself, in an idle moment and philosophical vein, why he should attend his parents' silver wedding celebration rather than the exciting party, I suspect he would not be stumped in the way he would be were an excited friend to stop him directly in the street and ask him what kind of party-pooper insists on going to the old folks' dreary get-together. Philosophical questions tend to strike people as odd; they are out of place and inappropriate if put to those who are attending silver wedding celebrations without a thought other than that this is the right thing to be doing. They are good questions, nonetheless.

In exactly the same way, citizens of the just state may happily go along with the regime which governs them, but if perchance the question of why they should accept the obligations imputed to them is put to them by a child or a fool or a philosopher they should be able to find an answer which gives good reasons for their accepting the authority of the state. If, just as likely, typical citizens of the modern world were to ask themselves why they should accept the regime of duties which the state imposes on them, in an idle moment or in circumstances where the issue is pressing because the demands of the state seem immoral or otherwise onerous, many of them just will not accept the fact of their membership of the polity as sufficient reason for them to accept what is demanded. They will require further good reasons to be provided.

Coda: Margaret Gilbert's theory of political obligation

Margaret Gilbert's (2006) book, A *Theory of Political Obligation*, is the culmination of research going back more than 20 years. It builds on her earlier work on social agency and joint commitment. Indeed, at the heart of it is the claim that the political obligations of members of a political society derive from their joint commitment to uphold the political institutions of that society. Since joint commitment is key to her reasoning, her approach comes very close to actual contract theory. Indeed actual contract theory is argued to be a special case of the plural subject theory that Gilbert favours (Gilbert 2006: 183, 215–37) which should be no surprise since actual contracts are perhaps the clearest, since most explicit, cases of a joint commitment. However, it is appropriate to tackle Gilbert's theory in the context of the 'communitarian' theories because the account of the joint commitments that she delivers to fund political obligations does not rely on actual contracts or specific agreements. Instead it appeals to a common understanding amongst members of a political society of the nature of their joint commitment, a common readiness on their part to be thus jointly committed, and a common knowledge amongst members that they have thereby acquired a political obligation to uphold the political institutions of their society. These understandings may simply have accumulated over time as members have developed a sense of their societal co-existence as a joint undertaking. No deliberation need have been given to the implications of what they were doing; no decisions need have been taken. Political obligations may, like Topsy, have 'just growed', being grounded in 'one's membership in a political society' (Gilbert 2006: 44).

I have no doubt that Gilbert has illuminated the very important phenomenon of group recognition and social identification amongst members of a functioning political union – the political modality of that inter-subjective recognition that Hegel characterizes quite generally (in the *Phenomenology*) as the '"I" that is "We" and "We" that is "I"' (Hegel 1977: ¶177). There are many domains in which we speak of common beliefs and values, common actions and common goals, in the language of the first-person plural as attesting a unitary subject. '"We" [the family] go to the Panto every Christmas'. '"We" [the football team] were last in the FA Cup Final in 1964'. '"We" [of the same faith] worship Jesus'. '"We" [the people] made a bad mistake in going to war'. Grammar proves little, but in these sorts of case it serves as evidence of a recognizable phenomenon – of persons who identify with some social union. This phenomenon also has many non-linguistic manifestations with which all of us are perfectly familiar since we are all of us accomplished practitioners. Gilbert has been a pioneer amongst contemporary philosophers in the study of social agency. The issue at hand is whether or not, or better, how far, does this expertise cast a light on the problem of political obligation?

Let us begin at the beginning, alongside Gilbert, with the simplest examples of joint action. The example she uses is that of a couple taking a walk together.[14] She argues that in undertaking a joint activity 'each participant has obligations towards the other participants to behave in a way appropriate to the activity in question' (Gilbert 2006: 114). Further,

Absent special background understandings, any given party, A, has an obligation to any other party, B, to obtain B's concurrence in any determination of the details of the joint activity. This includes A's exit from the joint activity. Alternatively, B, has a right against A that A obtains B's concurrence in any new determination of their joint activity.

(Gilbert 2006: 114–15)

In such cases of joint activity the parties may or may not actually agree to conduct it together. They may just fall into the activity. What is necessary is that it be 'common knowledge' between them that there is a readiness amongst them to engage in the joint activity (Gilbert 2006: 116–21). When folk act together in this fashion, concurrently assuming rights and obligations, they jointly commit to that activity as a common goal. Being jointly committed, the parties speak and act as a plural subject – as a 'We', not severally as a couple of 'I's. So far, so good. As parties to a joint commitment they have obligations of joint commitment to each other (and concomitant rights).

The account of social agency that Gilbert develops here (and first explicated in On Social Facts (1989)) is impressive and useful. But we should register a caveat before we see how it is developed into an account of political obligation. It is commonplace that persons who act together with a joint commitment may fall out just as they may fall in. One party may get fed up of walking together and just slope off. Such a one has not fulfilled an obligation – she has done wrong in some sense. She has failed to respect the standing of the other party. This may be a trivial failure but it may amount to (a little) betrayal nonetheless. Equally, it may be described as a breach of trust and the betrayer is answerable for it to those to whom the obligation of joint commitment is owed. Gilbert uses this language (of failure to respect, betrayal, trust, answerability and owing) heavily in her discussion of the implications of the concept of joint commitment (Gilbert

2006: 149–56) and she is right to do so, yet she does not want to say that the obligations of joint commitment are moral obligations. As obligations, they simply give the person who holds them sufficient reason to act (ibid.: 26–35).[15] Failure to meet a genuine obligation bespeaks minimally a failure of rationality, not a moral wrong.

I find this very mysterious. What kind of wrong is done to another person when one fails to act as reason dictates that one should? Some critics believe that Gilbert has gone wrong in speaking of obligations at all in the case of all jointly committed activity, particularly in the simple cases she discusses. I disagree. I believe with Gilbert that there are obligations here but the kind of obligation must be articulated. To speak of etiquette, good manners and politeness in this context does not fit the (sound) discussion of failure to meet obligations of joint commitment as matters of betrayal and breach of trust unless lack of etiquette, bad manners and impoliteness are themselves moral faults which they may well be in given circumstances. We must know the currency of normativity if we are to make sense of what has gone wrong when a genuine obligation has not been fulfilled. We cannot just insist that it is a genuine obligation nonetheless and leave a blank cheque to account for the debt of the wrongdoer. I believe that even in the simple case of the folk who go for a walk together, if there is a joint commitment then there is a *moral* obligation on the part of all participants to accomplish the activity as well as may be expected, subject to standard defaults and excuses. The moral obligation may not carry great weight. In cases of failure the sin to expiate may be quickly overlooked or forgiven. The charge may be merely that the guilty party was inconsiderate, but if such consideration is owed – as it is in cases of joint commitment – then the fault is moral.

In fact I charge that this refusal to identify the obligations of joint commitment as moral obligations contaminates the account of political obligation which Gilbert draws from it.[16] (That said: it is an open question how far the entire structure of Gilbert's theory of political obligation might be refashioned with moral obligation as its corner-stone.) The drift of her account goes as follows. Membership of a political society is a type of joint commitment. The goal of the plural subject members is to uphold the institutions of the polity. This furnishes their (wholesale) political obligation – to uphold political institutions – and these institutions and the specifics of what is necessary to uphold them determine the special (retail) political obligations of the members.

To understand this account, we have to see that membership of the political society is key to political obligation. What does membership require? It requires a joint commitment to uphold whatever kind of political rule is in place, which is to say: members express to each other a 'readiness for joint commitment in conditions of common knowledge' (Gilbert 2006: 256). In these circumstances a political obligation amongst members (citizens) to each other has been established. This is the point at which Gilbert's plural subject theory comes closest to the actual contract model.

Is this theory acceptable? Critics have challenged it on the same sort of ground that they have challenged actual consent theories. They have asked just what kind of behaviour constitutes a readiness for joint commitment and just what would count as evidence to validate the claim that there might be common knowledge amongst citizens. As soon as answers are given to questions of this kind (citizens regularly pay their taxes and obey the law, they approve the punishment doled out to criminals, they vote in elections, they watch the Queen's Christmas broadcast, etc.) the critics pounce. These activities may not be universal amongst citizens; they may not be signs of a joint commitment among those who do engage in them – they may signal simple prudence; those who do engage in them as a matter of habit and daily routine do not exhibit the common knowledge of the implications of their behaviour that the theory requires, and so on.

Even where citizens do seem to express a common readiness underpinned by common knowledge of each others' joint commitment, Simmons charges that Gilbert's theory rests on three different confusions. It confuses feelings of obligation with genuine obligations. (Such confusion is perfectly possible, but since it is a confusion amongst citizen members there is no reason to think that Gilbert shares it.) It confuses 'political acquiescence with positive obligation-generating acts or relationships' (Simmons 1996: 75). (Such confusion is also possible; it is more likely amongst observers rather than participants, but if Simmons has the latter in mind, again there is no reason to think Gilbert shares it.) Finally, as a description of the sentiments of the typical citizen members of a modern state, it confuses reasonable expectations with entitlements. Gilbert flatly denies that she is guilty of this confusion and to my mind her repudiation of all three confusions is reasonable (Gilbert 2006: 271–2).

All these confusions may occur as one attempts to describe the mind-set of citizens, but notice that these charges are addressed to claims that the Political Problem has been solved in the case of some particular regime. They do not address the impossibility of member citizens being in relationships of joint commitment in the manner required by Gilbert's theory. So they do not challenge her answer to what I framed as the Philosophical Problem. So far as the content of her theory goes it is unimpugned by all these suggestions as to what might be happening in the real world. If the contemporary world is plagued by such confusions and citizens' allegiance is poisoned by illusion and false consciousness, then so much the worse for a modern world that has only a few outlaws, anarchists and philosophers who can see clearly through the darkness. But I do not see that Gilbert's theory is thereby compromised.

I diagnose her chief problems elsewhere. Our walkers want to go for a walk together; they don't just want to go for a walk which they might as well do together as not. They are plural subjects with a genuinely common rather than a coincident goal. As Rousseau would have said, they exhibit a truly general will rather than a coincidence of particular wills. What can we say about the goals of the member citizens? What do they have a joint commitment to do, in the way that our walkers have a commitment to walking out together? They have a 'joint commitment to accept certain rules, rules that count intuitively as political institutions' (Gilbert 2006: 238–9). Fair enough – but what are these rules for? The walkers we might suppose, following Gilbert's splendid discussion, have as rules:

'Don't walk too far behind or ahead of your companion.' 'Don't pack in the walk without excuse or apology'. These rules govern the exercise of walking together and the fulfilment of the joint commitment. What activities do the political rules cover? What genuinely common goal (beyond the observation of the rules and the obligation to uphold them) do the citizen members share?

I think it would be a good, old-fashioned, category mistake to say at this point that the point of their joint activity is to fulfil an obligation to uphold the political institution as constituted by its rules. We should get an answer to the question by asking the further question: What are the rules for? Because the answer to this substantive question will tell us what the citizen members are doing other than, formally, obeying the rules, thus fulfilling their obligations, *whatever they may be.*

This is the answer I propose, fully understanding the controversies hereabouts, and it is as uncontroversial a specimen as I can devise in good conscience: the rules are intended to secure justice, that is: the well-being of all members severally, consistent with the achievement of liberty and equality for all.[17] Just as our walkers aim to walk together, so do citizens aim to promote justice as specified above. Justice is the goal of citizens and hence the promotion of it is the point of the rules constitutive of political institutions.

We have already noticed that for Margaret Gilbert obligations of joint commitment are not moral obligations. They are just genuine obligations. So political obligations, as obligations of joint commitment, are not moral obligations, either. It may be that one reason why she takes this view is that it would be very strange if political obligations were constrained by morality, since, as she sees matters, political obligation is *solely* a consequence of membership of a political society. And political societies may be grievously immoral. (Think of your own examples and the huge variety of reasons why this may be the case.) But, she claims, citizen members of a political society, *however unjust it may be,* have a political obligation to uphold the institutions of that society, since as members they have a joint commitment to it.[18] If political obligation were a type of moral obligation, this would mean that members of an unjust polity would have a moral obligation to uphold an immoral regime. Clearly there are two ways we can go when faced with such an absurdity. One way is Gilbert's way: to deny that political obligation is moral obligation. The other way is my way: to deny that one may have a political, that is, moral, obligation to an unjust regime. I have defended this view in Chapter 5 as the Justice Constraint.

I believe that Gilbert has blundered here and insist, as before, that whatever obligations may be entailed by the fact of membership of a political society (as this is explained by the ethics of joint commitment) must be conditional on the justice of that community. In other words, the joint commitment invoked by membership of a political society is conditional on the good reasons citizens otherwise may give for recognizing that society as just. Membership (by itself), joint commitment (by itself) whether amongst walkers or citizens can never generate mutual obligations if the activity they regulate is unjust or more broadly immoral. To repeat the old saw that I used in argument against Dworkin: there is no justice amongst thieves – and there are no obligations either.

Conclusion

We should summarize what we can learn from the communitarian challenge in its different guises. It advances a coherent account of the self-understanding of many citizens who accept that their membership of the polity requires them to accept a regime of citizens' duties. It is not a necessary feature of such an identification with the political institutions of their community that those who accept it have voluntarily chosen to be citizen members, although some may well have done so. This does not mean that there is no answer available to the citizen who, for one reason or another, questions whether membership entails political obligation or who seeks good reasons to ground the imputed duties. In fact, there must be good moral reasons available if the claim to authority and the imputation of citizens' duties is to succeed.

This is not a counsel of despair. In the second half of this book I have stated the philosophical credentials of a number of different arguments which I believe may demonstrate that the state is well-founded and that citizens should recognize their proper duties. Whether these reasons apply in the particular circumstances of the anxious or curious questioner who confronts his state with the ineliminable demand that it establish its legitimacy is an empirical issue, towards the settling of which philosophers have nothing further to contribute.

Chapter 12

Conclusion

We have examined what I dubbed 'communitarian' arguments – arguments which purport to yield 'associative' obligations as explicit in membership of the political community. My conclusion was that such accounts, valuable though they are as conceptual explorations of the hermeneutics or the phenomenology of political association, will not generate political obligations unless the communities they describe can be legitimated in accordance with one or more of the standard repertory of arguments designed to solve the Philosophical Problem of how states may be assigned authority and how duties may be imputed to citizens.

We have reviewed a number of arguments which aim to solve this Philosophical Problem of political obligation – arguments from consent and contract in a variety of forms, from fairness and gratitude as proper responses to the receipt of benefits from the state, from utility and from the natural duties of justice and (Samaritan) care for others. The conclusion that I drew was that the arguments were generally plausible as philosophical exercises, but that some put out more hostages to fortune than others. In the case of the argument from utility its success depended entirely on the independent question of whether utilitarianism as a normative ethic can be given acceptable foundations, and that is a hugely contested issue. In the same way, the normative version of the hypothetical contract argument depends entirely on how far one can articulate attractive and defensible independent values of equality and liberty. All of the other arguments have been revealed as conditional. How far they apply to the circumstances of some or most citizens will depend upon the particular facts of the matter which may or may not hold in the case of the citizens of some particular state. Needless to say, and despite the pretensions of some of our colleagues, authority over these factual matters, matters of history and current affairs, is not given to philosophers. These facts (and opinions concerning them which may be true or false) together with the independent cogency of other philosophical arguments asserting the value of, say, justice, will feed into an assessment of who owes which political duties or obligations (in each case to be specified) to their state or to their fellow citizens. This is how things should be if the philosophical issues in this domain can be properly represented in the slogan which I claimed expresses the dialectic of liberalism: 'the state proposes; the citizen disposes'.

Notes

1 Political obligations and citizens' duties

1 This term nowadays has a wider remit which is illuminating as it reflects back on its political source. When I write in personal references that students or staff have been good citizens, I trust that readers understand that these folk have demonstrated a certain spirit, a characteristic virtue of members of their respective communities who are concerned with and work for the good of their fellows. No doubt there is more to be said, but it can't all be stated in a note.

2 George Klosko (2005) takes the view that the task of a philosophical theory of political obligation is to lay out the philosophical basis of the belief that most citizens of modern liberal democracies actually espouse – that they have an obligation to obey the laws of their state. In Chapter 5, I dispute this sanguine view of philosophical methodology hereabouts, but I should restate now that I believe there are more things at stake in a theory of political obligation than the specific question of whether or not citizens have an obligation to obey the law.

3 I disavow any obligation to recompense purchasers who claim that they have been sold a pup on the basis of the sub-section title and the arguments that follow. This aggressive statement has been cleared by the lawyers engaged by my publishers to deter vexatious litigants.

4 Hart believes that '"duty", "obligation", "right" and "good" come from different segments of morality, concern different types of conduct, and make different types of moral criticism or evaluation' (Hart 1955: 288). There is a full discussion in Simmons (1979: 7–16).

5 I take it that obligations oblige their subjects, but that persons may be obliged to do actions which they have no obligation to perform. Thus it makes perfect sense for the bank-teller to say he was obliged to hand over the money to the robber. (This point was clearly made by H.L.A. Hart 1961: 80–1. Hobbes, as I read him, deliberately conflates the conditions of being bound by an obligation (or duty), i.e. being obligated, and being obliged.)

6 I say these duties are 'orientated towards' the state because I don't want to insist that these are duties *to* the state or *to* one's fellow citizens. This is probably false in the case of the disobedient officer. (I'm grateful to one of my referees for pointing this out.)

7 We shall see later in Chapter 10 that John Rawls adopts Hart's account of obligations and then claims that 'There is, I believe, no political obligation, strictly speaking, for citizens generally' (Rawls 1971: 114). But we should not deduce that he is a sceptic concerning the duties of the citizen since he sharply distinguishes obligations from duties and also believes that we have a 'natural duty' 'to comply with and to do our share in just institutions when they exist and apply to us' (Rawls 1971: 334). It is because I don't want to get involved in potentially misleading circumlocutions like this that I use both terms to mean the same thing.

8 Simmons (1979: 12–14, 16–23) dubs institutional duties 'positional' duties.

9　With minor alterations, what follows is Simmons' example (1979: 17–19). I'm not sure this is a good example. I suspect that US presidents have moral institutional duties independently of their taking an oath so that when they fall asleep (or worse) on the job they do two things wrong. Perhaps the clearer case is that of the goalkeeper mentioned above who is contracted to go to bed early before matches, but nips out to a club . . . and then has a poor game.

10　The literature on natural law and positivism is vast. For those who are new to these debates, as good a place as any to begin is *The Oxford Handbook of Jurisprudence and Philosophy of Law* (Coleman and Shapiro 2002), articles 1–4. A full modern defence of the positivist position is given in Kramer (1999).

11　The example is discussed in Hart (1958: 598) and Fuller (1958: 630). Hart corrects his account of the judgement in Hart (1961: 254 –5).

12　I suppose there might be such a redundant master law (the law-maker might be an ass) but it would lead to conundrums. Do all law-breakers break at least two laws – the particular law and the master law? And of course one should ask: what kind of obligation does the master law impose? A regress cannot be avoided.

13　Thomas McPherson argues for this position (McPherson 1967: 66–75).

14　As one of my referees pointed out, the state cannot *decree* that citizens have moral duties.

15　This is a hypothetical example, so you must suppose that our hero Emily has no *legal* defence against the charge of theft if, for example, that was brought by the vindictive hit-men in a private prosecution. We know that all actual legal systems contain this sort of (if not this particular) idiocy.

16　'The phrase '*prima facie* duty' must be apologized for' (Ross 1930: 20).

17　For a fuller discussion with further references, see Simmons (1979: 24–8). Subsequent literature has shown that Simmons was whistling in the wind when he urged that 'the prima facie – actual terminology be avoided altogether'.

18　This is a sloppy account of *pro tanto* reasons which I trust delivers the gist. This is a canonical statement: '*Pro tanto* reasons are manifestations of the conflicting values that may continue to exert their discrete influences over us even when we have arrived at all-things-considered judgements' (Hurley 1989: 137).

2　The state and its legitimacy

1　'This public person, formerly took the name of *city*, and now takes that of *Republic* or *body politic*; it is called by its members *State* when passive, *Sovereign* when active, and *Power* when compared with others like itself. Those who are associated in it take collectively the name of *people*, and severally are called *citizens* as sharing in the sovereign authority, and *subjects*, as being under the laws of the State' (J.-J. Rousseau, *The Social Contract*, Book I, Chapter VI [many editions]). Cited from J.-J. Rousseau (1973: 175). On the nature of government, see Book III, Chapter I.

2　For a useful list of defining features and general characteristics, see Dunleavy (1993).

3　See the Introduction to *Leviathan* for the 'Artificiall Man' and Part I, Chapter XVI for the 'Artificiall person' (Hobbes 1968).

4　Readers wishing to investigate these matters further should look at Searle (1995: 1–57) or for a summary version, Searle (1999: 111–34).

5　Dworkin (1986: 167–75).

6　As in the recent work of Margaret Gilbert, for example. See Gilbert (2006).

7　Leslie Green argues that 'we should at least distinguish the question of what justifies the rule of government – the problem of *legitimacy* – from the question of what justifies the duty to obey – the problem of *obligation*' (Green 2002: 520). This distinction is pressed by Greenawalt (1989) and Edmundson (1998). I can't deny that there is a distinction as stated. I do insist that there is a close relation between the solutions of the two problems of legitimacy and obligation.

8 For details of the operation, see Powers (2006), reviewing James Risen, *State of War: The Secret History of the CIA and the Bush Administration*. For the scholars' letter to Congress, see *The New York Review of Books*, Vol. 53, no. 2, 9 Feb. 2006, pp. 42–4. The charge of illegality was denied by the George W. Bush Administration.

9 *Charter of the United Nations* (1945) Chapter II, *Article* 4, cited from Brownlie (1995: 4).

10 This is a puzzling case. The temptation is to say that if a state (or government) is neither legally nor morally legitimate it is not properly a state, or it is a 'state' in some inverted commas sense – more like a regime of bandits, a scaled-up version of an Italian city-state ruled by *condottieri*. But this would yield some strange conclusions. If, as many judge, the Nazi state was guilty of constitutional usurpations, it was not legally legitimate. Likewise, there are plenty of plausible grounds for claiming that it was morally illegitimate – take your pick. One wouldn't want it to follow that one who believed that it was illegitimate in both normative modalities is committed to denying that Nazi Germany was a state (or that the Third Reich was a government).

11 For a variety of different classifications, see Knowles (2001a: 135–54). The classical statement is given in W.E. Hohfeld (1923). It has recently been used in an impressive analysis of rights in Wenar 2005.

12 Hobbes (1968: 269 [112]). I have outlined, as stated, 'one thread' of argument in Hobbes's argument. He is generally quite clear that citizens have duties to obey (no liberty to disobey) the absolute sovereign. His insistence that no rational subject could consent to the sovereign's exercise of his legitimate power to kill, wound or imprison him (or to conscript him for military service without the opportunity of substitution) severely damages his argument. Hobbes's willingness to detach the sovereign's right to rule from the citizen's duty to obey, to distinguish the legitimacy of the state from the political obligations of the subject, has been followed in recent times by a number of authors (notably Ladenson 1980; Greenawalt 1989: 47–61; Wellman 1996; Sartorius 1981; Edmundson 1998). The discussions in these texts do not map four-square on to mine at this point since these authors are primarily concerned with moral legitimacy.

13 These matters are much more complicated than I suggest. For a very full discussion of the notion of legal duty (and a careful defence of the 'positivist' position), see H.L.A. Hart (1982: Ch. VI 'Legal Duty and Obligation'). The fullest contemporary defence of legal positivism is Kramer (1999).

14 The European Convention on Human Rights (1953), *Article* 15, cited Brownlie (1995: 15).

15 I invite readers to work out how the state's right to punish may be construed in each of these three ways.

16 Here is an example: Wellman writes (before listing a number of philosophers who *agree* with him!),

> Political theorists seldom distinguish between political legitimacy and political obligation . . . [they] often suppose political legitimacy and political obligation to be inseparable insofar as they are logical correlates of one another. This is a mistake. The correlative of a state's right to coerce is not a citizen's moral duty to obey: it is a citizen's lack of right to not be coerced. Political legitimacy entails only the moral liberty to create legally binding rules, not the power to create *morally* binding rules.
> (Wellman 2001: 741 & n. 8)

Prime amongst the things that have gone wrong in this passage is the undefended assumption that the state's legitimacy is to be explained in terms of a Hohfeldian liberty-right as against a Hohfeldian claim-right – the second but not the first of which does entail correlative duties on the part of the citizen. To put the matter in straightforward terms: Wellman begs the question against an opponent who (following sound argumentation) concludes that political legitimacy is a matter of the state's creating moral duties by way of creating legal duties. As a final query, one should ask : Who might have the slightest interest in institutions that have a moral liberty-right (= no-duty-not-) to create legally binding rules which are not morally binding? What might such a legislature be like from the perspective of the citizen? We might have two very different worries about the state: first, it can create legal duties on our part that are legally sanctioned by the prospect of punishment; second, it can create moral duties that determine what is the right thing for us to do (by way of making law). The first is a problem for the amoralist criminal as well as the decent citizen, but the second is not; the amoralist criminal could not care less what morality requires. We should not just *assume* that claims of political legitimacy dictate nothing more than the prudential calculations that the amoral criminal is perfectly able to carry out.

17 Taylor (1994: 58), cited from Simmons (2001: 132). I am indebted to Simmons's discussion.

18 Simone Weil, 'La Legitimité du Gouvernement Provisioire' in *Ecrits de Londres*, cited in Winch (1972: 252). Rousseau makes a similar claim about 'the feeling for legitimacy':

> In a well-ordered city every man flies to the assemblies: under a bad government no one cares to stir a step to get to them, because no one is interested in what happens there . . . . As soon as any man says of the affairs of the State What does it matter to me? the State may be given up for lost.
>
> (Jean-Jacques Rousseau, *The Social Contract*,
> Bk III, Ch. XV, cited from Rousseau 1973: 240)

3 Political authority

1 For examples and references see Chapter 2, notes 12 and 16. This imputation assumes that one has legal or moral authority which can claim a right to determine political obligations, as explained in what follows.

2 The material is summarized in his article 'Obedience' (Milgram 1987).

3 It is likely that susceptibility to authority varies between communities. For evidence, this is what a soccer manager has to say:

> There is a story I like to tell. In Japan, if you tell the players to sprint at high speed into a brick wall, they will do it unquestioningly. Then, when they crack their heads open and fall to the ground, they look at you and feel completely betrayed. The English player runs at full speed into the brick wall, gets up, dusts himself off and does it again. He won't feel betrayed by his manager or ask himself the point of running into the wall.
>
> Now, the French player, like the Italian, will react differently. He'll look at you and say, "Why don't you show us first how it's done?" . . . [The English] do as they're told, they follow orders, they do not question authority and they never give up.
>
> (Arsène Wenger, as quoted by Gianluci Vialli,
> excerpted from *The Italian Job*, *The Times*, 24 April 2006)

4 A full discussion of the varieties of authority is given in Hurd 1999: Chs 3–6, from whom I have taken the terms 'practical' and 'epistemic' authority.

5 Heidi Hurd describes this as 'influential authority' (Hurd 1999: 65–6). If one believes that requests (or offers) can be authoritative quite independently of any threats associated with them, this variety of authority should be distinguished from the practical authority of the commander.

6 David Brink distinguishes three strands in Kant's claim that moral demands are categorical imperatives: (1) an *'inescapability* thesis' to the effect that the application of moral requirements 'to an agent does not depend on the agent's own contingent inclinations or interests', (2) an *'authority* thesis' such that moral demands 'are requirements of reason such that it is *pro tanto* irrational to fail to act in accordance with them, and this authority is independent of the agent's own aims or interests', and (3) a *'supremacy* thesis' which insists that the authority of moral requirements is always overriding (Brink 1997: 255).

   To clarify: in taking authoritative norms as 'binding' I mean that they are inescapable. I doubt, but it is moot, whether they ever have authority in Brink's sense, and I would deny that the norms of any practical authority (e.g. the legal norms of the state) are overriding, i.e. have supremacy. I'm grateful to John Skorupski for urging me to clarify these matters.

7 For a well-known discussion see M.B.E. Smith 1973. (Smith rejects the imputation of even a *prima facie* obligation.) This terminology is rejected in A.J. Simmons 1979: 24–8. For the detail of Ross's original distinction, which Simmons is correct to read as much confused, see Ross 1930: 19–20 and my discussion pp. 14–16 above.

8 Raz introduced the term 'exclusionary reasons' in *Practical Reason and Norms* (Raz 1975: 35–8) and continues to use the term in *The Authority of Law* (Raz 1979: 23–33). In *The Morality of Freedom* (Raz 1986), the term appears to have been dropped in favour of 'pre-emptive reasons'. I shan't attempt to track down the similarities and differences between peremptory, exclusionary and pre-emptive reasons. I do not accept Raz's view that exclusionary reasons may never be overridden when they conflict with a first-order reason, as we shall see later. The strongest claim we can make concerning exclusionary or pre-emptive reasons is that they have a very high exclusionary threshold. For further discussion, see Schauer 1991: 88–93.

9 This thesis of Hart's is disputed by Green (1988: 44–8). I doubt the thesis can be defended on conceptual grounds given the vagueness of the term 'social practice', the possibility of charismatic authority, and, as mentioned in what follows, possible claims to the effect that God's authority is unrestricted by any existent social arrangements. Let us draw in our horns: the forms of practical authority we shall discuss are all structures of social practice.

10 A similar point is made by Raz (1986: 62), Green (1988: 42) and Hurd (1999: 80-1).

11 Joseph Raz (1986: 78) counsels us to: 'Remember that sometimes immoral or unjust laws may be authoritatively binding, at least on some people'. Taking 'immoral or unjust laws' as laws that command citizens to do immoral or unjust actions, my position implies that Raz is mistaken.

12 Hobbes is best read as arguing that the sovereign does have the authority to put citizens to death or at grave risk, but that citizens have no duty to comply with such commands. Sovereign authority and citizens' duties are thus detached. The sovereign does no wrong to issue such a command and citizens do no wrong when they disobey. For Hobbes's complex discussion, and this quotation, see Hobbes 1968: 26–9, Ch. 21 [111]. In respect of sovereign commands of this limited type, the right to rule of the Hobbesian sovereign assigns a liberty-right. In all other cases, where citizens' lives are not put at risk, the right is a power to assign claim-rights.

13 Rousseau believes this:

   > Every man has a right to risk his own life in order to preserve it . . . The death-penalty inflicted on criminals may be looked on in the same light: it is in order that we may not fall victims to an assassin that we consent to die if we ourselves turn assassins.
   >
   > (*The Social Contract*, Bk II, Ch. V (Rousseau 1973: 189–90))

14 Following an observation by Jonathan Wolff, I accept that the category of the absurd, etc. is something of a ragbag, including as it does the absurd, the pointless, the out of

date and the blundering commands. I suspect that what commands of these types (and more) have in common is that *those who issue them*, so long as they are otherwise rational and not ethical monsters, would accept that it would not be sensible for subjects to follow them in the circumstances.

15   This example is used by M.B.E. Smith (1999: 94).

16   The nest of problems hereabouts is familiar from discussions of utilitarianism. We shall take up these issues again in Chapter 9 when we discuss utilitarian defences of the state's claim to authority. A full (and most sensible) discussion of these issues is to be found in Schauer 1991.

17   Joseph Raz makes a similar point, distinguishing a great mistake from a clear one (Raz 1986: 62). His argument is challenged by Heidi Hurd 1999: 85–6.

18   Raz 1986: 76. Raz does not endorse this claim himself.

19   '[T]hat King whose power is limited, is not superiour to him, or them that have the power to limit it; and he that is not superiour, is not supreme; that is to say not Soveraign' (Hobbes 1968: 246, Ch. 19 [98–9]).

20   For a full discussion see Hampton (1986: 197–207).

21   All quotations from J.S. Mill, *On Liberty*, Ch. I (Mill 1968: 67, 72–3).

4 Questions of justification

1   I shall discuss arguments from consent in great detail in Chapter 7. For the purpose of the present argument I just suppose that they have some initial plausibility.

2   'Subjective motivational set': This is Williams's term. He has in mind one of the subject's desires or projects as a member of such a set.

3   Which is not to say there might not be conditions on which sort of state might properly put forward arguments for the citizen to examine. I shall argue later that only a just state can possess the moral standing necessary to make claims on its citizens.

4   References to Kant cite the standard Royal Prussian Academy edition in square brackets.

5   For further discussion of these passages see Knowles (2002b: 193–7).

6   'Voluntarism' is the term used to characterize this position by Carole Pateman (1979), Patrick Riley (1982) and many subsequent writers. I couldn't find a rigorous definition or careful explication of the term in either of these important modern texts. Readers should note that a standard usage of 'voluntarism' (traceable to nineteenth century sources) gives the term an almost opposite meaning in the different but related context of moral philosophy. Thus J.B. Schneewind glosses voluntarism as the claim that 'God created morality and imposed it on us by an arbitrary fiat of his will' (Schneewind 1998: 8).

7   I argue that theories which derive citizens' duties from their active solicitation and receipt (acceptance) of benefits and the consequent application of a duty of fair play, (to be discussed in Chapter 9) should also be considered voluntarist accounts. Here the candidate voluntary act consists in the acceptance of benefits on the understanding that this entails a duty of fairness to support the system (the state) that provides the benefits.

8   I put things in this way because this thesis concerning fathers, familiar from Sir Robert Filmer's text *Patriarcha*, as refuted directly by Locke in his '*First Treatise of Government*' (many editions) was generally described as 'Patriarchalism' on the assumption or by argument that the domestic authority was the father, the head of the household. Hobbes, bless him, was not a patriarchalist. His story is witty and comical and true:

> For as to the Generation [of children] . . . there be always two that are equally Parents: the Dominion over the Child, should belong equally to both, which is impossible; for no man can obey two Masters. And whereas some have attributed the Dominion to

the Man onely, as being of the more excellent sex; they misreckon in it. For there is not always that difference of strength or prudence between the man and the woman, as that the right can be determined without War.

(Hobbes 1968: 253; Part II, Ch. XX [102])

(Numbers in square brackets refer to the pagination of the original (*Head*) edition.) As one should expect from Hobbes, the story continues in unpredictable ways.

9 We shall discuss this passage further in Chapter 8.

10 This is a Hobbesian blip which readers may properly reject on my account since I shall deny that genuine consent can be coerced. Hobbes says that 'Feare and Liberty are consistent' (Hobbes 1968: 262; Part II, Ch.XXI [108]), but he is wrong. Others disagree with my view, notably Margaret Gilbert who argues that genuine agreements may be coerced (Gilbert 2006: 75–82).

5 The scope and limits of justificatory arguments

1 M.B.E. Smith dubs an obligation on the part of all citizens 'generic'.

2 I am conscious that the typology of state arguments in virtue of the scope of the variables (*all*, *some*) in their conclusions is not fully articulated. Some scope ambiguities remain. Thus in (4) it is ambiguous whether all citizens should accept the same subset of duties or whether there is some subset of duties which is attributable to all citizens, though not the same subset to each – as in every girl loves a sailor. The ambiguity is even more apparent in (5) below.

3 Wolff (2000: 185) uses this term.

4 Klosko's views change between *The Principle of Fairness* and *Political Obligations* in ways that I don't fully understand. But, with apologies to Klosko, I shan't conduct a careful audit. Klosko's methodological stance is criticized in Green (1999).

5 Klosko now recognizes this point. See Klosko (2005: 13).

6 References should not be necessary, but readers who wish to consult a digest of the horrors should read Jonathan Glover, *Humanity: A Moral History of the Twentieth Century* (Glover 1999). Those who wish to keep their fingers on the pulse of the horrors of humanity (hopefully with practical intent) should note that, as I write, genocide is taking place in the Sudan. For details and further references, see Kristof (2006: 14–17), and the splendid *sleeplessinsudan.blogspot.com* (closed 1 Feb 2006) cited by Kristof.

7 We should remember in this context the lesson of Chapter 3 that immoral directives will constrain the proper domain and hence the proper exercise of authority. This will be of particular importance where the form that injustice takes is the violation of citizens' rights.

8 Rawls himself defends what I term the justice constraint: 'Obligatory ties presuppose just institutions, or ones reasonably just in the circumstances'. Of course he has his own account of what justice amounts to. See Rawls (1972: 112). On this account justice is operating as a *necessary* condition on legitimate authority and the proper imputation of citizens' duties. We shall see later (in Chapter 10) that Rawls believes that the justice of a state is a *sufficient* condition on the attribution of duties to citizens.

9 This distinction is drawn in a careful and sensitive discussion of these problems in Greenawalt (1989: 186–94).

10 For more detail on what follows, see Sorell (1986: 14–17, 127–44), and Waldron (2001).

11 Rawls discusses 'the publicity condition' in a number of places and contexts. It is obviously related to the concept of public reason as that concept is deployed in his post-*Theory of Justice* writings, but, emphatically, it is not the same concept. Rawls's use of this condition, linking as it does with a wide range of classic modern, as well as contemporary

sources, deserves very careful study. See, for starters, Rawls (1972: 130–3; 1993: 66–71; 2001: 120–2), and the indices to these volumes.

12 The point is controversial. Jeremy Waldron identifies a theme of 'respect for the individual intellect' in Hobbes's thought (Waldron 2001: 448).

13 Hegel (1991: §§279R, 281R). For a full discussion, see Knowles (2004).

6 The anarchist challenge

1 Readers who wish to pursue the study of anarchism are recommended to read Joll (1979) for a history of anarchism, Woodcock (1977) for an anthology of anarchist writings and Miller (1984) for a sympathetic critical study with suggestions for further reading.

2 Proudhon, P.-J. *General Idea of the Revolution in the Nineteenth Century* (English trans.), 1923: 294, cited from Miller (1984: 6).

3 This argument is put very clearly in Alan Carter (2001).

4 This argument was famously put by Robert Nozick in the opening chapters of *Anarchy, State, and Utopia* (1974).

5 The main lines of this deduction are usefully described in C.B. Macpherson's editorial introduction to Hobbes (1968: 30–41).

6 Chaim Gans dubs this kind of anarchism 'autonomy-based anarchism' (Gans 1992: 5–41).

7 David Leopold usefully stresses the distinction between 'ordinary' self-interest – which Stirner rejects – and self-interest as 'self-mastery' – which Stirner endorses. I'm not sure self-mastery is the right term; it has echoes of Protestant self-control which Stirner, with his emphasis on self-enjoyment, would eschew. 'Self-will' with its implication of wilfulness, which Stirner relishes, is a better characterization of the interest of the self-interested individual. That said, I should record how much I have learned from Leopold's essay on Stirner's anarchism (Leopold 2006).

8 Wolff recognizes this, stating explicitly that 'there are at least some situations in which it is reasonable to give up one's autonomy' (Wolff 1976: 15). But having made this sensible concession, he immediately takes it back. 'For the autonomous man, there is no such thing, strictly speaking as a *command*' – not even on a sinking ship where everyone else is obeying the captain's command to man the lifeboats '*because he is the captain*'. Incredibly, rather than jump to it, the autonomous man will reflect on what is the best thing to do (Wolff 1976: 15–16). Wolff is surely wrong on this point.

9 'By and large, political philosophers have supposed that utopia was logically possible, however much they may have doubted that it was even marginally probable. But the arguments of this essay suggest that the just state must be consigned the category of the round square, the married bachelor, and the unsensed sense datum' (Wolff 1976: 71).

10 A fuller discussion of Wolff and more arguments to this conclusion can be found in Horton (1992: 125–31).

11 Gans calls this position 'critical anarchism' (Gans 1992: 2, 42ff). Horton dubs it 'negative philosophical anarchism' (Horton 1992: 131–6).

12 This strategy, and this conclusion, are evident in the following passage from Simmons's essay *Justification and Legitimacy*:

> Because I subscribe to political voluntarism as the correct account of these transactional grounds for legitimacy, and because I believe that no actual states satisfy the requirements of this voluntarism, I also believe that no existing states are legitimate (simpliciter).
>
> (Simmons 2001: 155–6)

For reasons of the same sort, he argues in the concluding chapter of *Moral Principles and Political Obligations* that 'citizens generally have no special political bonds which require that they obey and support the governments of their countries of residence. Most citizens have neither political *obligations* nor "particularized" political *duties'* (Simmons 1979: 192).

13 I should make explicit a *tu quoque* (and equally cheap) element in this remark. Simmons (1979: 22) writes, with relaxed but heavy irony, of a Billy Budd case: 'He [the press-ganged American sailor] is no doubt "obliged" to obey, for British "military justice" has been renowned for centuries'. I suspect that American "military justice" (Guantanamo Bay, Abu Ghraib, 'rendition' and all that disgusting stuff) is even more renowned nowadays.

7 Consent and contract

1 Rainborough's contribution has been cited in many different philosophical (and, of course, political) disputes, concerning justice, equality and democracy, as well as our concern – the value of consent in vindicating claims to political authority and explaining citizens' obligations. Citizenship is now taught in English schools as part of the national curriculum. My modest proposal is that every schoolchild should be drilled to learn this quotation by heart. And every political philosophical tourist should visit the church of St Mary's, Putney (in London) where the great debates took place.

2 These terms have a history. Heidi Hurd speaks of 'moral magic' in Hurd (1996). Alan Wertheimer speaks of consent as 'morally transformative' in Wertheimer (2003: 119–21).

3 For obvious reasons, consent arguments have been carefully studied by authors who have written on the ethics of sex as well as medical ethics. On the first, first-rate studies include Pateman (1988), Archard (1998) and Wertheimer (2003). On the latter, see any textbook of medical ethics. The most complete source is Beauchamp and Faden (1986).

4 I cannot forbear to suggest how much careful argument is still needed to defend the necessity of informed consent in cases where doctors do what they must: treat their patients as best they can. 'Informed consent' is the curse that half-baked philosophy has thrown at the medical profession. For an example of how this nostrum can work against the public interest, see Knowles (2001b).

5 Harry Beran seeks to clarify the concept of consent 'by using the model of a promise' (Beran 1987: 5), but the concept of a promise itself stands in need of analysis. Simmons states that 'consent theory has fastened on the promise as the model for the grounds of political obligation' (but later questions the applicability of this model) (Simmons 1979: 70, 76–7).

6 According to J.L. Austin's admittedly rebarbative terminology, acts of consent and promising both have *illocutionary force*, being *performatives* of the *exercitive* and/or *commissive* kinds. See, for suggestive material, Austin (1962: Lecture XII) and much else.

7 If someone were to argue that acts of consent which are invalid do not amount to real or true consent – much as fake banknotes aren't really banknotes – hence implying that all consent is valid, I wouldn't know how to adjudicate the issue between us. Fortunately, I don't think the difference of analysis matters.

8 'The right of Dominion by Generation . . . is called PATERNALL. And is not so derived from the Generation, as if the Parent had Dominion over his Child because he begat him; but from the Childs Consent, either expresse, or by other sufficient arguments declared' (Hobbes 1968: 253; Ch. 20 [102]). This curious argument is worth close study (and not least, in its continuation, for an example of Hobbes' wit which is supreme amongst philosophers; thus, on those who claim that Man is 'the more excellent Sex': 'they misreckon in it. For there is not always that difference of strength or prudence between the man and the woman, as that the right can be determined without War'. Even this gloriously insinuating rebuke to men's preening prompts philosophically motivated, interpretative questions: thus 'Does Hobbes believe that right *can* be determined by war? That might = superior power is right?'.

I believe that the 'by other sufficient arguments declared' component clearly establishes Hobbes's aptitude for hypothetical consent arguments. We shall have more to say on this topic later.

9   For a very important practical example of this, see Knowles (2001b).

10 We shall examine this assumption later in this chapter.

11 With very, very, few exceptions concerned with national security, confidential personal information, and the like, and with obvious safeguards against the abuse of such exceptions.

12 The quotation is taken from a work of fiction, but the description is sadly true.

13 I should put my cards on the table: I take it that the detention and interrogation of hundreds of immigrants as 'terrorist suspects' in violation of their basic human rights and US law by Attorney General John Ashcroft following the terrorist attacks of 11 September 2001 was supported by those millions of electors who voted for George W. Bush in the 2004 Presidential election (and no doubt many more citizens as well). This support, interpreted as consent, is invalid given that the deeds were immoral.

14 Resolution of the House of Commons in the Convention, 28 January 1689, cited in Glassey (1977: 165).

15 A most useful source for studying the early history of the social contract tradition is Lessnoff (1986).

16 Or 'Civil Society', 'Community' 'Government', Body Politick', 'Political Society', Commonwealth': he uses all these terms through §§95–9 of the *Second Treatise*.

17 This reading of Locke is widespread among modern commentators – to whom I am indebted. See, e.g. Simmons (1993: 68–9) and authors cited at his footnote 25.

18 Unsurprisingly, this too is a really vexed question among expert interpreters of Locke. Readers of Locke's other philosophical writings should not be surprised by this dialectical versatility. Locke's aggressive philosophical temperament explains his using any argument against any opponent *ad hominem* if he thought it might work, notwithstanding its inconsistency with other things he has to say elsewhere. My colleague, Paul Brownsey, explained this to me years ago.

19 This interpretation of Part Two of Rousseau's *Second Discourse* as conjectural history is controversial. Some readers take a different view of Rousseau's injunction in the introductory paragraphs:

> Let us begin then by laying all facts aside, as they do not affect the question. The investigations we may enter into . . . must not be considered as historical truths, but only as mere conditional and hypothetical reasonings, rather calculated to explain the nature of things, than to ascertain their actual origin . . ..
> (Rousseau 1973: 50)

They do not accept that Rousseau is doing history in the *Second Discourse* – and it is certainly true that he is doing other things as well. Without giving my reading the careful defence that it needs, I claim that Rousseau is suggesting here that his account of the state of nature in Part One (rather than the history of mankind after nature has been left behind in Part Two) is derived from 'mere conditional and hypothetical reasonings', though he does believe that both are (likely to be) true accounts. His use of the term 'hypothetical' in this passage, and also at the end of the Preface where he writes of 'the hypothetical history of government', should not lead readers to believe that Rousseau is articulating a hypothetical social contract as I shall explain that term in what follows.

20 I should caution that it is not always explicit exactly what such persons are giving their consent *to*. The only occasion on which I was asked to give (unpaid) practical advice, on the basis of my expertise as a professional political philosopher, was when a candidate for citizenship had reached the final stage – as it then was – of signing the form. He asked whether or not, as a republican hostile to the monarchical principle he could sign the form with its explicit reference to Her Majesty in good faith. I

explained that in signing the form he was taking on exactly the same set of citizens' duties avowed by myself and all other born citizens, and that this set did not include a specific duty to accept the monarchical principle. Sophistry succeeded. The aspirant citizen signed on the dotted line and remained both a citizen and a republican in good conscience. I think I was correct, but I haven't checked the position with a constitutional lawyer.

21 Government ministers in the UK have been prone to record secret dissent from cabinet decisions in their diaries (if we can believe the diaries) and have later published their evasion of collective responsibility.

22 Peter Singer uses the example of buying drinks in rounds to make a different point. He says that the person who accepts drinks bought in rounds has not actually consented to buy a round in turn, hence *ex hypothesi* cannot have tacitly consented, since tacit consent is a form of actual consent. This is a mistake which we shall take up when we discuss the consent involved in democratic participation. See Singer (1974: 49–50).

23 In my undergraduate dissertation I concluded that Locke had blundered and that Plamenatz was obviously correct. In my *viva* in the University of London I was brought up short by Richard Wollheim who asked me: why so? Wollheim, I suspect, had his tongue firmly in his cheek, but I'm still not sure whether he (as cited) or Plamenatz is correct. (Locke himself says that one who simply goes about his business does not become '*a member of that society*' (§122), although he is subject to the laws.)

24 Plato emphasizes this point, too, when he quotes the Laws of Athens as stating 'we have brought you into the world and educated you, and given you and all your fellow-citizens a share in all the good things at our disposal' (*Crito* 51c). On my reading it is unclear whether Plato is citing Socrates' acceptance of these benefits as a mark of his tacit consent or whether he is describing the benefits as an appropriate occasion for gratitude (or both).

25 Carter (2001) challenges the claim that citizens on balance receive benefits from the state.

26 This example was drawn to my attention by Helen Higgins.

27 My student David Colledge urges me to say what we should think of the obligations of the ignoramus who, *ex hypothesi*, has not consented since she has not understood that this is what she was, or would be taken, as doing. I think it is clear that if the ignorance is excusable, the ignoramus has not consented and the duties of the citizen cannot be imputed to her. But what if her ignorance is negligent or otherwise culpable? What if, carelessly, she hasn't worked out how to behave? Then I think she should be treated *as if* she had consented. Notice that in this case we need to supplement the argument from quasi- or tacit consent in order to deal with culpable incompetents. And notice too, since incompetents who have not been educated to understand the implications of their actions may be excused for their non-compliance, this condition imposes a clear duty on the state to educate its citizens in the duties of citizenship.

28 This is the theme of Part II of Singer's book.

29 The story is told by Singer (1974: 53–4).

30 Many people in the UK withheld their poll-tax in 1989–90 whilst willingly paying a progressive income tax. There's no inconsistency here. They consented to one tax but not to the other.

8 Hypothetical contract

1 This is a very good example of the tendency, noted by Plamenatz, for those who think that the only legitimate authority derives from consent to find consent in the most implausible places.

2 See Hampton (1986, 1997).

3 It is discussed with very great care in Kraus (1993).

4 It is fair to say that Hampton was well aware of these difficulties: readers should study her texts with very great care to see whether or not she overcomes them.

5 See Rousseau's speculative account of the fraudulent contract in the *Second Discourse on the Origins of Inequality* (Rousseau 1973: 97–9).

6 There is a huge literature. For the authors mentioned see Rawls (1972, 2001), Grice (1967), Richards (1971) and Scanlon (1982, 1998).

7 In Macpherson (1962) and very briefly in the editor's 'Introduction' to Hobbes (1968) C.B. Macpherson argues, correctly, that Hobbes is describing his own social world in these chapters, but incorrectly identifies that social world as a bourgeois market society wherein the competitive power relations are predominantly economic.

8 Kant probably had a slightly different thought in mind. He was quite clear that his own version of the contract argument was entirely hypothetical, so in speaking of the establishment of the state he was not giving an account of the state's origins. On his account the solution of the problem is possible for a race of devils because he is taking them to be rational. His account is meant to be entirely *a priori*. It is not predicated on any characteristics of human nature other than man's rationality and respect for the moral law. Kant's 'devils' are rational and do their duty when they see it.

9 I should make it clear that this interpretation of Hobbes is a matter of very great controversy. For a review of the issues (and, to my mind, for a clear resolution of it) see Watkins (1965: 75–99).

10 In point of scholarship, I shall be even more slip-shod: I shall present a composite picture, drawing on elements of both of these authors' theories in an opportunistic fashion. This is legitimate because my prime aim here is argument construction rather than careful interpretation. I shall call this the Locke–Rousseau argument simply to give these authors their due: there is nothing new under the sun, though matters have perhaps not been said in quite this way before.

11 They are implied however, notably in Book I, Chs 2–4, where Rousseau denies that political authority derives from natural inequalities, from the right of the strongest, or from voluntary servitude of the sort attributed to slaves by philosophers of the time. From these arguments one can learn that men value equality and prize liberty.

12 John Rawls recognizes this. See Rawls (1972, §§ 11, 26, 39, 82).

13 This story has its origins in Hobbes's *Leviathan*, Rousseau's *Second Discourse on the Origins of Inequality*, and James Mill's democratic reworking of Hobbes in his *Essay on Government*. It echoes elements of Nozick's argument in (1974) Part I. In recent times, Jean Hampton has done most to revivify this traditional style of argument. See Hampton (1986, 1997).

9 The provision of benefits: arguments from fairness and gratitude

1 A useful, philosophically motivated, schematic account of the typical benefits provided by the modern state can be found in Klosko (2005: 22–50).

2 Rawls describes the principle as 'the principle defining the duty of fair play' (Rawls 1999: 118).

3 This exact sentence is to be found in Rawls's (1958) paper 'Justice as Fairness', describing one of the elements of the conception of fairness that Rawls first broached in that essay. It is also reproduced in his (1963) paper 'The Sense of Justice'. Rawls acknowledges his debt to Hart, but strangely does not put the citation in quotation marks in either place. See Rawls 1999: 60 and 99n.4.

4 We should also notice that this example engages the value of fairness in another respect, that of the distribution of the burden. Those who use the system should volunteer in some ordinal measure equivalent in frequency to the use they make of

the system – those who use it more often volunteering more frequently. I put to one side, for the moment, the question of whether there might be grounds for thinking that all members of the club whether or not they do or would seek to benefit from the system have a duty to volunteer.

5   I owe this example to Helen Higgins, who sent off the importunate gourmet with a flea in his ear.

6   Klosko (2005: 6, 67) argues that the lesson of Nozick's examples cannot be extended into the space of political obligations because the benefits received from the PA system in particular are of very little value. This is obviously true. Indeed, in respect of the detail of the story, Nozick's example is a complete mystery to me.

7   The term is Simmons's (1979: 130), as is 'readily available'. Klosko distinguishes 'excludable' and 'non-excludable' goods (1992: 35–6) and then treats this distinction as if it is much the same as Simmons's 'open'/'readily available' distinction. This is very misleading where the crucial issue concerns not whether citizens are excluded from the provision of some good but whether or not they actively solicit it when it is readily available (i.e. not excluded) to them. He lists as one of the functions that the state performs in modern societies '6. The state provides a wide range of excludable goods, for example, cultural institutions, national parks, public schools, etc' (Klosko 2005: 23). Since I don't suppose that in describing these as excludable goods he has in mind the state's power to ban certain folks from theatres, national parks and schools, given his account of excludable goods as goods that 'can be provided to some members of a given community while being denied to specified others' (Klosko 1992: 35), I conclude that he has thoroughly muddled the two very different distinctions.

8   Note again, Klosko, that it would be infelicitous to describe the pensioners' bus pass as an excludable benefit. They no doubt think of it as exclusive and a justifiable privilege!

9   I say 'commercial' rather than 'contractual' to avoid confusion with contract arguments of the kinds discussed in Chapters 7 and 8. Simmons attributes this view to many citizens, 'even in democratic political communities, these benefits are commonly regarded as purchased (with taxes) from a central authority, rather than accepted from the cooperative efforts of our fellow citizens' (Simmons 1979: 117). Greenawalt (1989: 135) explains why this cannot be the whole story about citizens' views on the matter.

10 Exactly the same tensions, conflicts and confusions have developed between universities and their staff and students. Are staff simply employees who relate to the management of the university as to their bosses – or collegiate fellows serving an institution? Are students clients making commercial (contractual) demands on their service provider or pupils in a pedagogical relationship with their teachers? Or both, in both cases?

11 In Klosko's latest work he takes up these factual questions directly and demonstrates that ordinary people are not as obtuse as Simmons suggests. See Klosko (2005: 223–43).

12 A number of philosophers have replied to Simmons that, au contraire, most citizens do in fact understand the moral consequences of their willing receipt of benefits from the government (Arneson 1982; Gans 1992: 61–2; Dagger 1997: 73–5; Greenawalt 1989: 135–6). Dagger states that, 'against this [Simmons's] view we may set the plausible counter-assertion that, as a matter of fact, far more people than he recognizes satisfies one or other of the two conditions' (Dagger 1997: 73–4). Since this is a factual matter, we do not need to take a view, though we should report the research conducted by Klosko (see n. 11 above).

13 We shall have to treat this case as hypothetical since the details as reported turned out to be false!

14 J.-J. Rousseau, Discourse on the Origins of Inequality (1973: 93).

15 Claudia Card notices the inaptness of speaking of debts of gratitude, claiming that the idea is paradoxical, hence metaphorical (Card 1988: 115–27).

16 'We are presumed to have a kind of control over our actions that we do not have over our feelings; we can, at least normally, try to act in specified ways where we cannot try

to have certain emotions or feelings (in the same way). And surely part of the point of a moral requirement is that its content be the sort of thing which we can, at least normally, try to accomplish' (Simmons 1979: 167).
17 This argument is rejected in Walker (1988). Walker's paper is unusual in modern times in that it defends the gratitude argument. Most writers see it as a soft target.
18 See Walker (1988: 196).

10 Utility, justice and Samaritan duties

1 The terminology of formal theory and value theory was first introduced in Lyons (1965).
2 Arguably this approach does not address the problem of political obligation at all since it prescinds entirely from the fact that the state claims authority. I suspect this objection is sound, but shall take it no further since I have not placed any restrictions on the facts concerning consequences that the calculator may take into account. If she considers whether or not failure to comply will weaken the authority of the state and its laws, or weaken the citizen's disposition to comply with positive duties, and reviews the effects of these possibilities, she will not be ignoring the claims of authority. But she will not be taking the demands of authority to be pre-emptive and content-independent in the sense discussed in Chapter 3.
3 I shall not discuss utilitarian value theory. For convenience's sake, and to honour the classical utilitarians, I shall take the good to be happiness – pleasure net pain. For the purposes of our discussion, I believe that nothing hangs on this.
4 Ideal rule utilitarianism has been supported most prominently by R.B. Brandt (1959) and (1979). A recent defence of the theory is to be found in Hooker (2000).
5 The best-known criticisms are those of J.J.C. Smart and David Lyons. In what follows I adapt the examples discussed in Lyons (1965).
6 The term 'rule-worship' was introduced in this context by J.J.C. Smart (1956).
7 'Rule of thumb' is the jargon for this type of rule. In his great article 'Two Concepts of Rules' John Rawls dubbed such rules 'summary' rules and usefully discussed their properties. That term has not caught on. See for details Rawls (1955).
8 There is a first-rate discussion of these problems – indeed of the whole realm of decision-making in accordance with rules – in Schauer (1991). On this issue see 104–11.
9 To my knowledge the distinction between this category of 'institutional' rules and rules of thumb and the importance of this distinction was first made by John Rawls (1955). (Rawls dubbed what I call institutional rules 'practice' rules.) I don't believe that the usefulness of this distinction in the defence of utilitarianism has been fully appreciated. Ironically Rawls himself failed to see that it disarmed many of the criticisms of utilitarianism that he himself made in A *Theory of Justice* (1972) after he moved to pastures new. In the title essay of *Utilitarianism as a Public Philosophy* (1995), Robert Goodin reasserted the strength of the utilitarian position in this domain.
10 'The rules of equity or justice depend entirely on the particular state and condition in which men are placed, and owe their origin and existence to that utility' (Hume 1975, Sect. III, Part I: 188); also

> What is a man's property? Anything that is lawful for him, and him alone, to use. But what rule have we, by which we can distinguish these objects? . . . . the ultimate point, in which they all [sources of rules] terminate, is the interest and happiness of mankind.
> (Part II: 197–8)

11 See Sagoff (1988) and O'Neill (1993) for strong criticisms.
12 This is true especially in his essays. See Hume (1963).

13 'Finds oneself': it is important for this argument that the citizen hasn't chosen or
    selected the state towards which the purported duties are directed, since this might
    obscure the dialectic. This is not to say that the argument from justice, if successful,
    might not supplement arguments from citizens' consent.

14 'Natural duty' is a term of art. Christopher Wellman, citing A. John Simmons,
    explains natural duty approaches as aiming to 'derive the duty to obey the law from
    a more inclusive moral duty to promote some more impartial value like justice or
    happiness' (Wellman 2004: 98, citing Simmons 2003).

15 For details and references see Chapter 5, pp. 76–7.

16 I say this state is just *ex hypothesi*. In fact since the state as described is engaged in the
    systematic deception and manipulation of the subjects it is doubtful whether it would
    be admitted as just under any substantial specification of how the just state must be
    constituted other than Plato's own.

17 There are vexed real-world problems which are in part shaped in this way, as in the
    attempts by some in the Northern provinces of Nigeria to impose Sharia Law on all
    citizens in their locality whether or not they are Muslims.

18 I confess: given the varieties of subjectivism I can't devise an argument from consis-
    tency that will pin this conclusion on all of them. We know there are some who reject
    whatever account of reason might yield consistency arguments.

19 Simmons (1979: 30–5, 147–56; 2001: 47–8, 68–9). This criticism is endorsed by
    Dworkin (1986: 193).

20 Jeremy Waldron suggests that this wide reading of the principle is the only explana-
    tion of the duty that officials of one regime have to uphold the just institutions of
    another regime, arguing that such a duty is the only explanation of one's intuitions
    that it was quite wrong of officials of the French state 'to obstruct the investigation of
    the Rainbow Warrior affair, to counsel their operatives to perjure themselves, and to
    interfere with their punishment' Waldron 1993: 10). Inept French secret agents were
    brought to trial in New Zealand after they blew up the Greenpeace ship Rainbow
    Warrior in Auckland harbour in 1985. (For full details of the shameful shenanigans,
    follow the references in Waldron's article.)

21 Waldron terms what I have called a 'self-referential' principle a 'range-limited'
    principle (Waldron 1993: 12–15).

22 Simmons continues to argue in this vein in Wellman & Simmons 2005: 161–5.
    Readers can judge whether or not the argument here improves on the original.

23 Notice that the applicability of a role need not be a matter of territoriality. If a British
    citizen goes abroad and assists the war effort of his country's greatest enemy, in the
    manner of William Joyce, alias Lord Haw-Haw, self-styled 'Jew-Baiter No. 1', in World
    War II, this will see him guilty of treason under UK law. Contrariwise, the citizen of
    Libya may find that he is liable for conviction under Scots law if he puts a bomb in
    an aircraft that blows up over Lockerbie in Dumfriesshire.

24 Waldron disputes this, arguing that 'Certainly, if we are to use range-limited princi-
    ples, we must have an argument justifying our use of them' (Waldron 1993: 14). The
    implication is that we need an argument to justify limiting the range of application of
    the relevant principle, in this case the principle of justice. This is a worry that philoso-
    phers who deal with the problem of global justice frequently press: is one who speci-
    fies the terms of justice which apply to the basic structure of her own society
    committed to using the same principles when addressing the issue of justice between
    societies? And Waldron has this problem in mind when he says that 'the assumption
    that justice may be confined within the borders of a single society is unsatisfactory'
    (Waldron 1993: 13), contrasting the difference in wealth between citizens of New
    Zealand and Bangladesh. I think the assimilation of this genuine problem with the
    problem of whether justice is a sufficient condition for political obligation is just too
    quick. Even in the former case, it is an open question whether the principles of jus-
    tice within a state apply to intra-state relations. (We can easily imagine someone

arguing that whereas a conception of justice as constrained equality should operate within well-off states, a conception of justice as responsiveness to dire need should operate between societies.) In the case of the different problem of political obligation, it is certainly a good question whether or not (and if so, why) a citizen of one state has any political obligation to another state, but it is not the same question as pertains to her relation to her own state. We should not require consistency across circumstances that are demonstrably different. I conclude that the burden of proof here lies with the philosopher who claims that consistency requires that if justice is a ground of obligation within a state it is also a ground of obligation across states. Such a one should explain why two very different problems require the same solution.

25 Rawls himself makes these points in a strong and sensitive discussion of civil disobedience (Rawls 1972: 363–91).

26 I'm told that this is not a hypothetical example, that there are communities in the home of the brave and the land of the free where the only place one can smoke cigarettes legally is within one's own home. If so, come back de Tocqueville and speak up about the tyranny of the sickeningly moralizing majority, the nanny state that does an injustice to the most intrusive and manipulative nanny. I say this last because I cannot believe that these extreme paternalistic injunctions are motivated by a real concern for the best interests of the poor benighted smoker. Do they not express contempt, the happy discovery of a vulnerable minority that those of our fellows who are natural condemners may seek out and persecute?

27 Wellman (1996, 2001, 2004; Wellman and Simmons 2005).

28 Readers of the Wellman literature should note that the deal has got worse. In Wellman (2004: 108 n. 15), he writes, 'the sacrifice of political obligation is analogous to a third party coercing you to trade your hundred-dollar bill for thirty ten-dollars bills'.

29 In Wellman (2005) the names are switched in a confusing fashion. Alice (victim: 2001) becomes Beth (2005); Beth (rescuer: 2001) becomes Amy (2005); Carolyn (car-owner: 2001) becomes Cathy (2005).

30 Georgia Testa tells me this is an odd way to describe the normative position. If Carolyn has a claim-right (of ownership, hence exclusive use, of the car), she doesn't lose it when the urgency of Beth's situation gives Alice a liberty to use it. Rather her right is legitimately infringed because it is over-ridden by the weight of reasons favouring Alice's use of it. This is surely correct.

31 '[T]he RIGHT OF NATURE is . . . the Liberty each man hath, to use his own power, as he will himselfe, for the preservation of his own nature' (Hobbes 1968: 189; Ch. XIV [64]). This concept of liberty-right was called by Hohfeld a 'privilege', by others a 'bare liberty'. See Hohfeld (1923) and, for a glossary of this terminology, Knowles (2001a: 138–45).

32 I conjecture that Wellman stresses the permissibility of the state's exercise of its coercive powers when he is arguing directly for the legitimacy of the state and trying to distance himself from arguments for citizens' political obligations. Thus he writes 'A state may permissibly limit a person's liberty because this restriction is necessary to provide the crucial goods of political stability to that person and others' (1996: 214, author's italics). Here the Samaritan duty (= liberty-right) is attributed to the state.

33 This view of the implications of the example strikes me as very odd. If Cathy has a duty to loan her car, surely her duty is to drive it (in normal circumstances where, e.g. she is sober).

34 Simmons writes:

> Wellman seems in the end to be employing a version of a duty of rescue (or mutual aid) that is quite idiosyncratic and morally suspect. The duty actually used in his arguments concerning a duty to obey the law is not the same as the moral commonplace to which Wellman appeals in his examples [the duty to rescue folks in immediate danger]; and indeed the specific form of Wellman's duty seems to be inspired primarily by his argumentative needs, not by independent reasons to believe such a duty exists.
>
> (Simmons, in Wellman and Simmons 2005: 182–3)

I share Simmons's suspicions, but this isn't yet to convict Wellman of error. Simmons, to be fair, goes on to articulate several grounds of objection.

35 We should notice that the considerations of fairness which are introduced at this point differ from those which are central to the duty of fairness or fair play discussed by Hart, Rawls and Klosko and reviewed in Chapter 9 above. This latter duty is incumbent on those who solicit benefits. Wellman introduces fairness as a principle to govern the distribution of responsibility for the communal task of benefiting others.

36 The alternative view, for which Renzo has some sympathy, is that we revise our chauvinist intuitions and endorse the extension of Samaritan duties beyond the national domain.

37 See Wellman (2000). Renzo vigorously disputes the implication that this strategy can rescue the Samaritan account (Renzo 2008).

11 Communities and citizenship

1   A.J. Simmons identifies Edmund Burke as a classical source of the views we are examining. See Simmons (1996: 65, 73–4, citing Burke 1886: 164–7).

2   For details, see Knowles (2002b: 6–10, 64–6).

3   G.W.F. Hegel (1991). In respect of ethical life generally see §149, 'The individual finds his liberation in duty'. Applying this thought to family life, he writes of marriage partners, that 'In this respect [they give up 'their natural and individual personalities'] their union is a self-limitation, but since they attain their substantial self-consciousness within it, it is in fact their liberation' (§162). If the domestic arrangements which Hegel presents are judged to be inhibiting and constraining, as they are for women under Hegel's portrayal of their proper social role, then those who suffer under them could perfectly well challenge the specification of their duties. They may not in fact do so; in which case they may be self-deceiving or, more likely, victims of false-consciousness, embracing an ideology which limits rather than promotes their personal growth. On Hegel's account of the historical dialectic of ethical life, if a form of social life is ethically flawed, limiting rather than expressing freedom, it will go under and stronger institutions, more true to human nature, will emerge.

4   Hegel (1991: 20). For an explanation of this (in)famous slogan see Knowles (2002: 67–77).

5   This account of Hegel's position is a caricature. Although there are further elements in his theory of the state which support the claim that he rejects the problem of political obligation, notably his rejection of liberal individualism and the contract theory, I am prepared to defend my conclusion. If Hegel's defence of political obligation has a conspicuous flaw it is his failure to meet the publicity constraint discussed in Chapter 5 above. For fuller discussion of these issues see Knowles (2002: 303–27; 2004: 41–53).

6   In virtue of which Carole Pateman has dubbed this 'the conceptual argument' (Pateman 1979: 27–30, 103–33). Gilbert (2006: 7–9) dubs this the analytic membership argument'.

7   Dworkin also speaks of these obligations as 'fraternal' obligations (Dworkin 1986: 198–9).

8   Emphasis in original here and in subsequent extracts.

9   It has been put to me that this is an empirical point. I agree, and to make matters worse I must confess that I can't back it up. That's because I can't imagine what such a feeling might be. I invite the reader to consider whether they can identify such a feeling.

10 That said, Dworkin does not believe a community will meet or sustain their responsibilities 'unless its members by and large actually feel some emotional bond with one another' (Dworkin 1986: 201). Simmons argues, correctly I believe, that this is a fatal concession (Simmons 1996: 78).

11 In point of 'honor', Dworkin speaks to the example of daughters who marry against their father's wishes (Dworkin 1986: 205). I read in *The Times* (30 January 2008) this

headline: 'Pregnant Muslim bride who married in secret dies on trip to Pakistan', followed by some grim details. Given what regularly happens in the real world in the sort of conflicted circumstances described by Dworkin, a world wherein 'honor' requires killing rather than apologies and explanations, I should say that his example contains at least one nuance too many.

12 Notice that on this view a commitment to justice is integral to the genuine political community – which makes it hard to see how, in a political context where other associative obligations are regulated by the state, there could be the sort of conflict of justice and obligation that Dworkin believes might arise.

13 I can think of an objection to this conclusion which does not help Dworkin's position at all. It may be that a robber-band – thieves, murderers, the lot – constitutes a genuine or true community on Dworkin's account. Obligations are special and personal, manifesting equal concern for fellow gang-members: 'All for one and one for all!' For the purposes of argument, to be blunt in face of Dworkin's subtleties, I claim that no special, personal, obligations of concern, equal or otherwise hold amongst the murderous bandits. There may be roles and rules galore. None of them has moral force. The greatest violation of these rules – betrayal – may be a noble act. If this is true the implication is obvious: whatever normative force is possessed by the obligations constitutive of associations depends entirely on the independent moral worth of those associations. Since the list of associations crucially includes the state, this conclusion is true of the state as well. But then we should expect that the moral worth of the state as independently established, itself constitutes sufficient grounds for its claim to legitimate authority and the citizens' obligations to it.

14 Gilbert uses this example in a number of earlier articles as well as in 2006. For ease of reference I shall discuss her final account as given in Gilbert (2006).

15 For details, see Gilbert (2006: 26–35).

16 In Chapter 1 I committed myself to the view that political obligation is a type of moral obligation.

17 This how I explain the 'object' of the general will as explained by Rousseau. And this is what I believe the state should secure for its citizens. This is as brief a conspectus as I can offer of the just state. But the details, even at this level of generality do not matter. If you disagree, just substitute your own. My point is that there should be some such substantive specification of the point of having political institutions.

18 'Plural subject theory can allow that the members of a political society with unjust laws may be morally required to do all they can to subvert them. It can allow that, at the same time, the members of this society have standing obligations that run in a contrary direction [presumably to uphold the unjust laws!]. These are obligations of joint commitment. They are obligations of membership' (Gilbert 2006: 265). I ask, bemusedly: How much weight do these obligations of joint commitment carry if members of an unjust society are, (not 'may be') morally required to subvert them? I answer: No weight at all – and wonder, as before, what sort of obligations these might be.

Bibliography

Anscombe, G.E.M. (1978) 'On the Source of the Authority of the State', *Ratio*, 20: 1–28 [reprinted in G.E.M. Anscombe, *Collected Philosophical Papers, Vol. III: Ethics, Religion and Politics* (1981) Minneapolis, MN: University of Minnesota Press].

Aquinas, St Thomas (1991), *Summa Theologiae: A Concise Translation*, ed. T. McDermott, London: Methuen.

Archard, D. (1998) *Sexual Consent*, Boulder, CO: Westview Press.

Arneson, R. (1982) 'The Principle of Fairness and Free-Rider Problems', *Ethics*, 92(4): 616–33.

Austin, J.L. (1962) *How to Do Things with Words*, Oxford: Clarendon Press.

Baghramian, M. and Ingram, A. (eds) (2000) *Pluralism: The Philosophy and Politics of Diversity*, London: Routledge.

Beauchamp, T.L. and Faden, R. (1986) *A History and Theory of Informed Consent*, New York: Oxford University Press.

Beran, H. (1987) *The Consent Theory of Political Obligation*, London: Croom Helm.

Brandt, R. (1959) *Ethical Theory*, Englewood Cliffs, NJ: Prentice Hall.

—— (1979) *A Theory of the Good and the Right*, Oxford: Clarendon Press.

Brink, D.O. (1997) 'Kantian Rationalism: Inescapability, Authority and Supremacy', in G. Cullity and B. Gaut (eds) *Ethics and Practical Reason*, Oxford: Clarendon Press.

Brownlie, I. (ed.) (1995) *Basic Documents in International Law*, 4th edn, Oxford: Oxford University Press.

Burke, E. (1886) 'Appeal from the New to the Old Whigs', in *Works of Edmund Burke*, Vol. 4, Little, Brown.

Card, C. (1988) 'Gratitude and Obligation', *American Philosophical Quarterly*, 25: 115–27.

Carter, A. (2001) 'Presumptive Benefits and Political Obligations', *Journal of Applied Philosophy*, 18: 229–44.

Coetzee, J.M. (2007) 'Diary of a Bad Year' (excerpt from a forthcoming novel), *The New York Review of Books*, 54(12), July 19: 20.

Coleman, J. and Shapiro, S. (eds) (2002) *The Oxford Handbook of Jurisprudence and the Philosophy of Law*, Oxford: Oxford University Press.

Dagger, R. (1997) *Civic Virtues: Rights, Citizenship and Republican Liberalism*, Cambridge: Cambridge University Press.

Daniels, N. (ed.) (1975) *Reading Rawls*, Oxford: Blackwell.

Dunleavy, P. (1993) 'The State', in Goodin and Pettit (eds) (1993): 611–21.

Dworkin, R. (1975) 'The Original Position', in Daniels (ed.) (1975).

—— (1986) *Law's Empire*, London: Fontana.

Edmundson, W.A. (1998) *Three Anarchical Fallacies: An Essay on Political Authority*, Cambridge: Cambridge University Press.

—— (ed.) (1999) *The Duty to Obey the Law*, Lanham, MA: Rowman & Littlefield.

Frey, R.G. and Wellman, C.H. (eds) (2003) *A Companion to Applied Ethics*, Oxford: Blackwell.

Fuller, L. (1958) 'Positivism and Fidelity to Law', *Harvard Law Review*, lxxi: 630.

Gans, C. (1992) *Philosophical Anarchism*, Cambridge: Cambridge University Press.

Gilbert, M. (1989) *On Social Facts*, London: Routledge [reprinted 1992, Princeton, NJ: Princeton University Press].

—— (2006) *A Theory of Political Obligation: Membership, Commitment, and the Bonds of Society*, Oxford: Clarendon Press.

Glassey, L. (1977) 'The Lawyer, the Historian and the Glorious Revolution', in E. Attwooll (ed.) *Perspectives in Jurisprudence*, Glasgow: University of Glasgow Press.

Glover, J. (1999) *Humanity: A Moral History of the Twentieth Century*, London: Jonathan Cape.

Godwin, W. (1971, 1st pub. 1793) *Enquiry Concerning Political Justice*, abr. & ed. K. Codell Carter, Oxford: Clarendon Press.

Goodin, R.E. (1995) *Utilitarianism as a Public Philosophy*, Cambridge: Cambridge University Press.

Goodin, R.E. and Pettit, P. (eds) (1993) *A Companion to Contemporary Political Philosophy*, Oxford: Blackwell.

—— (1997; 2nd edn 2006) *Contemporary Political Philosophy: An Anthology*, Oxford: Blackwell.

Green, L. (1988) *The Authority of the State*, Oxford: Oxford University Press.

—— (1999) 'Who Believes in Political Obligation?', in Edmundson (1999): 301–17 [reprinted from Narveson and Sanders (eds) (1996): 1–17].

—— (2002) 'Law and Obligations', in Coleman and Shapiro (2002): 514–47.

Greenawalt, K. (1989) *Conflicts of Law and Morality*, New York: Oxford University Press.

Grice, G.R. (1967) *The Grounds of Moral Judgement*, Cambridge: Cambridge University Press.

Hampton, J. (1986) *Hobbes and the Social Contract Tradition*, Cambridge: Cambridge University Press.

—— (1997) *Political Philosophy*, Boulder, CO: Westview Press.

Harrison, R. (ed.) (1980) *Rational Action*, Cambridge: Cambridge University Press.

Hart, H.L.A. (1955) 'Are There any Natural Rights?', *Philosophical Review*, 64: 175–91 [reprinted in Goodin and Pettit (2006): 281–8, from which citations are taken].

—— (1958) 'Legal Positivism and the Separation of Law and Morals', *Harvard Law Review*, lxxi: 598.

—— (1961) *The Concept of Law*, Oxford: Clarendon Press.

—— (1982) *Essays on Bentham*, Oxford: Clarendon Press.

Hegel, G.W.F. (1977, first pub. 1807) *Phenomenology of Spirit*, trans. A.V. Miller, Oxford: Oxford University Press [cited by paragraph number].

—— (1991, first pub. 1821) *Elements of the Philosophy of Right*, ed. Allen W. Wood, trans. H.B. Nisbet, Cambridge: Cambridge University Press [cited by paragraph number].

Hobbes, T. (1968, first pub. 1651) *Leviathan*, ed. C.B. Macpherson, London: Penguin Books [cited by page reference to this edition; then part and chapter numbers plus a page reference in square brackets to the original edition].

Hohfeld, W.E. (1923) *Fundamental Legal Conceptions as Applied in Judicial Reasoning*, New Haven, CT: Yale University Press.

Hooker, B. (2000) *Ideal Code, Real World: A Rule-Consequentialist Theory of Morality*, Oxford: Oxford University Press.

Horton, J. (1992) *Political Obligation*, Basingstoke: Palgrave.

Hume, D. (1963, first pub. 1758) *Essays, Moral, Political and Literary*, Oxford: Oxford University Press.

—— (1965, first pub. 1739) *A Treatise of Human Nature*, ed. L.A. Selby-Bigge, Oxford: Oxford University Press.

—— (1975, first pub. 1751) *An Enquiry Concerning the Principles of Morals*, ed. L.A. Selby-Bigge, 3rd edition, Oxford: Clarendon Press.

Hurd, H.M. (1996) 'The Moral Magic of Consent', *Legal Theory*, 2: 121–46.

—— (1999) *Moral Combat*, Cambridge: Cambridge University Press.

Hurley, S.L. (1989) *Natural Reasons*, Oxford: Oxford University Press.

Joll, J. (1979) *The Anarchists*, 2nd edn, London: Methuen.

Kant, I. (1996a) *Practical Philosophy*, trans. and ed. Mary J. Gregor, intr. Allen Wood, Cambridge: Cambridge University Press. [References to Kant also cite in square brackets the volume and page number of the Prussian Academy edition in accordance with common practice.]

—— (1996b) 'An Answer to the Question: What is Enlightenment?', in Kant (1996a).

—— (1996c) 'Toward Perpetual Peace', in Kant (1996a).

—— (1998) *Critique of Pure Reason*, trans. & ed. Paul Guyer and Allen W. Wood, Cambridge: Cambridge University Press.

Kim, S. (2003) 'A Visit to North Korea', *New York Review of Books*, 50(2), Feb 13: 16.

Klosko, G. (1992) *The Principle of Fairness and Political Obligation*, Lanham, MD: Rowman & Littlefield.

—— (2005) *Political Obligations*, Oxford: Oxford University Press.

Knowles, D. (2000) 'Conservative Utilitarianism', *Utilitas*, 12: 155–75.

—— (2001a) *Political Philosophy*, London: Routledge.

—— (2001b) 'Parents' Consent to the Removal and Retention of Organs', *Journal of Applied Philosophy*, 18: 215–27.

—— (2002a) 'Gratitude and Good Government', *Res Publica*, 8: 1–20.

—— (2002b) *Hegel and the Philosophy of Right*, London: Routledge.

—— (2004) 'Hegel's Citizen', *Bulletin of the Hegel Society of Great Britain*, 49/50: 41–53.

Kramer, M. (1999) *In Defense of Legal Positivism: Law without Trimmings*, Oxford: Oxford University Press.

Kraus, J.S. (1993) *The Limits of Hobbesian Contractarianism*, Cambridge: Cambridge University Press.

Kristof, N. (2006) 'Genocide in Slow Motion', *New York Review of Books*, 53(2), Feb 9.

Ladenson, R. (1980) 'In Defense of a Hobbesian Conception of Law', *Philosophy and Public Affairs*, 9: 139–54.

Leopold, D. (2006) '"The State and I": Max Stirner's Anarchism', in *The New Hegelians: Politics and Philosophy in the Hegelian School*, ed. D. Moggach, Cambridge: Cambridge University Press.

Lessnoff, M. (1986) *The Social Contract*, London: Macmillan.

Lewis, D. (1969) *Convention: A Philosophical Study*, Cambridge, MA: Harvard University Press.

Locke, J. (1960) *Two Treatises of Government*, ed. Peter Laslett, Cambridge: Cambridge University Press. [There are many editions. References are given to the *Second Treatise*, chapter and section number.]

Lyons, D. (1965) *Forms and Limits of Utilitarianism*, Oxford: Clarendon Press.

Macpherson, C.B. (1962) *The Political Theory of Possessive Individualism: Hobbes to Locke*, Oxford: Oxford University Press.

McPherson, T. (1967) *Political Obligation*, London: Routledge & Kegan Paul.

Markwick, P. (2000) 'Law and Content-Independent Reasons,' *Oxford Journal of Legal Studies*, 20: 579–96.

Milgram, S. (1974) *Obedience to Authority*, London: Tavistock.

—— (1987) 'Obedience', in R.L. Gregory (ed.), *The Oxford Companion to the Mind*, Oxford: Oxford University Press.

Mill, J.S. (1968) *Utilitarianism, Liberty, Representative Government*, London: Dent, Everyman Library.

Miller, D. (1984) *Anarchism*, London: J.M. Dent.

Narveson, J. and Sanders, J.T. (eds) (1996) *For and Against the State*, Lanham, MD: Rowman & Littlefield.

Nozick, R. (1974) *Anarchy, State, and Utopia*, New York: Basic Books.

O'Neill, J. (1993) *Ecology, Policy and Politics*, London: Routledge.

Pateman, C. (1979) *The Problem of Political Obligation*, Chichester: John Wiley & Sons.

—— (1988) *The Sexual Contract*, Oxford: Polity Press.

Pitkin, H. (1965) 'Obligation and Consent', *American Political Science Review* LIX, no. 4, and LX, no.1 [reprinted in, and cited from, P. Laslett, W.G. Runciman and Q. Skinner (eds) (1972) *Philosophy, Politics and Society*, Fourth Series, Oxford: Blackwell].

Plamenatz, J. (1992) *Man and Society*, Vol. 1 (new edition, rev. by M.E. Plamenatz and R. Wokler), London: Longman.

Plato, *The Republic* (many editions); cited universally by paragraph numbers.

—— (1959) *Crito*, tr. H. Tredennick, London: Penguin Books; cited by paragraph numbers.

Powers, T. (2006) 'The Biggest Secret', *The New York Review of Books*, 53(3), Feb 23: 9–12.

Rawls, J. (1955) 'Two Concepts of Rules', *Philosophical Review*, 64(1): 3–32 [reprinted in Rawls (1999)].

—— (1958) 'Justice as Fairness', *Philosophical Review*, 67(2): 164–94 [reprinted in Rawls (1999)].

—— (1963) 'The Sense of Justice', *Philosophical Review*, 72(3): 281–305 [reprinted in Rawls (1999)].

—— (1964) 'Legal Obligation and the Duty of Fair Play', in S. Hook (ed.) *Law and Philosophy: A Symposium*, New York: New York University Press [reprinted in, and cited from, Rawls (1999)].

—— (1972) *A Theory of Justice*, Oxford: Clarendon Press.

—— (1993) *Political Liberalism*, New York: Columbia University Press.

—— (1999) *Collected Papers*, ed. S. Freeman, Cambridge, MA: Harvard University Press.

—— (2001) *Justice as Fairness: A Re-statement*, Cambridge, MA: Harvard University Press.

Raz, J. (1975) *Practical Reason and Norms*, London: Hutchinson.

—— (1979) *The Authority of Law*, Oxford: Clarendon Press.

—— (1986) *The Morality of Freedom*, Oxford: Clarendon Press.

Renzo, M. (2008) 'Duties of Samaritanism and Political Obligation', *Legal Theory*, 14: 3.

Richards, D. (1971) *A Theory of Reasons for Action*, Oxford: Clarendon Press.

Riley, P. (1982) *Will and Political Legitimacy*, Cambridge, MA: Harvard University Press.

Ross, Sir D. (1930) *The Right and the Good*, Oxford: Oxford University Press.

Rousseau J.-J. (1973) *The Social Contract and Discourses*, trans. G.D.H. Cole, rev. J.H. Brumfitt and J.C. Hall, London: Dent, Everyman Library.

Sagoff, M. (1988) *The Economy of the Earth*, Cambridge: Cambridge University Press.

Sandel, M. (1984) 'The Procedural Republic and the Unencumbered Self', *Political Theory*, 12: 81–96 [reprinted in Goodin and Pettit (2006): 239–47].

Sartorius, R. (1981) 'Political Authority and Political Obligation', *Virginia Law Review*, 67 [reprinted in Edmundsen (1999): 143–58].

Scanlon, T.M. (1982) 'Contractualism and Utilitarianism', in A. Sen and B. Williams (eds) *Utilitarianism and Beyond*, Cambridge: Cambridge University Press: 103–28 [widely reprinted].

—— (1998) *What We Owe to Each Other*, Cambridge, MA: Harvard University Press.

Schauer, F. (1991) *Playing by the Rules: A Philosophical Examination of Rule-Based Decision Making in Law and in Life*, Oxford: Clarendon Press.

Schneewind, J.B. (1998) *The Invention of Autonomy*, Cambridge: Cambridge University Press.

Searle, J.R. (1995) *The Construction of Social Reality*, London: Allen Lane, The Penguin Press.

—— (1999) *Mind, Language and Society*, London: Weidenfeld & Nicolson.

Simmons, A.J. (1979) *Moral Principles and Political Obligations*, Princeton, NJ: Princeton University Press.

—— (1993) *On the Edge of Anarchy: Locke, Consent and the Limits of Society*, Princeton, NJ: Princeton University Press.

—— (1996) 'Associative Political Obligations', *Ethics*, 106: 247–73 [reprinted in, and cited from, Simmons (2001)].

—— (2001) *Justification and Legitimacy*, Cambridge: Cambridge University Press.

—— (2003) 'Civil Disobedience and the Duty to Obey the Law', in Frey and Wellman (eds) (2003): 50–61.

Singer, P. (1974) *Democracy and Disobedience*, London: Oxford University Press.

Smart, J.J.C. (1956) 'Extreme and Restricted Utilitarianism', *Philosophical Quarterly*, 6: 344–54 [reprinted in P. Foot (ed.) (1967) *Theories of Ethics*, Oxford: Oxford University Press].

Smith, M.B.E. (1973) 'Is There a Prima Facie Obligation to Obey the Law?', *Yale Law Journal*, 82: 950–76 [reprinted in, and cited from, Edmundson (ed.) (1999): 75–105].

Sorell, T. (1986) *Hobbes*, London: Routledge.

Stirner, M. (1915, first pub. 1844) *The Ego and His Own*, trans. S.T. Byington, London: Jonathan Cape.

Taylor, C. (1994) 'Alternative Futures: Legitimacy, Identity and Alienation in Late Twentieth Century Canada', in M. Daly (ed.) *Communitarianism: A New Public Ethics*, Belmont, CA: Wadsworth.

Waldron, J. (1993) 'Special Ties and Natural Duties', *Philosophy and Public Affairs*, 22(1): 3–30.

—— (2001) 'Hobbes and the Principle of Publicity', *Pacific Philosophical Quarterly*, 82: 447–74.

Walker, A.D.M. (1988) 'Political Obligation and the Argument from Gratitude', *Philosophy and Public Affairs*, 17: 191–211.

Watkins, J.W.N. (1965) *Hobbes's System of Ideas*, London: Hutchinson.

Weber M. (1946) 'Politics as a Vocation', in H.H. Gerth and C. Wright Mills (trans. and eds) *From Max Weber: Essays in Sociology*, New York: Oxford University Press.

Weil, S. (1957) *Écrits de Londres et dernières lettres*, Paris: Gallimard.

Wellman, C.H. (1996) 'Liberalism, Samaritanism, and Political Legitimacy', *Philosophy and Public Affairs*, 25: 211–37.

—— (2000) 'Relational Facts in Liberal Political Theory: Is There Magic in the Pronoun "My"?', *Ethics*, 110: 537–62.

—— (2001) 'Towards a Liberal Theory of Political Obligation', *Ethics*, 111: 735–59.

—— (2004) 'Political Obligation and the Particularity Requirement', *Legal Theory*, 10: 97–115.

—— (2005) 'Samaritanism and the Duty to Obey the Law', in Wellman and Simmons (2005).

Wellman, C.H. and Simmons, A.J. (2005) *Is there a Duty to Obey the Law?*, Cambridge: Cambridge University Press.

Wenar, L. (2005) 'The Nature of Rights', *Philosophy and Public Affairs*, 33: 223–53.

Wertheimer, A. (2003) *Consent to Sexual Relations*, Cambridge: Cambridge University Press.

Williams, B. (1973) 'Deciding to Believe', in B. Williams, *Problems of the Self*, Cambridge: Cambridge University Press: 136–51.

—— (1981) 'Internal and External Reasons', in B. Williams, *Moral Luck*, Cambridge: Cambridge University Press: 101–13 [reprinted from Harrison (ed.) (1980)].

Winch, P. (1972) 'Man and Society in Hobbes and Rousseau', in M. Cranston and R.S. Peters (eds) *Hobbes and Rousseau*, New York: Anchor Books.

Wolff, J. (1996) *An Introduction to Political Philosophy*, Oxford: Oxford University Press.

—— (2000) 'Political Obligation: A Pluralistic Approach', in M. Baghramian and A. Ingram (eds) *Pluralism: The Philosophy and Politics of Diversity*, London: Routledge.

Wolff, R. (1976) *In Defense of Anarchism*, New York: Harper & Row.

Woodcock, G. (1977) *The Anarchist Reader*, London: Collins Fontana.

Woodhouse, A.S.P. (1938, 2nd edn 1974) *Puritanism and Liberty: Being the Army Debates (1647–9) from the Clarke Mss.* (ed. Woodhouse), London: J.M. Dent.

Index